WHAT YOUR HORSE WANTS YOU TO KNOW

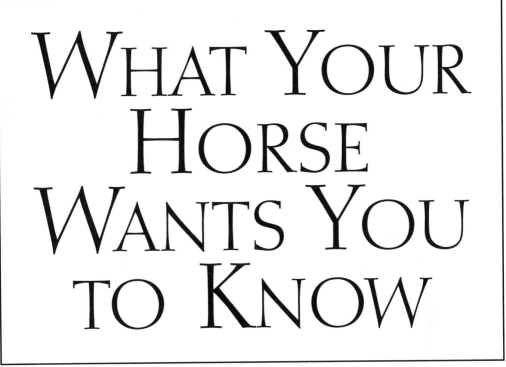

WHAT YOUR HORSE WANTS YOU TO KNOW

WHAT HORSES'

"BAD" BEHAVIOR MEANS, AND

HOW TO CORRECT IT

Gincy Self Bucklin

HOWELL
BOOK
HOUSE

Howell Book House

Published by Wiley Publishing, Inc., Indianapolis, IN

For general information on our other products and services or to obtain technical support please contact our Customer Care Department within the U.S. at 800-762-2974, outside the U.S. at 317-572-3993 or fax 317-572-4002.

Wiley also publishes its books in a variety of electronic formats. Some content that appears in print may not be available in electronic books.

Library of Congress Cataloging-in-Publication Data:

Bucklin, Gincy Self.

    What your horse wants you to know : what horses' "bad" behavior means, and how to correct it / Gincy Self Bucklin.

    p. cm.

    Includes index.

    ISBN 0-7645-4085-8 (alk. paper)

    1. Horses—Behavior. 2. Horses—Training. 3. Human-animal communication. I. Title.

    SF281.B83   2003

    636.1'0835—dc21

                                    2003004634

Manufactured in the United States of America

10 9 8 7 6 5 4 3 2

All drawings by Heather Holloway

Book design by Melissa Auciello-Brogan

Cover design by Jose Almaguer

Book production by Wiley Publishing, Inc. Composition Services

To Harris Howard Bucklin Jr.
Finest of horsemen, and best of husbands
This book is lovingly dedicated

CONTENTS

ACKNOWLEDGMENTS

I have learned about horses and training from many sources during my life, the most outstanding of whom were my mother, Margaret Cabell Self, Mike and Ruth Miller of Sleepy Hollow in Tarrytown, New York, William Hillebrand and Sally Swift. And, like all of us, I learned the most from the horses themselves. It took me a long time to learn to listen to them, but they never gave up, and I'm getting better at it.

I would also like to acknowledge the help and support for this book that I received from my daughter Karen Stoddard Hayes—the real writer in the family—and all the people on the Riding With Confidence and Horseman Off-Topic e-groups, who so generously gave of their thoughts and ideas when I was stumped.

Gincy Self Bucklin
Narragansett, Rhode Island
February 2003

PREFACE

A surprising number of horse owners are afraid of their horses! They aren't frightened all the time, but maybe they don't go on trails, or mounting is tricky, or they don't *really* like to canter. Other owners seem to spend a lot of time being angry with their horses, or disciplining them. When you think about the nature of the horse, you have to wonder what went wrong. Horses, as a group, are by nature somewhat lazy (they will sleep as much as 20 hours a day), gregarious (as herd animals, they enjoy interaction with their fellow creatures) and peaceful (as vegetarians, they don't have to fight with each other or attack other animals to get food). If horses are laid-back, friendly and nonviolent, what's to be afraid of or angry about?

Nearly all of the trouble is of our own making.

First, *we don't communicate well!* That is, we don't make clear to the horse, in ways that he can understand, what *we* want; and we don't listen, or don't try to understand, what *he* wants. The horse becomes confused and makes "mistakes" that are frequently perceived as deliberate: "What's wrong with you? You know better than that!" Both horse and handler have become frustrated and angry.

By focusing on communication, rather than simply "training," we change our attitude toward the horse from insisting on obedience to creating an atmosphere of mutual cooperation. This gives the horse far more confidence and eliminates much of the tension that lies behind so many "disobediences." The horse discovers that what we want is really the pleasantest and easiest thing for him to do in any situation, and we discover that making things easier for the horse leads to far more successful and satisfying training.

Second, *we don't understand the best ways to teach the horse.* We ride a young horse toward a jump. He approaches it somewhat tensely and unevenly balanced. Rather than risk a fall, he stops. We punish him for stopping! The next time, not only is he worried about his balance, he is also worried about being punished. If he does jump it will be an awkward leap, probably much higher than necessary to compensate for his insecurity. We tell all our friends what a big jump he has in him. He tells all his friends he hates jumping!

With the spread of knowledge through better worldwide communication—more books, Internet access, television, etc.—the understanding of how to deal with other species has undergone a revolution. Knowledgeable trainers have moved away from the belief that the horse is inferior in intelligence and incapable of learning except through punishment. Instead, they have studied how the horse perceives humans and how he learns. They understand the importance of good relationships and positive reinforcement—marking the good behavior rather than the bad. The result is that the horse himself becomes part of the solution rather than part of the problem. Instead of worrying frantically about how to avoid punishment, he looks for ways to earn rewards.

Third, *we're in too much of a hurry.* A horse is not born knowing all the things we want him to know. It takes time for him to learn them, and people are not always patient. They send a young horse to a trainer for a month and think he should be perfectly trained when he returns. The trainer may be under pressure to get the horse ready for competition, so he skips the true essentials to put a superficial gloss on the horse. We are also not patient enough with ourselves. Riding and handling horses well are not skills that are learned in a hurry, but people want to ride on trails and canter and jump and often expect the horse to cope with their inadequacies. The horse tries to tell them he can't do it, but they insist, and soon you have a frustrated or frightened animal and a rider who thinks he has a problem horse.

The purpose of this book is to guide you in solving some of the problems you may be having with your horse, and to improve your understanding both of the problem and of the horse himself. This book deals almost entirely with problems you meet on the ground, because riding problems often result from inadequate riding skills, which are a separate challenge. However, many riding problems are best solved on the ground first.

Each chapter describes a different problem, telling you first of all what the horse is trying to communicate to you, as well as what he may think you are saying to him. Only when you know what the *horse* thinks the problem is can you help him solve it.

Then I will offer you a variety of possible ways to deal with the problem. The solutions are mostly based on using one or more of four training systems: clicker training, Parelli Natural Horse-man-ship, round pen training and Tellington-Jones Equine Awareness Method, all of which are explained briefly in the Introduction. I have found all of these systems to be fairly easy to learn, and there is a good support system for each one in books, tapes and on the Internet (see Appendix A). With reasonable care, the novice whose intent is good can use them without harming or abusing the horse.

Finally, I will tell you what *not* to do, which is often equally important.

You should begin by reading the Introduction, to get an overview of the things you need to know to use the book. There will be page references throughout the text to bring you back to a specific tool or training method.

Introduction: What You Need to Know to Help Your Horse

THE RULES

Rule Number 1

Look after your own personal safety first, then your horse's.

And, of course, the safety of anyone nearby. Working with horses is different from working with smaller animals. Even a horse who doesn't want to hurt you may do so by accident. He has so much size and power and quickness that a slight miscalculation on his part can result in serious injury to someone. I have known some very experienced horsemen who stood too close and were nailed by a horse who was just playing and got a little careless. Don't be careless yourself.

Rule Number 2

The most important factor in having a horse who wants to please you is genuine caring on your part. Horses are very forgiving of the people who truly love them, even when those people make mistakes that are frightening or even painful.

This is a book about dealing with things horses do that don't please you. This means that to some extent you're going to be "training" your horse. Or trying to. In the process, you're going to make mistakes. We all do. But if your horse's welfare and feelings have top priority, you're not going to make many unforgivable mistakes.

Rule Number 3

Make learning fun for both of you.

Look for ways to make the horse feel successful, not frustrated or angry. All the training systems described later on, and used throughout the book, have an element of fun and accomplishment. If you get bored or frustrated, change games. If you aren't having fun, the horse won't either. Use a lot of praise and smiles. When you smile it makes you feel happy, and the horse senses that and feels happy too.

RULE NUMBER 4

"If it doesn't even begin to work, try something else." (Morton W. "Cappy" Smith)

Helping your horse solve his problems is largely a matter of trial and error, especially when you're just learning. As you gain experience, you make better guesses about what will work, but they are still guesses. The trick is to see the error early on and be willing to try something else, not be chained to one way of doing things. That's not the same as chopping and changing until the horse is confused. It simply means that you try something for awhile. If you see improvement right away and the horse seems comfortable with it, you know you're on the right track. If nothing much seems to be happening, stay with it a bit longer—sometimes the road to understanding has a few bumps and curves in it. If it upsets the horse a lot or makes the behavior worse, it's probably wrong.

RULE NUMBER 5

Be patient, persistent and consistent.

Patience. Take the time it takes. Don't try to get it all done in one day. Only if you are willing to spend the time doing the basic stuff—what a house painter calls the prep work—will you get the best results. That doesn't mean you have to keep doing the same boring things over and over. It does mean that as you go forward and see weaknesses, you must have the patience and the persistence to go back and fix what isn't right. Horses, like children, have a lot of patience and persistence when they're trying to get their own way. So you have to be just as patient and persistent. And as you are persistent in asking for what you want, so you are also consistent. You don't tell the horse one thing one day and change the rules the next. That's how children, and horses, turn into spoiled brats. You also have to have the judgment to make this fit with Rule Number 4!

RULE NUMBER 6

Always ask yourself "Why?"

Don't make the "just" assumption. The horse is "just being a stinker" or "just wants to annoy me" or "that's just the way he is." Horses have reasons for everything they do. Sometimes it takes a long time to determine the reason. Sometimes you don't know for sure, but you make an educated guess. In the case of sudden behavioral changes, always look for a physical cause—something that is creating pain or the potential for pain.

TALKING HORSES

I had a horse who I had been jumping pretty regularly. One day, about halfway through our jumping session, I asked him to jump through a three-foot combination—two fences with one stride between—which he had been doing successfully for some time. To my surprise and annoyance, he refused to jump the second fence. After a short battle—I wasn't going to "let him get away with it" —I got him over the two fences. The next day he was dead lame! It seems he had strained his back a little at some point, and the effort of jumping two fences in quick succession was more than he thought he could do. He was right. I was wrong. It cost me time and money, and his trust. So we learn.

RULE NUMBER 7
Beware of shortcuts and quick fixes.

A horse doesn't develop a bad habit or a bad attitude in a day, and you aren't going to fix it in one or two training sessions. Physiologically, it takes three times as long to change a habit as it did to develop it in the first place. The real "shortcut" is to learn as much as you can, so you can find the true cause of the problem and choose the best method for solving it. Sometimes the right solutions are simple and quick, but if they're not, trying to cut corners will end up taking longer, or may mean not arriving at all.

RULE NUMBER 8
Always quit when you're both ahead.

It's so tempting to do it "one more time" when things are going well. Besides risking failure, you also take away from the horse's feeling of success, which is what makes him want to do it again tomorrow.

RULE NUMBER 9
You don't always have to win.

Sometimes the best thing to do when you're getting nowhere is simply leave it alone, rather than making a big issue of a particular problem. Work on other, totally unrelated things that the horse and you can enjoy together. After a few weeks of this, if the problem comes up again, the horse's whole attitude toward you and it may have changed to the point where he no longer sees it as something to worry about.

RULE NUMBER 10
If you don't know, ask.

If you have a problem that you can't solve, find someone who *knows* and ask for help. If there is no one in your area, try the Internet or the library. Just be sure the person you ask is someone whose skills and techniques you respect. And don't make the mistake of running around and asking everyone you meet what they think. You may get 20 different answers and end up more confused than before.

THE TOOLS

What It's All About: Building a Good Relationship

The big difficulty we and horses have in communicating with one another is that they are prey—potentially someone's lunch—and we are predators whom they instinctively perceive as someone who wants to eat them. If you walk straight at a horse, looking at him as you do so, his *instinct*, even if he knows you well, is to turn away, ready to run, since your body language is saying that you want to catch (and eventually kill and eat) him. So your first goal with a horse is to communicate that even though you look like a predator, you really don't want to have that relationship with him.

What kind of a relationship *do* you want with your horse? Pretty much the same relationship you want with a friend or a spouse—a give-and-take relationship, a partnership. But partnership doesn't mean you are equal all the time. In any given situation where there are decisions to be made, one of you will nearly always be more qualified than the other. If it's a question of which trail to take to reach an objective, you're the one who knows, but if it's a question of where to put his feet to get over a bit of trappy ground, the horse has a better feeling for that. You each have to respect the other's judgment and be willing to give up control when the other partner is the expert.

But now we run into another horse attribute: Horses are herd animals. In the wild, the lowest-ranked member of the herd is the one most likely to lose out, whether it's getting the best food or being pushed out to where a predator can get him. It's called survival of the fittest, and is one of the ways nature ensures that the best animals survive. But that means in his relationships with other horses, a horse is constantly challenging, trying to improve his rank. Once he has decided you're not a predator but a friend, and therefore a member of his herd, he tries to make you a lower-ranked member than himself. Since he is bigger and stronger than you, he doesn't see why he shouldn't be able to do this.

Consequently, before you can be partners, you have to gain the horse's respect so that he will give you control when it's appropriate. Since most of the time you work in situations where you know more about what's going on than he does, he has to give up control most of the time to you. You have to be "lead mare," the herd boss.

A lot of trainers try to gain this respect solely by being bossy, aggressive, demanding, making the horse toe the line. That's what the lead mare does. But there appears to be an innate trust between horses in a herd that does not apply to our relationship. In other words, the lead mare can apparently be tough and bossy with the other horses and they still love and trust her. You have to create that love and trust first. Then, when you ask for respect as well, the horse will not perceive it simply as tyranny. Think of the teachers you had in school. If you felt the teacher liked you and she gave you a bad mark on a paper, you tried to do better. On the other hand, if you felt she *didn't* like you and she gave you a bad mark, you figured it was just because she didn't like you. In addition, the teachers whom you felt liked you, *but who also expected—and got—respect and politeness* from the students at all times, are the teachers you remember and hold in the highest regard.

First, you build trust. You show the horse that you respect his needs and feelings. You will see in the descriptions of Parelli, clicker training and Tteam that there are a number of ways to do that. Then you can use those same training systems, with the addition of round pen training, to gain respect and even greater trust. (Round pen training is also used to gain initial trust, but it takes a more experienced horseman.) A horse who trusts and respects you will listen to you, and that's what you need to start with. When a horse trusts you, he gives up control to you, even in situations that are threatening. The horse who isn't willing to give up control is the one who spooks violently or bolts when something unusual or unexpected occurs. A horse who trusts you says, "Oh! What was that? Oh, you say it's okay? Fine."

One situation where building a relationship can be difficult is with stallions, and some mares in heat. Many people have beautifully behaved stallions, but working with them does require greater experience and sensitivity than with the average gelding. Mares in heat are sometimes so tense and uncomfortable that you just have to be very forgiving. There are hormones and homeopathic remedies that work in many cases to make the mare more comfortable.

The classic green rider–green horse combination produces another difficult situation. This is compounded if the rider is a child. Parents give the child a young horse as though it were a puppy or a kitten, but puppies and kittens don't weigh a thousand pounds, and you don't try to ride them, either. Older riders who rode as children decide to go back to it, and get talked into a young horse because their perception of their skills is skewed by memory and childhood fearlessness. It is possible, if the horse is kind and the rider is sensible, very patient and has a good advisor, to work these relationships out, but they should be avoided if possible.

Communication From You to the Horse Your Body: The Natural Tools

We all know about the natural aids: hands, legs, seat, weight and voice. But those are not the only natural ways in which we communicate with a horse. Our whole body talks to the horse all the time. Two things are taking place; the first is something I call muscular telepathy, which describes a phenomenon we see in all creatures that move around in groups, whether herds of horses, flocks of birds or schools of fish. Let's take a school of fish, several hundred all swimming along together. Suddenly they all shoot off, upward and to the right, almost simultaneously. Now you know the lead fish didn't say to the second fish, "When I get to that piece of red coral, I'm going to go up and to the right. Pass it on." Of course not! But something is going on that enables the fish to move together effortlessly and without running into one another. At some level, their bodies talk to each other, hence "muscular telepathy." This ability is not restricted within species; our bodies talk to our horses' bodies and theirs to ours. Therefore, by releasing tensions in our own bodies we can communicate relaxation and confidence to the horse.

TALKING HORSES

I originally learned about muscular telepathy at a Centered Riding clinic some years ago. As an instructor, I was assigned a student on a longe line. We were told to choose some area of the horse's body that we wanted to change. The horse carried his head high with his neck somewhat upside-down, so we chose the back of his neck. Then the two of us, student and instructor, were to focus on the backs of our own necks and do whatever exercises seemed appropriate to release any tensions we might have in that area. So we worked on that for five minutes or so. Then we were to focus on the horse's neck and, while continuing to maintain relaxation in our own necks, imagine the horse's neck releasing and relaxing as well. To our astonishment, the horse immediately released much of his tension and dropped his head!

Since then I have learned that if we allow ourselves, we can feel what is going on in the horse's body because we can find the same tensions in our own bodies.

There is a corollary to muscular telepathy that was only discovered fairly recently. It was always thought that emotions began in the brain, and the body reacted. Research now indicates that it works the other way around. For example, your body sees, hears or senses something scary and responds by holding its breath, tensing abdominal muscles to create a protective fetal position and preparing to flee. The brain looks at this and says, "Gracious, I must be frightened!" Then along comes someone who is relaxed and confident, who smiles cheerfully and says, "Hey, it's okay." You find yourself returning the smile, and suddenly you are no longer frightened. Her body transmitted its emotion (cheerful/smile) via muscular telepathy to yours (you smile), and changed your emotion from fearful to cheerful.

You have probably known people who never seem to be concerned when riding and whose horses never seem to act up. My husband is such a person. Horses who were nervous wrecks with other riders would just trudge along with him. If they happened to spook at a bird, it was as if he didn't even notice. He just went with the motion and calmly continued on his way. The lack of tension in his body was transmitted to the horse via muscular telepathy, and gave the horse the confidence and thus the relaxation we all look for. "Well," you may say, "good for him, but *I* can't do that." *Yes, you can.* It takes practice and it doesn't happen overnight, but you can learn. Here's how.

The Five Steps and Grounding

The five steps are a group of exercises derived from Centered Riding, yoga, tai-chi and similar mental and physical disciplines. Together they put your body into the mode it would normally be in when you feel relaxed and confident. When you sense trouble during ground work, either in yourself or in your horse, by doing the five steps you fix your body in "confident" mode, and your brain then says, "Ah, now I feel more comfortable." Your horse copies you and finds himself feeling secure as well. The more you do this, the more confidence both you and your horse develop.

Grounding is the ultimate result that the five steps lead you to. I have been using the terms "relaxed" and "confident," but "grounded" is more correct and specific. Grounding is what all good athletes are doing when they are performing well: the tennis player receiving a serve, the baseball player at bat, the skier in a downhill race and you when you were playing dodge ball in grammar school. Remember that stance you had? Alert, balanced, ready to move your body in any direction to avoid the ball, but with your feet firmly connected to the ground, without tension. By contrast, not being grounded is what you experienced when you tried to skate the first time!

Grounding is also essential for the horse, both physically and emotionally. Grounding makes him feel he can handle any situation, and this, in turn, makes him calm and confident.

TALKING HORSES

When I was taking a Parelli clinic, I was impressed with how easily our clinician seemed to handle every horse, no matter how uncontrolled the horse had been with his owner. I watched him carefully to see what he did differently, and the thing that caught my eye was that he always looked solidly grounded. This meant that not only could he move quickly and athletically whenever necessary, but the feeling I got was that if a bomb went off, his feet would never leave the ground.

The five steps can be practiced in any order, but I find this order works best for most people. If you find one step more difficult than another, you can practice it more, but don't dwell on it to the point of making yourself tense about it.

Step 1. Growing

Growing stretches and straightens your body, and thus makes it more flexible, just as stretching out a Slinky makes it more flexible. It also releases tensions in the front of your body, which tends to shorten up in stress situations (sort of like returning to the fetal position).

Bring your relaxed left hand up in front of your nose, with your thumb toward you. Now reach up with your left arm, following it up with your eyes and head until your arm is *vertical* above your shoulder, with your fingers slightly flexed. Next bring your head and eyes back down so you are looking straight in front of you, but as though you were looking over granny glasses. Continue to reach up with your arm, stretching as far as you can, until you feel a pull at your waist. Bring your arm down slowly, but leave your body up there.

Repeat with your right arm, but this time when you finish bring your hand down to the top of your head, directly between your ears and behind your nose. Tap a couple of times, then, bringing your arm down, imagine there is a string on the top of your head that is attached to a big balloon, or, if you prefer, imagine a lock of your hair is caught in a nail above your head. Allow the balloon, or the pressure on your hair, to pull your body upward.

Think of a cardboard skeleton—a Halloween decoration. Its head and torso hang from a string, and then its arms and legs hang from the torso.

Step 2. Shakeout

Shakeout releases all sorts of small tensions throughout your body that you would normally not be conscious of. You see many athletes shaking out just before a competition.

From your "growing" position, allow your arms to dangle, then begin to shake your fingers as though you had water or sand on them that you were trying to flick off. Continue up your arms with the same shaking motion, doing your hands, wrists, forearms, elbows, arms and finally your shoulders.

Now do your feet, one at a time, beginning with the foot, then the ankle, shin, knee and thigh. Be sure to shake them vigorously, not rotate or wiggle them up and down. You can imagine that they are saltshakers and you are shaking salt everywhere.

Finally, bend over from the hip, as far as is comfortable, with your knees lightly flexed and your arms dangling, and shake all over like a dog. (Hint: The sillier you feel, the better you're doing it!)

Step 3. Breathing

Correct breathing is *the* essential skill. Hold your breath for 10 or 15 seconds and see how tense you become throughout your whole body. Horses hold their breath when they are tense, too. Correct breathing consists of a fairly short inhale and a long, slow exhale—at least twice as long as the inhale. Take a quick, gasping breath. Even the sound is scary. Now breathe a long sigh. Whew! That's better! When horses breathe out that long sneezy sigh, which we call blowing out, we know they're relaxed. Horses who never blow out are always a bit tense.

Correct breathing comes from the diaphragm, not the chest. Your shoulders should not lift when you inhale, and your upper chest should not expand until the end of the inhale. Place your hand on your stomach, just about at your waistline. Breathe in through your nose, if possible, fairly rapidly. Feel how your hand is pushed out by your diaphragm. Also feel how your chest expands in back as well as in front. Then immediately start breathing out through your mouth, letting the air out slowly, but not so slowly that you are trying to hold your breath. Then breathe in again. Try to let the breaths flow smoothly from one to the next, so that you are always breathing either out or in.

If you have trouble learning to breathe from the diaphragm instead of the chest, try this. Lie on your stomach on the carpet. Lift your shoulders by crossing your forearms on the carpet underneath your shoulders. Your forearms will be next to each other with each hand touching the opposite elbow, and your upper arms will be vertical. Now practice your breathing again. You will be able to feel your diaphragm moving, and the position of your arms will keep your shoulders still.

Step 4. Soft Eyes

The easiest way to understand soft eyes is to experience them. To find soft eyes, begin by staring at some object in front of you, not too far away. Try to block out everything else and just focus on that. Now your eyes are hard. Continue to look toward the object, but instead of focusing on it, allow yourself to see all around it. Notice how much you can see without moving your eyes. Your eyes are not focused directly on any one thing. They are soft. It feels as though not only can you see all around you on the outside, but on the inside as well.

Soft eyes are especially important in riding, but have their uses on the ground too. First, they are much less threatening to the horse than hard eyes, which is the focused look of the predator about to attack (think of a cat stalking a bird). But more importantly, they help you with your awareness of yourself in space, and they turn on your right brain.

When you are in left-brain mode, your thinking is *linear*, like these directions. Step one, step two and so on. Right-brain thinking is *holistic*; it takes all the steps and puts them together into a unit. For example, when you learn to mount, you have to think, "put my hand on the saddle with the reins in it, hold the stirrup with my other hand and put my foot in, put that hand on the mane, straighten up, push off, stand up, swing my leg over, sit down gently, pick up my stirrup"—or whatever method you use. That is all left-brain linear thinking. But after a while you don't think about it, you just do it, and all the steps flow together effortlessly. That's right-brain holistic thinking.

Left brain is verbal, right brain is not. So when you take a lesson and the instructor is talking to you, you're in left brain. When you ride by yourself, you can go into right-brain mode and everything comes together. That's why so often a person rides better when no one is around.

Left brain is controlling, right brain is not. So left-brain riding often frightens the horse. It tends to be rather white-knuckle if anything a little disturbing happens, while right brain just says, "I'm cool; piece of cake." One of the reasons instructors say "eyes up" when the horse is acting up is because when riders are frightened they virtually always stare with hard eyes at the horse's neck. When they look up, their eyes become softer and they are better able to follow the horse.

Horses' eyes can also be soft or hard. A horse who is being worked by a sympathetic trainer will usually have a soft eye. He is secure about giving up control for the moment and just working comfortably and holistically. A horse who is being worked abusively will have a hard eye because he feels the need to maintain control—another reason why abusive training is less successful than supportive training.

You can practice soft eyes very effectively while driving your car, especially in heavy traffic. The combination of being more aware of what's happening around you and thinking holistically about how to deal with those crazy drivers makes the commuting experience a little more bearable. You will then find it far easier to use soft eyes when you're having a problem with your horse.

Step 5. Longitudinal Centering (Teeter-Totter)

Unless your body is centered over your base, you can't keep your balance without tension. Teeter-totter develops your awareness of whether or not you are truly centered.

This exercise must be done *very* slowly, so that you are constantly aware of your balance and the tensions being created or released. Stand on a carpet in your stocking feet. Place your feet a few inches apart, so that they're under your hip joints and your knees are straight but not locked. Using soft eyes, without looking down, keep your body straight and gradually rock forward from your ankles until you start to lose your balance and have to take a step. Then rock just as slowly backward the same way. Now do the same thing again, but this time stop *before* you have to take a step. Next, rock forward again, but this time see if you can feel when your feet start to tense up, and stop. Then rock back until the balls of your feet are just *beginning* to come off the ground. Stay there, and notice the tension in your lower back, buttocks and thighs. Finally, come forward slowly, just until the tension disappears, and stop. Now you should be exactly centered over your feet, with no tension. Try to keep that centered position while you breathe, and shake out your arms.

Now sit down and lift up one foot so you can touch the bottom of it. Put a finger in the hollow under your second toe, then slide your finger straight down over the ball of your foot until you come to another little hollow. This spot is a bit sensitive, and is the point the martial arts people call the "bubbling spring." That's where your foot connects with the ground. Try the teeter-totter again, and you'll notice that as long as that "bubbling spring" is on the ground, you are fairly secure. But when it lifts up, you've lost your balance and will have to take a step to keep from falling.

Putting It All Together: Grounding

Stand again on a carpet in your stocking feet. Run through the five steps. Now think about your feet and how they feel on the ground. Then curl your toes up tightly, followed by the muscles in your feet, and continue all the way up your legs into your buttocks. Hold the tension and think about how your feet feel on the ground. Now let go of the tension, starting with your buttocks and going downward, breathing out as you do so. Try to feel all the tension and release it all. Notice how your feet feel on the ground now. They should feel as if they have grown roots. Smile.

As you become more aware of your grounding, you will become aware that when you start to tense up, the first thing that goes is your grounding. And when you reground, the tension leaves.

Practice the five steps as much as you can, not just when you're around your horse. They will help your confidence in any situation that makes you tense, from driving on the turnpike (you can ground into your seatbones, too) to an interview with your boss or your ex. By practicing them over and over, you fix them in your muscle memory so they will be there automatically when you need them. When you are working with your horse, by constantly—and, in time, automatically—running through the five steps and regrounding, you build your horse's confidence in himself as well as his trust in you.

Necessary and Useful Skills

Praising

You need to use this skill a lot! It's how the horse knows he did the right thing. Doing the right thing, so that others are happy with you, is more than just a moral behavior. To a herd and prey animal, it's survival. If you please the other members of your herd, they let you stay and protect you. If you don't, they drive you away. You can watch horses teach this concept to bratty younger horses. Mares teach it to their foals in a no-nonsense way, and older herd members teach the younger ones.

Thus, praise is one of your most successful tools, and should be the easiest to use. Praise can take the form of words, touch or treats. Usually you use all of these at different times. Allowing the horse to stop the exercise is also a form of praise—not because the horse hates the work and wants to stop, but because you are essentially saying, "Hey, you won!" which makes the horse feel happy and successful. This also carries over to the next training session, when the horse remembers and associates feelings of success with the work.

Praise should always be accompanied by a smile. This is not always easy to do when you're concentrating. It takes practice. But you will find that the more you smile for your horse, the more you will enjoy yourself.

Things to know about praise:

- It must occur close enough to the action you want to mark that it is easy for the horse to figure out what he did right (see Clicker Training, page 27).

- It must be sincere. Use it as a tool, not an emotion. If you've ever had the experience of someone telling you that you were "just absolutely *wonderful*" and spouting on at length about something you knew wasn't all that great, you know that insincere or overdone praise tends to be more aggravating than pleasing.

- It should not be used to calm a horse who is exhibiting undesirable behavior.

⋂ If you are using treats as part of praise, you have to be selective with
your words. Many horses learn to associate the words "good" or "good
boy" with a treat, and will stop whatever they're doing. They can also
associate treats with your tone of voice or even your thought, which is
why many people don't like to use treats. I find that if I say something
like "Gooooood, that's it," followed *immediately* by a cluck or some
other signal not to stop, they soon learn to wait for a specific signal to
stop and get a treat.

Bothering

Bothering is a term Parelli uses to describe how you ask the horse to do something
that he doesn't offer on his own. Think of trying to get someone to move over so
you can get by in a crowded room. You say, "Excuse me," and wait a couple of seconds, then do it again, maybe a little louder. Eventually the person notices and
moves over. Immediately you stop bothering them, smile and thank them. If you
don't get a reaction after a reasonable time, you might tap them lightly on the
shoulder or back, to attract their attention, but unless you are looking for a fight,
you would never escalate your actions to the point of aggression.

The essence of bothering is repetition. Think Chinese water torture—a drop
of water falling on your head every second. Supposedly, it will drive you crazy
after awhile, and you will do anything to get it to stop.

Bothering generally takes the form of tapping or gentle prodding, or even
gesturing. For it to be effective, it must stop the instant the horse begins to
respond, and be followed by praise.

Punishment

Punishment is *very rarely* used. Only if the horse does something deliberate,
unprovoked and calculated that is not the result of fear or defensiveness and is
simply not acceptable, should you punish him. If you have the right kind of relationship with your horse, simply snarling at him and walking away is punishment enough, or perhaps a sharp slap. Here are a couple of examples.

Example 1: You have been out of town on business for 10 days. When you
return, you go to see your horse. You go in to talk to him and he gives you a
sharp nip, which is contrary to his usual behavior (horses tend to get offended
at perceived neglect). Your instant response: "Owwww! That *hurt!*" You back
away and sulk. The horse's response should be a very apologetic look, dropping
his head, etc. At which point you say, "It's all right, I still love you. But let's be
more careful, okay?" If he raises his head and gives you a "gotcha" look, walk
away and stay away for five or 10 minutes. When you come back he should look
somewhat submissive and welcoming, and you can then smile and pat him as
though nothing had happened.

Example 2: You are grooming your young horse and he starts to paw. You
ignore it until he stops for a few seconds, then you praise. A few minutes later
the whole scenario is repeated. Then a third time, and you notice he's watching

you pretty carefully and his pawing is also getting a bit close to striking. You know your grooming is not the cause, nor is he acting tense or impatient in any other way. He's had his turnout, as well. This is an entirely new game he is playing. Again you wait for him to stop, and praise when he does. But the fourth time, when his foot comes off the ground to start his little game again, he receives a noisy, though not painful, slap on the neck, and a sharp "That's enough!" The horse's response should be to jump a little, look at you rather surprised, perhaps lick and chew after a moment, "Oh, I guess you really don't want me to do that, do you? Duuuuuh." *His "apology" is followed by immediate forgiveness from you.* Smiles and pats.

Punishment should not inflict real pain. The horse will either block it out, or become frightened and forget what the punishment was about. It should be as brief as possible, just long enough for the horse to react with an "Oops. Wrong thing to do." If it doesn't immediately cause the desired change in behavior and attitude, you've missed something, so don't keep trying.

And, most important, *punishment is always the very last resort!* If you're wrong, you've treated the horse unfairly, and you can't take it back.

Control With Your Center

The body's center is more than just a place. On the one hand, it is your physical center of gravity. Its location is low in your pelvis, near your spine at the point where it curves furthest forward. To balance, your center must be over your base, as you saw in the teeter-totter exercise (page 10).

However, your center is also a center of energy, and it therefore affects those around you. Thus, it is one of the principal tools you can use to tell the horse the direction in which you want him to move. Think of playing tag with someone. If you run to her left, she will move to her right to get away. If you get in front of her, she'll turn and go the other way. Your center is blocking her center. Horses, as prey animals, are very conscious of how a predator's center is moving in relation to theirs as the predator tries to catch them.

If you are working close to a horse who is standing still or moving very slowly, the movements you make should be quite small. For example, if you are asking the horse to step to the side with a foreleg and he starts to back instead, you should move perhaps one step to get behind *his* center a little bit, so he stops backing up. If you are far away from the horse and he is moving rapidly, your movements may have to be much greater, as when you are free-longeing and want the horse to stop and turn around when he is galloping. You may have to run across the arena to get far enough ahead of him so that he has time to stop.

As you move, your projected path will tell the horse to stop, turn or keep moving. It takes a fair amount of practice to move your center in relation to the horse's center so that you give clear directions, rather than confusing him. This way of using your center is called using your *active* center. Many of the problems people have with longeing, free-longeing and round pen work are the result of using their centers incorrectly—being in the wrong place at the wrong time.

You can also use your center passively. When you are in front of someone and you stand aside to let them go through a doorway, you have let your center be passive. When you play follow the leader, the leader's center is passive. He invites the others to follow him, but he doesn't chase them as in tag. When you lead a horse, your center is passive as long as he is following obediently. But if he tries to get past you, your center becomes active to block him. When you are working a horse either free or on the longe line, your center is active, telling him to move; but if you allow your center to become passive he will gradually slow down and stop.

As you become more aware of how your center affects your horse, you will find that your ability to control him without being aggressive improves enormously.

Dingo

Dingo is a Tteam technique to teach the horse to move forward in response to a light signal.

Stand by the horse's head facing more or less forward, with the lead held in your left hand and a long stick in your right hand. First stroke the horse with the stick on the *top* of his croup gently but firmly several times, to let him know you aren't going to hurt him. If he is afraid of the whip, you need to do some desensitizing (see friendly game on page 30). Then tap the horse lightly on the croup with your stick: tap—*tap*—**tap.** As you tap, face as much forward as you can and walk in place a little to give the horse the idea. Wait three seconds and if you get no response, tap again a little harder. Look for any response whatsoever from the horse—perhaps an ear or tail flick or the head raised—and thereafter continue to tap at the level that indicated the horse was somewhat bothered. *Do not focus on the horse's head.* You can glance back at his croup when you are tapping with the stick, but immediately turn again to look in the direction you want to go. If you get a step forward, praise, wait, then ask again. If the horse responds at the first or second tap of the sequence, of course stop tapping.

If you don't get movement after several tries, add a cluck and a soft leading tug with the line, but don't keep pressure on it. Look for a weight shift or any other indication that the horse is thinking about moving, and praise. If you still get no response in the way of movement after five or six more taps, tap and then immediately lead the horse's head strongly to the left. This will force him to move a foot to catch his balance. Instantly smile and praise him enthusiastically, take the stick away and give him a treat. Do this several more times until the horse is taking the first step by himself, showing that he has made the connection between the tap, taking the step and receiving the treat. Then ask him to take an additional step before he receives the treat. Continue to shape the behavior by gradually asking for additional steps until the horse is following easily.

Lowering the Horse's Head

One of the most useful skills for gaining the horse's respect is to teach him to drop his head. This is a submissive pose, indicating the horse feels relaxed and

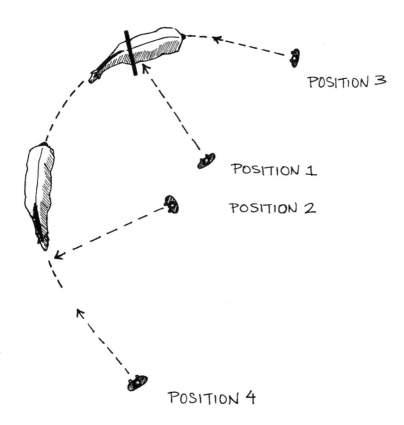

POSITION 3

POSITION 1

POSITION 2

POSITION 4

POSITION OF CENTER DURING
LONGEING AND FREE-LONGEING.

Position 1: Correct position for maintaining the horse's gait. The projected path is toward a point slightly behind the horse's center.

Position 2: Most common mistake. The handler's body is turned so that the projected path is ahead of the horse's center, blocking his movement.

Position 3: Position for sending the horse strongly forward when free-longeing. Positions between 1 and 3 will send the horse forward more or less, depending on the angle.

Position 4: Position for blocking, to stop or prepare for a turn. Positions between 2 and 4 will block the horse more or less, depending on the angle.

willing to accept direction. He gives up control to the trainer when he drops his head. A frightened horse will raise his head and look past you as though you weren't there, staring around in a panicky way with hard eyes. When you get him to drop his head, his eyes go soft, his emotions calm down and he begins to listen again.

TALKING HORSES

Lowering the head seems to be common to many creatures. In humans, a submissive posture always includes a bowed head. Think of prayer. Submission is not always a bad thing, and is not the same as slavery. In a partnership relationship, it is simply the willingness to give up control when it's appropriate. Perhaps that's why we nod our heads when we agree.

Head lowering is created by pressure just behind the poll, which can be done in any one of several ways. One method is to stand beside the horse and run your hand up his neck as far as he will allow, then press or tap or squeeze on top of his neck—but don't try to *push* the horse's head down. Look for a softening of the horse's resistance first, rather than an actual drop of the head. As soon as you feel that little yield, praise and slide your hand back down his neck. Wait a moment and repeat. You can also use the clicker when you feel the yield. Continue, asking for a little more as the horse becomes more confident, until his head is below yours, and eventually his poll is below his withers.

The second method is done using the halter—either a Parelli halter or a flat halter with a 30-inch chain or zephyr string (page 17). Squat in front of the horse and place your hands gently on either side of the halter nose or, if you are using a chain, holding the halter nose with one hand and the chain with the other. Gently pull down and again look for the yield, or softening of resistance, then relax the pressure and praise.

You can also combine both methods. Using a flat halter and chain, stand to the left of the horse's neck, and apply the chain with your left hand and pressure with your right hand on the top of his neck. Whatever method you use, as you work with the horse, try not to tilt your head back to look up at him. This is the equivalent of him raising his head, and sends a mixed signal. Instead, look up with your eyes only.

Teaching the horse to be led with his head behind your shoulder (see Leading: Rushing Ahead While, page 87) is another exercise in submission training.

Horse-Handling Gear

Halters, lead ropes, sticks and working space are the basic ground gear you need to work with all but the most advanced horses. There are also some more specialized tools. Like all equipment, these tools can be kind or abusive, depending on how you handle them. Your horse's overall physical health is also a factor that must be considered, and supported when necessary.

TALKING HORSES

One of my Internet friends ground trains her horses on her 75-acre farm with no equipment. If they don't like what she's doing, they leave, and may or may not come back later, so she is always forced to find out what works best from the horse's viewpoint. As a result, her horses are extremely cooperative and trusting. She has my greatest respect and admiration!

Halters

Halters are either flat and made of leather or nylon, or round and made of single or double rope. The material may be soft, smooth and flexible, or hard and abrasive. The significant pressure points are around the nose and across the poll. The narrower and rougher the material, the more opportunity for abuse. However, if the material is too friendly, the horse can become disrespectful.

Flat halters are usually made so that they can be unfastened either at the crownpiece or the throatlatch. If unfastened at the throat latch, they are easy to slip on and off. They have rings on the sides so that it is easy to fasten crossties to them. Some halters are made with a breakaway arrangement, so a horse can be safely left with his halter on.

Rope halters only unfasten at the crownpiece, and only have a ring or loop under the jaw. Being narrower, when used with just a lead rope, they offer more control than a flat halter.

The halter should be fitted so that the nosepiece does not rest so low that it presses on the unsupported bone at the lower end of the horse's nose, nor so high that it rubs against his cheekbones. It should be large enough around the jaw that the horse can open his mouth comfortably, but not so large that he could get a foot caught in it. Unlike the throat latch of a bridle, the halter throat latch should lie fairly close to the horse's throttle. (Also see Appendix B for information about halters.)

Lead Ropes and Chains

Lead ropes are made of natural or artificial fibers. Cotton is soft to the hand, but tends to rot and break over time and is easily shredded by a mouthy horse. Sisal is tougher, but is very rough on your hands. Braided nylon and Dacron are soft and flexible, but will burn your hand more easily if the rope pulls through it suddenly.

A good length is eight to 10 feet for ordinary work. Too short and you have to let go if the horse makes any trouble at all; too long and you are constantly getting tangled in it. The Parelli rope is 12 feet, which is useful for the games. A figure-8 knot (page 189) at the end of the rope keeps it from slipping through your hand, and can be undone easily if necessary.

Lead chains are used with a flat halter to add extra control. They usually come with a leather or nylon strap or a braided rope. The leather strap is nice to handle when broken in, but can be rather clumsy when stiff and new. For ordinary work the chain should be about 18 inches. That is long enough to run across the horse's nose if necessary, but if it is attached to the jaw ring you don't have too much chain in your hand. For more refined work, the chain should be 30 inches, which gives control of the horse's poll as well.

You can also create a lead that offers more control than just the flat halter, but is less severe than a chain. This is especially useful if a horse has been badly abused with a chain. Linda Tellington-Jones calls this a *zephyr lead*, and it consists of a length of soft quarter-inch braided line with a snap on one end and a ring or loop on the other, to which you can attach an ordinary lead rope. The zephyr lead can be used instead of the chain, and acts very much like a Parelli halter.

Attaching Ropes and Chains to the Halter

For general leading purposes, taking an obedient horse from here to there, the lead is attached to the center ring under the horse's jaw. This gives a straight pull forward and creates some pressure on the poll, as well. If you attach the lead to the side ring, the halter will tend to twist and get in the horse's eye, and you won't get even pressure on the poll.

If you have a lead with a long chain, it is not safe to run the chain through the halter ring and back to the ring at the end of the lead. Instead, run the extra chain through the jaw ring, then through the side ring from inside to outside, then up to the upper ring.

TALKING HORSES

You see long chains doubled through the jaw ring all the time, because holding the chain in your hand is awkward, but it is all too easy for the horse to put his foot through the loop in the chain. In fact, the very first time I tried this, that's what happened. Fortunately the horse didn't panic, but stood quietly while we got him undone. I think it scared me worse than it scared him!

When you want to use the chain for additional control, the Tteam method of attaching a chain to a flat halter is safe, effective and humane—totally unlike the usual, potentially abusive method. It requires a 30-inch chain rather than the usual 18-inch one. Begin by running the snap through the left ring on the halter noseband, from outside to inside and then up. Next, bring it down across the outside front of the noseband, then through the right ring from below, inside to outside. Finally, bring the snap up and fasten it to the upper ring on the right side.

With the chain positioned this way, when you apply pressure, it never goes directly on the horse's sensitive nose, especially not on the lower end where the nose bone is unsupported. Instead, the pressure is mostly on the halter noseband,

and also on the crownpiece, which gives it a head-lowering effect. Thus you gain more control than with the halter alone, but without creating serious discomfort, which can lead to rearing and fighting.

If you are using a shorter chain, you have the choice of putting it on in the same nonthreatening way, but taking it only as far as the other nose ring and fastening it there (which will give you more stopping power), or of running it from underneath the first ring through it from inside to outside, then up to the upper ring on the same side (which will give you more head-lowering effect).

Never use a chain across the horse's nose if you are trying to get him to come forward. The harder you pull on it, the more it stops him. If you are working with a horse who is resisting going forward by trying to spin around, use a separate rope on the jaw ring to lead him, and only use the chain when he tries to break away. I do not recommend running the chain *under* the horse's jaw at any time. The effect is to make the horse rear, which is hardly desirable.

Sticks

Whether you call it a wand, a carrot stick, a crop or a whip, the first thing to know is that it is not intended as an instrument of punishment. A stick is nothing more than an extension of your arm, so you can signal the horse more clearly. It should be comfortable for you to hold, have good balance and not be so flexible that you sting the horse with it accidentally. The handle should have a knob of some sort so it doesn't slip out of your hand, and should be made so that if you use it to tap the horse, it isn't too uncomfortable for him. It's handy to have a loop on the end to which you can attach things like plastic bags, to accustom the horse to odd things waving around. The Parelli carrot stick with a removable lash is useful for many different training exercises, though it's a tad long and heavy for many women.

Spaces

You need space to work a horse in. Most of the time for ground work the space doesn't need to be very large. Round pens are good not only for round pen work, but sometimes for other situations, because they have no corners the horse can hide in. Paddocks or corrals, square or rectangular and not less than 40 nor more than 80 feet on a side, are useful where you need straight lines or a corner. You can round off the corners by using barrels or rails to give you something approaching a round pen, when needed. Rings or arenas are necessary, especially if the horse doesn't have a large turnout area with good footing. They should be not less than 60 by 100 feet—larger for a larger horse—to allow him room to lengthen and stretch himself without fear of falling or running into a wall.

Special Tools

The Twitch. A horse who has had very good handling and training will rarely need anything more than a halter and lead to control him, but there are times when we need more control. Perhaps you have only had the horse a short time and need to do something essential to him that he won't allow. Or perhaps he needs a treatment that is painful, and you're concerned about having to hurt him. A twitch is a kindness in such a case.

Twitches have an undeservedly bad reputation. Of course they can be used abusively, but so can almost anything else you can name. For example, a twitch should *never* be applied anywhere except to the horse's lip (certainly not to the ear or tongue!), nearly always his upper lip. If there is an injury on the upper lip it can also be applied, carefully, to the lower lip with the same effect.

A correctly applied twitch works by releasing endorphins (natural tranquilizers produced by the horse's own body), which relieve tension and mild pain. It does *not* work, as so many people think, by "causing so much pain that the horse stands still." I have yet to meet a horse who stood still because he was in severe pain, unless he was also in shock and near death. Further, before the days of tranquilizers, when the twitch was one of the few tools a vet had to control a horse during minor surgery, you could walk up to any horse in my stable and put a twitch on him with very little protest, take it off after 10 minutes, and put it back on as many times as you needed to without any problem. I doubt if a horse who was being caused "severe pain" by the twitch would allow it to be put back on a second time!

Before ever using a twitch on your horse, however, you need to get him accustomed to the idea of having something around his upper lip. (Do *not* crosstie him when you are doing anything—especially around his head—that he may not like. A hard hat would be a good idea, too.)

Rubbing the lip with the flat of your hand is the first step. Most horses enjoy this, and will wiggle their lips around enthusiastically. Next, take the end of the lip, which is sort of like a big soft button, grasp it in your hand and hold gently for a moment, then release. Gradually increase the length of time you hold the lip and the degree of pressure until the horse will allow his lip to be firmly held in your hand for 30 seconds or so. (None of this will do any good if the horse doesn't trust his handler!)

When the horse accepts having his lip held, he can then be introduced to the one-person twitch—a small, aluminum twitch that looks like a jar opener with a string on the end. Let him look at it and sniff it first, then rub it over his nose so he finds out it won't bite him. Putting the twitch on is the part that fusses the horse, so that should be done as quickly as possible, but without being so hasty that you frighten the horse with fast moves.

Assuming you are right-handed, stand on the horse's right side, hold the lead shank in your left hand and slip the twitch over your right wrist. Grasp as much of his upper lip in your right hand as you can, then use your left hand to slip the open twitch over the lip until it is above the "button." Quickly but smoothly close the twitch and hold the handles firmly closed.

Once the twitch is on, the horse may toss his head around a bit, but when he finds that the twitch won't come off and doesn't hurt, he will stop. Don't allow him to rub against anything or he may rub it off, which you don't want. If he shakes it off, steady him and quietly put it on again.

When he settles down, wind the string around the handles to keep them closed. Fasten the clip to the side halter ring, making sure you don't lose the tension on the twitch. Let him wear it for a minute or two while you scratch him or groom him or something else he doesn't mind. Then remove it, again being as quick as possible. As soon as it is off, rub his upper lip with the flat of your hand to restore circulation. (It also reminds him that touching his upper lip is still okay.) Reward him and put him away.

Practice with the metal twitch regularly until he will let you put it on and stand with a minimum of fuss. The metal twitch is adequate for any work where the horse just needs reminding and a little distraction, rather than restraint.

For control in more difficult situations a wood-and-rope (*not* chain) twitch is necessary. If you only have one horse, chances are you will only need strong restraint when you also need a vet, who has the wood twitch and knows how to use it. Your training with the metal twitch, if you did it right, will make the vet's job with the wood twitch much easier.

If you do want to use a wood twitch, you'll probably have to make your own, but it isn't difficult. The best handle is a short (about two feet long) axe handle, which is oval (not round) in cross section, so it can be held easily without untwisting on you. You can buy them in hardware stores. Drill a hole large enough to accept a piece of soft cotton clothesline or quarter-inch braided rope, just far enough from the end so that the wood won't split. Run the line through and make a loop about six or eight inches long. Tie it off (use a good square knot, see page 190) and slide the knot up close to the handle. (If you're not sure about the length of the loop, try it on the horse before you cut it completely off.)

The easiest way to handle the wood twitch is to have one person slip the loop over her right hand, and then take the horse's lip and slip the loop over it, just as with the metal twitch. Then, a second person twists the handle to tighten it (it's easiest to use two hands to twist it.) However, if you have no helper and the horse is reasonable, you can put the butt of the handle under your right arm to steady it while you twist with the left. Another reason you want the oval-shaped handle is because you can hold it this way without it slipping. You have to twist it quite a number of turns, until the twists start to double up on themselves. Most people make the twitch too loose at first, rather than too tight, and the horse promptly shakes it off.

The wood twitch can be tightened more firmly than the metal one. The longer handle gives more leverage for controlling a fussy horse, and at the same time enables the handler to stand far enough away to be safe if the horse blows up. Whichever twitch you are using, *it must be removed at least once every 15 minutes* and the horse's lip rubbed to restore circulation. After a few minutes it can be reapplied.

Besides teaching the horse to accept having his upper lip held on to, the most important part of preventing him from fighting the twitch is putting it on *before* he gets upset. Very often a person will start something with the horse that upsets him, and he starts to resist. She then tries to make him behave by punishing him, which of course upsets him more. Then, when the horse is thoroughly frightened and angry, the handler approaches him with the twitch and tries to grab him by the nose. Since the horse is by now convinced the handler is trying to kill him, he reacts with either aggression or panic, endangering everyone including himself.

It is much more effective if you have the twitch ready any time you think the horse might not like what's happening to him. Then you put it on before you both get upset. Let's say you're are going to clip his ears. You don't expect him to mind, because he allows you to handle his ears with no problem. But when you start clipping, every time you bring the clippers near his ears he tosses his head in spite of your helper trying to keep it steady. After you have tried for a few minutes, with calmness and patience, to get him to hold still, and you aren't succeeding, quietly put the twitch on. You can then go ahead and clip his ears (unless he has been badly abused some other time, in which case you should forget it, at least for the moment). Thereafter, each time you clip his ears, start without the twitch, but put it on when it becomes necessary. If the rest of your handling is correct, you should find that you no longer need the twitch after a while.

If the horse has been badly mishandled with the twitch and is very reluctant to have it put on, you should probably not attempt it unless you are very experienced. A horse who is frightened about his head will rear and strike out with his front feet. Since you are, of necessity, standing almost directly in front of him, you are in extreme danger. A broken shoulder or a fractured skull is a real possibility.

Anyone, no matter how experienced, should wear a hard hat when working with a twitch on a nervous horse. Even if the horse allows the twitch to be put on without difficulty, the holder should *never* stand directly in front of him. A horse being held in any kind of restraint will sometimes explode without warning. The work area should also be clear of any obstacles that could injure either the horse or the handlers.

TALKING HORSES

I used to have a pony, Timmy, who just hated the vet. All vets. Once the vet entered the stable, Timmy became impossible to deal with, although he was normally a well-behaved little person. So we developed a system. When the vet came to give shots, or anything that required him to handle Timmy, we would watch for his car. Luckily, Timmy lived at the other end of the stable. As soon as the car appeared, we would go and put the twitch on Timmy, who was perfectly comfortable with it for things like having his ears clipped. The vet would come in and do Timmy first. With the twitch on, Timmy stood calmly and quietly for his treatment. The vet would finish, we would remove the twitch, and Timmy would go and hide in the corner of his stall, not coming out until the vet had left the farm.

It is important to understand that it is not the twitch itself that bothers the horse; it is the fear of being restrained when he feels threatened. Some horses are really claustrophobic about being restrained. In these days of tranquilizers, it is not necessary to risk life and limb. If the horse will accept restraint quietly—and the twitch is usually the most effective and humane method—then use it. If not, don't fight it. This is one time when you don't "say no to drugs."

War Bridle

This is an awful-sounding name for something that, if applied and used correctly, is perfectly safe and kind, because the horse is the one who decides how hard to pull.

Like the wood twitch, it is a build-it-yourself kind of tool. The best thing to use is a piece of clothesline, but two pieces of baling twine tied together with a square knot work just as well, and can nearly always be found wherever there are horses. Smooth, soft rope is not as desirable, since you want to be able to cause a bit of discomfort. The total length should be about 14 to 16 feet. Tie a bowline (page 189) in one end of the rope to make a small loop perhaps one and a half inches long. Pass the other end through the small loop to make a large loop, slightly larger than the horse's head is long.

As with the twitch, if at all possible you should prepare the horse by handling the area where the war bridle will be applied, which is under the horse's upper lip, over his upper gum. Most of the training systems recommend working with the horse's mouth anyway, to get him accustomed to the bit and to release the sort of mouth tensions that often lead to nipping. Slip your hand up under the horse's upper lip and rub back and forth over the gums. If the gums seem dry, try wetting your hand first. Most horses think this is kind of fun, but be careful the wiggling upper lip doesn't push your fingers down between his teeth—not that he will bite you on purpose, but even a little bit of pressure is pretty uncomfortable on your hands. Playing with his gums regularly will mean that when you put on the war bridle, he will not find it especially threatening.

To put on a war bridle, first place it behind his ears, but not on top of the halter crown, with the small loop just below his left ear and the big loop hanging just below his mouth. Hold the leftover rope in your right hand. Then take the bottom of the large loop in the palm of your left hand as though it were a bit, slip your fingers under his lip and over his gum and hold the rope there for a second while you take up the slack with your right hand. Only take just enough pressure so the horse can't wiggle it off with his lip and get it into his mouth (just like he tried to do with your fingers). If he does, just ease the rope a little and put it back on his gum again.

The war bridle asks the horse to come forward with pressure on his poll. For some reason, the pressure on his gum does not give him a conflicting command to go backward, as would pressure on his mouth or nose. You simply hold a slightly uncomfortable pressure and wait for the horse to step forward in an effort to relieve it. When he does, ease the pressure immediately—though not enough to allow him to spit out the rope—and smile and praise. If he attempts to get away by rearing or running backward, try to maintain the same pressure, not escalate it, and follow him until he comes down or stops going backward. You can always walk forward faster than a horse can walk backward.

Never pull painfully hard or jerk on a war bridle. Quiet patience will bring the right result. Aggression and inflicting pain will not.

Nutritional and Physiological Aids

More often than not, unacceptable behavior is caused by pain or physiological or nutritional problems. Always look for these as possible solutions if you see an unusual change in behavior, or if you have a behavior that doesn't respond to any reasonable training techniques.

Mineral balance is a very common cause of tension, especially the phosphorus–calcium–magnesium ratio. This should be in a ratio of one part phosphorus to two parts calcium to one part magnesium, with the horse getting phosphorus from concentrates and calcium and magnesium from hay. Unfortunately, horses often get too much grain, and the hay (because of the land it grows on and improper fertilization) lacks calcium and magnesium. These minerals are the principal components of limestone, which is one reason why Kentucky and Virginia are so highly regarded as horse breeding country. Much of the local soil contains high amounts of limestone, which is absorbed into the grass and hay. Lack of calcium causes muscle cramps and tension, while lack of magnesium causes jitteriness and irritability.

Homeopathy has been the subject of a great deal of study into its effect on horse behavior, especially fear and tension. Many people have been surprised and pleased by the changes in their horses after using this simple and quite safe form of treatment. Arnica Montana for bruises and stiffness is a very common homeopathic remedy. Bach Flower Essences are similar to homeopathics. Rescue Remedy is a Bach Flower Essence used for any stress situation.

Feed supplements, which can be found in catalogs and feed stores, can improve a horse's behavior by improving his total health, or by homing in on a particular weakness. Consultation with your veterinarian is one of the better ways to decide about supplements.

Acupuncture has been found to be very successful in diagnosing and treating pain and dysfunction. Horses in pain are likely to be irritable and often fearful, because they feel unable to escape in time of trouble.

Chiropractic is gaining more credibility as serious trained practitioners enter the field. Used with applied kinesiology (muscle testing) as a diagnostic technique, many sources of pain can be identified and corrected, with overall positive results in behavior as well as performance.

Massage incorporates a number of different techniques. It has been my observation that while most people swear by their own particular practitioner, many methods have shown good results in diverse situations.

Whatever approach you choose, what is most important is that you explore all the options when you have a problem, rather than limiting yourself and your horse to only the traditional training methods.

From the Horse to You

Receiving communication from the horse means you must learn how the horse talks to you and what he is saying. This is not an easy task, and requires many years of experience. Even skilled horsemen sometimes misinterpret the horse's actions. So all you can do is make educated guesses based on what you see, and then judge from the results you get whether or not you guessed right.

We can begin by learning some of the more obvious ways a horse shows his feelings. A horse who is relaxed and confident carries his head fairly low, that is, his poll (see "Parts of the Horse" in Appendix B) is not more than slightly above his withers. Part of the reason for this lies in the way the horse sees. Our vision is similar to the inside of a sphere, but a horse's vision is a comparatively narrow horizontal band. Think of a large hula hoop floating around him. When his head is down, he can see things right in front of him but he can't see distant objects. So if he hears a sound that worries him his head comes up, as does his field of vision, so he can see farther away. When he is comfortable with what's going on, his head is down so that he can see where to place his feet or where the juiciest grass is. A horse who trusts his handler's judgment is willing to let the handler do the looking around.

When a horse is relaxed, his ears are in a neutral position, neither pricked forward nor flattened back, and are quiet, not constantly flicking back and forth. A horse's ears are tied to his eyes, in the sense that his ear is always turned to where the eye is focused. If the horse is relaxed and meditative, his eye is focused inward—a soft eye—so his ears are as well.

Unless he has reason to move, his feet are still, and he may be resting a hind leg by cocking his foot up onto the toe. His tail is hanging down softly, and is not clamped into his buttocks. If he swishes it because of flies, it will be a fairly slow, sweeping movement. There won't be any obvious wrinkles around his eyes or mouth. If he's really relaxed, his lower lip may droop away from his upper lip.

If you come into his space politely, he will reach out with his nose and give you a greeting sniff. If you know where to scratch him, he will respond with movements of pleasure, stretching his neck out and flapping his lips, and if you stand in range of his head, he will probably try to return the favor by scratching you back!

If you are working with him and he is being attentive and confident, his eyes and ears will be either toward you, or soft, depending on whether he is listening for directions or processing what is happening. If he is thinking about something and trying to figure it out, he will blink his eyes rapidly or lick his lips or chew. (If you try it yourself, you will find that each of these actions makes you internalize your thinking.) When you finish a ground exercise he will come toward you, but not in the least aggressively. He will have a kind look and will look directly at you, not over your head or past your shoulder. This is called "giving you both eyes," showing interest and submission.

If he starts to get frustrated or confused you may see wrinkles around his mouth or eyes. Then his head will come up, indicating that he no longer wishes to submit, and his ears may sour. His movement may get more rapid, or he may stop altogether. He may turn his head away and refuse to meet your eye.

If he gets really angry with you, or really frightened, he will try to get away from you, either by running away or, if that is not possible, driving you away from him. If he is frightened he will tend to kick, and probably not with his ears back, except as necessary to follow you if you are behind him. His tail will be firmly clamped to his buttocks. A frightened horse doesn't want to do anything aggressive, but if pressured and trapped, he will kick even someone he cares about.

TALKING HORSES

A horse must clamp his tail to his buttocks in order to kick with both hind legs. The old horse traders used to demonstrate how gentle a horse was by taking his tail and draping it over their shoulders, then sitting on the horse's hocks. Of course, with his tail held away from his buttocks, the horse couldn't kick anyway!

An angry horse will flatten his ears, raise his head and perhaps show the whites of his eyes. If you persist in threatening him, he may charge at you and try to bite, or wheel at the last moment and kick out. Not something you want to experience! Usually, however, if you have a good overall relationship with the horse, he will let you know he's annoyed but will not attempt to hurt you directly.

If you listen to the quiet things your horse says, he won't have to "shout" with undesirable behavior.

THE SCHOOLS

There are currently four excellent systems for building a good relationship with your horse through ground work. They are clicker or positive reinforcement training, Parelli Natural Horse-Man-Ship, round pen training and Tteam (Tellington-Jones Equine Awareness Method). They are all good systems. Each one of them seems to work best for certain people, certain horses or certain situations.

Whichever methods you decide to use, you must be willing to spend the time to learn them and understand them if they are to be of any use to you or your horse. That might sound tedious, but of course it doesn't all have to be learned at once. You and the horse can have a lot of fun and learn a lot from each other by spending 10 or 15 minutes on ground training before every ride. It is important, however, to follow all the steps in any system you're working with, at least until you have a very thorough understanding of it. Shortcuts just confuse and frustrate the horse.

All four systems have some things in common. First, they do not train using abusive punishment, although some of them involve causing the horse a certain amount of mild discomfort. They emphasize gentle but firm, nonconfrontational handling.

Second, they all require a high degree of observation on the part of the trainer, both of how the horse is responding physically and of his attitude. The best training methods are based on the trainer either offering a positive reward such as a treat, or stopping something that is annoying (*not* painful), such as tapping with a stick, when the horse responds. *You have to learn the physical skill of noticing the exact moment that the horse responds, and instantly responding.* Parelli talks about the "try." You have to notice when the horse is beginning to get the idea and starts to *try* to do it. If you are quick to see the try, the horse will continue to build on his behavior in that direction. If you miss it, he'll figure he's wrong and try something else. It takes a lot of practice!

Third, to some extent they all use the concept of advance and retreat. This is an extremely important concept when you are dealing with a nervous animal. It involves exposing the horse very briefly to the thing that frightens him—so briefly that by the time he realizes it's there, it's already gone. The frightening thing may be touching a part of his body that he doesn't like touched. It may be walking in his direction if he is afraid of being caught. It may be starting to mount. Whatever it is, you start, and then stop before he has time to worry about it. Or you start, and when he shows that he is beginning to feel a little uncomfortable, you back away.

One analogy most people find useful is a first date. Two people go out and seem to enjoy each other's company. Toward the end of the evening, one of them makes a little pass. If the other person indicates discomfort, the first person may do one of two things. The first is to immediately back off. "I hear you and I respect your decision." After a while, if things still seem congenial, another pass is made. This time, since the one who made the pass has shown a willingness to back off as soon as asked, the other person is confident about accepting the increased closeness. "I am pretty sure that if I ask you to stop at any time, you will." However, if, when the first pass is made, the recipient's discomfort is ignored and the pass continues or even escalates, the reaction is a feeling of fear and being trapped. "You're not listening to me. You don't care how I feel, only about yourself." Trust and confidence are damaged, and will not return easily, if ever.

Observing the horse's reactions to *your* behavior, and giving him reason to believe he can trust you not to do things to him that he can't deal with, are the basis of successful training. Notice that I say, "things he can't deal with." It is *his* expectations that are important, not yours. Often we think that because most horses can deal with something, all horses can. Not true. Every horse is an individual, with his own makeup and his own history. Whatever training method you are using, you have to observe the responses you are getting and not second-guess your horse.

The four training systems I have mentioned are explained briefly here, and their application to many common problems will be discussed throughout this book.

Clicker Training

Clicker training, also called positive reinforcement training, is based on a system originally developed to train marine mammals. Obviously, you can't put a halter on a dolphin or chase him with a longe whip, so a way had to be found to get the animal to *want* to perform the desired task. The theory is simple. You begin by teaching the animal that when he hears a certain sound, that sound will be followed by a treat. The sound can be anything, but the most effective for training is the sharp click produced by the child's toy that we used to call a cricket—a piece of spring steel set in a box that makes a click sound when pressed with your thumb.

Once the animal has made the association between the click and the treat, the next step is to teach him that *he can control the click.* This is the whole basis of clicker training. Rather than compelling the animal to perform, you allow him to choose to do so by choosing to get a reward. In essence, he is in control. If he does the right thing, *he* can get *you* to give him a treat. Thus it is an extremely unthreatening training method, and very forgiving. At the very worst, the animal may get frustrated if the trainer is incompetent, but he never feels frightened.

Targeting is the way you teach most animals, including horses, that they can control the click, and thus the treat. You usually begin with the horse in his stall, with a breast chain or something similar to keep him from walking out. Standing outside the stall and using almost any object of moderate size, such as a brush or the plastic top of a supplement tub, you hold it in front of the horse a foot or so away. Out of curiosity, he pokes his nose out and gives it a sniff, touching it in the process. When he touches it, you click, followed by a treat. Then you hold it up again. Again he touches, click, treat. Usually after a few times he decides to see if he can avoid the target and just get to the treat, so you back out of reach, but keep holding the target where he will bump it, even if by accident. After awhile—in many cases, an amazingly short time—the horse makes the connection. "All I have to do to get something tasty is to touch this stupid thing with my nose. Gloryosky! The world is my oyster!"

The next step is the hard one. It cannot begin until the horse clearly understands, after plenty of practice, that he *can* get that treat any time he tries. Then you have to "shape" his behavior, that is, he must learn that there are different ways to get a treat besides just targeting, so he has to learn to try different things—to experiment, as it were. Say you decide to teach him to hold the target instead of just touching it. You hold up the target. He touches it. Nothing happens. "What's this? I touched it and it didn't work. The magic button is broken!" He touches it several more times; still nothing. Then he changes his behavior just a little bit. Instead of bumping it with his nose, he wiggles his upper lip around on it. Click! Treat! Hmmmmm.

He tries again, touching, nothing happens, maybe tries some other things, but none of them work. Eventually, the upper lip wiggles again on the target, and bingo! Once he is consistently wiggling his lip, then you start withholding the click until he takes a further step. Maybe opening his mouth a little. Gradually, you shape his behavior until he holds the target in his mouth. Some horses will learn this in half an hour; others may take days. Or you might have to try to teach him some other behavior that is more natural to him, such as touching the target when it is different places, and eventually walking to where it is and touching it.

Since clicker training is based on the horse offering the behavior in the first place, you have the most success asking for the sort of behavior he will offer naturally. If he is pawing, eventually he will stop for a moment and you can click for that and then shape the behavior to teach him not to paw (see Pawing From Nervousness, page 119). However, if you want to *teach* him to paw (say, so he can "count"), and he doesn't offer that behavior naturally, you have to use some sort of stimulus, like a tap with a stick, to start him picking up a foot, and shape from there. What you're really doing here is adding a different training method. No problem. Clicker and the other methods work very well together.

The other aspect that makes clicker training so horse friendly is that when you get unwanted behavior, you simply ignore it, unless it is deliberately aggressive. Thus the horse's mistakes are never stressed, so he doesn't worry about making mistakes. It has been shown that if you can entirely remove fear from the learning process, the speed of learning increases geometrically. By *not* punishing the horse's mistakes, you enable him to learn correct behavior much more quickly.

Two other elements are essential to success with clicker training. First, you have to find treats that the horse likes. If you are in a long training session and you keep feeding the same treat, eventually he gets tired of it, so you need a variety of treats. You also need what are called jackpot treats. These can be either a special treat or just a large amount of the treat you are using. Jackpots are used when the horse does something extra special. Serious clicker trainers use a fishing or photographer's vest, with lots of pockets for different treats.

Second, clicker training takes a lot more physical coordination on your part than you might think, especially when you are using your hands to signal the horse in some way. For the horse to understand what you want, you have to mark the exact behavior you want at the exact time it happens. Trainers like the clicker because the noise is so sharp that it marks very accurately. However, if you are something of a manual klutz, it can be hard to click at the exact moment. Many people, therefore, will use a word such as "good" or "yes" to mark the correct action. It is not as accurate as the clicker, and so not as refined, but it works for many situations.

Overall, especially if you are a novice, clicker training is often the best place to start in solving most problems. Even very aggressive horses often respond very well to the clicker. However, you might have trouble with a disrespectful horse who enjoys being bossy.

Parelli Natural Horse-Man-Ship

Parelli training (developed by Pat Parelli) is based on the premise that the horse just wants to be comfortable. If we make him a little uncomfortable, he will eventually try to get the discomfort to stop. When he does the right thing, we stop making him uncomfortable. Insofar as possible, whatever is making him uncomfortable should not be so irritating that he gets angry, because that would defeat the purpose by making him uncooperative, rather than wanting to please.

The Parelli system at the level we are concerned with consists of seven games, which are based on games horses play with each other. We will discuss only the first four games in detail. They must be played in order, since each depends on lessons learned in the one before. Like clicker training, Parelli should be fun for both horse and trainer. If either of you is bored or irritable, you need to change your plan for the moment.

Using the Parelli system involves some special tools: the Parelli halter and 12-foot rope; the carrot stick, so called because even though it looks like a stick, it can be as rewarding as a carrot; and the savvy string, which is essentially a lash for the carrot stick that extends its range without being painful if it hits the horse a little hard. The tools are fairly expensive, but they are very well designed and, in my experience, are easier to use and more comfortable for both the horse and the handler than most copies or homemade substitutes.

Friendly Game

The first game is called the friendly game. Although I am explaining it here as a Parelli exercise, the same or very similar techniques are used by all the training systems we are discussing. It is the way you show the horse that, no matter how threatening you may seem, you are still, and always, his friend, and have his best interests at heart. You play it using your hands, the stick, the rope and eventually any object the horse might perceive as threatening—sometimes using one, sometimes another, depending on how your horse responds and on his level of training. At the beginning, some horses are more comfortable with your hands, others don't want you that much in their space and so are more comfortable with the stick.

Begin with the horse in his Parelli halter and 12-foot line. Using advance and retreat and holding the line, you start touching the horse, first in less sensitive places like his shoulder, then moving on to more difficult areas—which depend on the individual horse and his response. As long as the horse stands quietly, you touch a bit, then stop, smile, praise, wait a little and go on to a new place. If, however, he starts to try to escape your touch by moving away, keep the touch on him and hold him in a small circle around you with the rope. As soon as he starts to slow down or stop, you remove the touch, smile and praise. Then you do it again. Pretty soon the horse discovers that (a) you're going to be persistent, (b) running around is tiring and (c) you don't seem to have any intention of actually hurting him.

Gradually the horse learns to accept your touch with hand or stick all over, even in sensitive areas like the ears, the sheath or bag, the flanks and under the tail. He learns to accept the savvy string, first all over his body, including wrapping it lightly around his legs so he learns not to panic about that, then swung around in gradually more noisy and frightening ways. When you first do this, you swing the stick and string around, but with your back to the horse, so it is obvious that you aren't after him. If he moves, you keep swinging until he stops, then smile and gently lay the stick against his neck or shoulder so the lash falls softly against him. "See, it doesn't hurt!" And you smile. As the horse develops confidence, you can make more noise and use it in areas that appear threatening, and the horse will learn to accept it, will become braver and will develop greater self-confidence.

Porcupine Game

The second game is the porcupine game, which teaches the horse to move away from pressure. Parelli has an excellent system for applying pressure of any sort, whether actual physical contact or more psychological. It calls for four steps: hair, skin, flesh, bone. At first the pressure is so light that it only affects the hair. (The horse can feel this, just as he can feel a fly landing on him.) *After giving the horse time to react* (about three seconds) you move on to the next level. The second pressure affects his skin, the third gets down into his muscle and the fourth really gets in there to the bone. The fourth level can be fairly uncomfortable, but it doesn't take the horse long to find out that (a) he can relieve the discomfort by moving away from it, and (b) if he moves before you get to the bone stage, he'll never feel discomfort.

Naturally, as soon as the horse shows a "try" (see page 26), you stop the pressure, praise and smile and start from phase one again. It is exciting and rewarding to see how quickly a horse learns to respond to the lightest touch. This works extremely well with horses who appear to be sullen and stubborn. These horses are made so by being punished unfairly for not reacting, often because they have not gained full coordination and are thus unable to do so! Giving them time to work it out, and the knowledge that *they* can control the amount of discomfort by their response, often results in a major attitude change.

Using the four levels of pressure, in the porcupine game you ask the horse to back by pressing on either side of his nose with your fingers. Be sure your fingers are resting on bone, not on his nostril passages. If you use the stick, place it in the center of his chest. It is important to think in terms of *pressing* on the horse's body, so that he moves away from that pressure, rather than *pushing* him back, which will immediately create resistance. It's a subtle difference, but psychologically very important. As soon as you feel the try, change the pressure to a rub with either hand or stick, depending on which you were using, accompanied by a smile and a word of praise. As well as praise, the rub reminds the horse that your hand or the stick doesn't really hurt, and is also the signal to stop. If the horse backs more than you want, continue to rub until he stops. Then gradually shape the behavior to get as many steps back as you want.

After you have used the porcupine game to get the horse to back, ask him to step to the side with his front legs, away from you. Place one hand on his muzzle and the other on his shoulder. I like to hook a finger through the halter so that if he decides to spin too quickly, I can keep up. It is just as much of an evasion for him to spin more and faster than asked as it is not to move at all. Use the four levels of pressure with both hands, but now you have to pay attention to which part of him you want to move. You only want him to yield a small amount with his head, since if he turns it too far he will have trouble moving his feet. So once he yields with his head, ask him to yield at the shoulder.

Don't forget to go through all four levels of pressure each time you ask. It is all too easy to jump to a higher level because you get impatient. If he starts to back up, move more toward his rear. If he starts to move forward, move forward to block him. Watch his feet and look for the slightest movement to the side to reward. Be sure to rub with both hands when he steps over, both as a reward and as a signal to stop.

TALKING HORSES

It can be confusing when the same action is both a reward and a command. In the case of rubbing, a little light rub or pat says, "Good. No more pressure. You're finished. You can stop." If the horse doesn't stop, you continue rubbing, which now becomes a bit aggravating and says, "I'm going to keep doing this until you stop what you're doing." When the horse stops, the rubbing stops as well, and he gets a smile and praise.

It is easiest for the horse to learn to step over with his front legs if he carries his head slightly in the direction his feet will be moving. However, when he steps over with his hind legs, it's easiest if he bends his neck quite far in the *opposite* direction. Using a combing action on the rope (page 33), gently bend his head around until it is looking slightly toward the rear. Then apply pressure with your fingers on his hindquarters about six inches above and behind his stifle joint. There is a nice little hollow there. Be sure not to lean into him, which would throw his weight onto the other foot and make it hard for him to move. If necessary, use a little poking motion rather than steady pressure to get that first yield.

The horse should learn to step over in both directions with both front and hind legs. Be sure you teach him to cross so that the crossing leg always passes in *front* of the other leg. He will nearly always find one set of legs easier to move, and one direction easier than the other. Practicing on both sides makes him better coordinated and builds his confidence.

Driving Game

The next game is the driving game, which teaches the horse to respond to gestures rather than actual pressure. Again, the horse learns to move backward and sideways with each set of legs. And again, we use four levels of pressure, but now it becomes four levels times four stages, or 16 levels total. The first level is a small gesture with, say, the hands toward the horse's face, to ask for the back, *followed by a one- or two-second wait.* The second level is a little larger gesture, the third is a little bigger yet and the fourth is a sharp little rap on his nose with your fingers. If none of these has any effect at all, then you go to the second stage. Each of your levels in the second stage is stronger than the same level in the first stage. And so on through four stages. But I have to think that if you had to progress through all those stages to get any response at all, you should wonder whether maybe you're doing something wrong, either in your observation of the horse or in your training at the previous levels.

The driving game, like the porcupine game, can be done using the hands alone, the hands holding the rope in a little loose bridge that can be swung up and down or back and forth, or the stick, moved in a vertical plane toward the place you want the horse to move from (the horse's nose, for example, if you are asking for a back).

An essential aspect of the driving game is teaching the horse to yield his hindquarters to the carrot stick and savvy string when you are standing near his front end, so that he swings his head around and faces you. This is a natural reaction as well as a gesture of submission, and also helps with horses who tend to break away from a pull on the rope or who are difficult to catch. Eventually you should be able to look at his hindquarters and gesture toward them to have him face you.

Yo-Yo Game

The fourth game, the yo-yo game, is the last one we're going to talk about and is a very important and useful game. It teaches the horse to respect your space when asked and to yield to forward pressure on his head. Thus it works well on both bratty horses and panicky ones.

You begin by facing the horse from a couple of feet away, using a little porcupine to get him to back away, if necessary. Hold the end of the rope in your hand, with the tail coming out by your little finger. The four phases of pressure in the yo-yo game are finger, wrist, elbow and arm. You're going to use the rope to get the horse to respond. Be prepared to stop the instant the horse starts to yield and step back.

First give your horse a firm look—it's called the "mother-in-law look." With your wrist straight, extend your index finger, then shake it (point it once sharply) at the horse four times, about one second apart. Shake, wait, shake, wait, shake, wait, shake, wait. Think of your mother shaking her finger at you and saying, "How many times have I told you not to . . .." Maintaining the same rhythm, with the back of your hand toward the horse and your forearm horizontal, flip your hand (using only your wrist) four times toward the horse. If you were close to him, you would bat him on the nose with your knuckles, but in this case, the movement of your wrist is just going to make the line start to wiggle a little. Next, still with your forearm horizontal, swing your whole forearm at him, from the elbow, four times. Now the rope is swinging pretty actively. Finally, use your whole arm, from the shoulder, to swing the rope vigorously back and forth at the horse's head. If necessary, be quite aggressive in your attitude and swinging, and continue until the horse yields and starts to step back. Smile and praise. Now start over from the beginning with the mother-in-law look and the pointing finger, and repeat as far as you need to get more backing. Continue until the horse has backed about four or five feet, then allow him to stand there for 5 or 10 seconds.

Next, take up the slack in the rope and comb it to ask him to come to you. Combing consists of drawing your hands toward you, alternating hands as though you were gathering in the rope. But instead of pulling the rope in, you allow your hands to slide over it toward you, so that instead of a rigid pull, you have a very soft elastic pressure on the rope as you change from one hand to the other. In addition to the combing, make yourself welcoming by squatting or bending down, smiling and using soft eyes. Again, be willing to wait as long as it takes for the horse to decide to yield and come toward you, and be effusive in praise at the first sign of compliance.

Continue practicing the yo-yo game until the horse will back away at the first wiggle of your finger and come toward you at the lightest pressure from the rope. A horse who has learned this game well is neither going to walk all over you at feeding time nor panic and pull away when tied.

Round Pen Training

Round pen training is perhaps the easiest training system to abuse, so it must be used with care. It is based on the horse's need to be part of a herd, and thus to bond with whoever is with him. Using a soft rope to chase the horse, the trainer asks the horse to move around the pen, since in horse relationships the one who can make the other one move is the dominant individual. If the horse responds by racing around trying to control the situation by controlling his own movement, he can be kept going for a while, then blocked using the trainer's center and the rope, and sent back the other way. The demands are gradually increased until the horse is stopping and changing directions at the will of the trainer. Gradually the horse begins to realize that the trainer is in control, and he starts to pay serious attention. The experienced trainer recognizes this and offers the horse the opportunity to stop and approach him in a submissive manner.

Properly handled, round pen training shows the horse that he must give up control to the trainer to find comfort and support. The trainer then offers protection and kindness. This can be a very quick and effective method with a domineering horse. However, if the trainer's object is primarily to "show the horse who's boss," the horse will recognize this and become either frightened or sullen. In either case he will not show submission, and the careless trainer may then continue to run him until he risks causing physical damage.

TALKING HORSES

A group of us on the Internet were discussing horses who bully other horses in the field. One woman, who runs fairly large groups of horses, told about a particularly aggressive mare she acquired. She used all the usual preparatory techniques to make the initial introduction go smoothly, but the mare still entered the herd with a lot of dominance issues. In the herd were four large draft mares. They couldn't run as fast as the new mare, but between them they were able to keep her moving continuously for days, under their control, driving her away until she finally realized that if she wanted to be part of the herd she would have to do so on their terms. Thereafter she fit in perfectly and never gave any more trouble. Like most good training methods, round pen training was invented by the horses themselves!

Tteam (Tellington-Jones Equine Awareness Method)

Tteam is a very unusual training system. It is really more about bonding and also includes many healing techniques. It has many different aspects, but the ones that concern us here are Ttouch, which creates awareness and relaxation, the leading and some of the leg exercises. The latter two are found in the appropriate chapters in this book.

There are many variations on Ttouch, but the basic element is a small, single, complete circle, made by pressing one or more fingers gently but firmly on the skin so that as the fingers move in a circle, the skin slides over the underlying flesh. To get a sense of this touch, begin by touching your closed eyelid lightly with one finger, enough so that you can feel the touch, but there is no pressure. Now touch the back of your other hand with the same degree of pressure. On a scale of 1 to 10, this is considered a 1. The pressure you usually use on a horse is a 3. Touch your eyelid again, but this time press in hard enough so that you depress the eye itself, but not enough to be uncomfortable. Again, transfer this pressure to the back of your hand. This is a 3. Now imagine a small clock face on the back of your hand, with your finger at six o'clock. Move your finger and the skin underneath it slowly in a clockwise direction, saying to yourself, "six o'clock, eight o'clock" and so on, until you get back to six again, then go a little further and finish at seven o'clock, to make sure you close the circle.

Most commonly when you use the Ttouch, you use all the fingers on your hand. When I first learned about Tteam we used just the three middle fingertips, slightly overlapping, and I still find this very easy and comfortable to use. There are a number of different ways to use your hands, all with unique animal names—clouded leopard, python lift and the like—to be found in the Tteam texts.

When you are doing Tteam, you only make one circle in one place on the horse, then move to another place nearby and make another circle, continuing to move around the area you are working on. You can return to the same place over and over, but never for more than one circle at a time.

These circles, which are based on a technique called Feldenkrais, awaken certain brain waves and draw the attention of the brain to the area being touched. They stimulate, relax and heal—and many more things in the hands of experts. If you aren't into alternative healing, they may sound like some sort of crazy witchcraft, but they work surprisingly well in many situations.

TALKING HORSES

When I had a large lesson program in New England, there were days in the winter when it was too cold to comfortably spend an hour and a half in the arena. One such day, I put two rather tense horses on the aisle and assigned four students to each horse. They were to use Tteam touches all over the horse for 10 or 15 minutes. The students had not been doing Tteam for very long and were a bit skeptical. In the beginning, there was some nervous laughter and talk, and the horses' heads were up and they were fidgeting. I walked quietly around, making an occasional correction of technique. Gradually I became aware of a total change in the atmosphere, not only of the horses being worked on, but the people doing the work and the other horses in the stable. The best way to describe it is to say that peace descended on the whole group. When we went out to ride later on, riders and horses were relaxed but alert, in spite of the cold, and we had an unusually good lesson. I think that experience made converts of all of us.

The best thing you can do for yourself and your horse is to read up on these systems, and any others that interest you. Watch tapes and attend clinics if possible (see Appendix A for some suggestions). The more tools you have for problem solving, the more likely you are to be able to solve problems and the better you'll be able to understand your horse. Go for it!

BATHING: AFRAID OF THE HOSE

It's a hot day and Denise has been walking her horse, Timmy, for the last 15 minutes of her ride, but he is still hot, sweaty and sticky, although his breathing is normal. Denise decides this would be a good opportunity to give him a bath, so she takes off his tack, puts on his halter and lead rope and takes him over to the hose. She turns the water on, but when she picks up the hose and starts to spray Timmy, he runs backward away from her. She has to drop the hose to keep him from getting away, and when she tries to lead him back he wants no part of it. She ends up sponging him off with a bucket, but it is time consuming and she doesn't feel as though he is really clean.

WHAT YOUR HORSE WANTS YOU TO KNOW

∩ *That's weird, and cold and scary.* Even though it seems like cold water would feel good on a hot day, cold water on a hot body just feels cold. That, combined with the experience of having something coming out of nowhere and hitting his body—the horse doesn't even realize at first what it is—is pretty disconcerting.

WHAT TO DO ABOUT IT

∩ First use the friendly game (page 30) to introduce the horse to the hose, with the water turned off. After he has looked at the hose, felt it on his body and accepted it, he should see it being dragged and flipped around as one does when using it. Allow him to move around if he wants to, but keep doing whatever made him move until he stops, or begins to stop, then stop your motion as well. This tells him that standing still works better than running around. After a moment, run the hose across his body again in a nonaggressive way, smiling, to remind him that the hose doesn't hurt and your intention is not to hurt, either.

∩ If at all possible, use warm water at first, rather than cold. Leaving the hose sitting in the sun will make at least the first few minutes of slowly running water nice and warm. In any case, when you use the hose the day should be warm and the horse should not be extremely hot.

∩ Turn the water on so it is running slowly. Hold the hose away from the horse at first, so he can see it. When you bring it toward him, keep your eyes soft and your approach casual. Smile. Let him put his nose up to it and see what it is, and let the water run over his lips so he licks it and finds out what it is, but be careful it doesn't get into his nostrils. Next, using advance and retreat (page 27), let the water run on his front feet and lower legs first, allowing him to move but praising him when he stands. Be careful he doesn't step or get tangled in the hose if he moves.

Gradually move up to his chest, back to his hind legs, up the underside of his neck, across his barrel and over his back and croup.

⋂ Unless he seems to be enjoying his shower, wait until another day to do the remainder of his head, between his hind legs and under his tail, using warm water on the latter two if at all possible. When using the hose on his head, be very careful not to get water in his ears, which, besides being very uncomfortable, can lead to ear infections.

⋂ Let the horse tell you if he is enjoying his shower. Most horses learn to love it if given a chance, but if you are pushy and inconsiderate you may make him fidgety and uncomfortable instead.

WHAT NOT TO DO ABOUT IT

⋂ When you're trying to get the horse to like something, try not to think you're going to "win" and *make* the horse accept it.
⋂ Don't be impatient. Even though you know the shower will feel good, it may take him some time to figure it out.

BITING PEOPLE

Tom is getting ready to ride his new horse, Red. He is near the stall getting his grooming tools organized when Jane comes by, leading her horse, Billy, through the stable on her way out to ride. As she passes Red's stall door, his head snakes out over the door with his ears flat back. His mouth is open and he snaps viciously at her shoulder! Fortunately, Billy sees him coming and jumps to the side, pulling Jane with him. She is unhurt but upset by the incident. Tom apologizes and promises to do something about it. He is quite surprised by Red's behavior, since he had not seen it when he was looking at Red in his previous home.

True biting, as distinguished from nipping, is intended to hurt! Since horses are not naturally aggressive in most situations, something pretty serious is going on. Besides charging at the stall door, other times the horse may bite are when the girth is being fastened up or tightened, or when he is eating.

WHAT YOUR HORSE WANTS YOU TO KNOW

⋂ *I feel extremely threatened!* Because he is in new surroundings, the horse may fear that he will be driven away. He feels he has no friends and no one to protect him. He has almost surely been treated roughly, so he expects this treatment wherever he goes.

⋂ *I have to show myself as very strong in order to survive.* Horses who have been abused by clumsy or uncaring people sometimes decide the only way to survive is to be stronger and more aggressive and "do it first."

○ *I'm number one and you're number two. Now get out of my way!* This is comparatively rare, luckily, but you do occasionally meet with a horse who has no respect for humans at all. This is, of course, the result of bad or nonexistent training.

WHAT TO DO ABOUT IT

○ Try to determine the base cause of the biting. That is, what is the horse afraid of? Is it people coming into what he considers his personal space? Or perhaps someone approaching directly from the front, or carrying something that could be viewed as threatening? In any case, those threats should be removed as far away as possible, then gradually reintroduced through training.

○ Build trust first. Clicker training (page 27) has been shown to be very effective with horses who are defensive, since it involves nothing threatening. It is also the safest, because you can work with the horse from outside his stall, where you are safe. After teaching the horse the concept of right action–click–treat, reintroduce the threatening situation, but at a distance. Use the advance and retreat concept (page 27) to bring the person, whether it's you or someone else, closer to the horse's space, clicking and treating when he accepts their move, backing off when he doesn't.

○ If the horse reaches a point where he no longer wants to bite, and seems willing to trust you, begin some Tteam (page 34) mouth work, gently and carefully inserting your fingers in the corners of his mouth, rubbing his gums and tapping his tongue. Horses, like people, hold a lot of tension in their jaws and mouth, and mouth work helps to relieve some of this tension.

○ Safety is a major issue. A horse can cause serious damage with his teeth. Therefore, until you can solve the problem you must make sure others are safe. If the horse bites from his stall, a stall guard should be placed so that he cannot get past it with his head, and a warning notice should be placed on the door. If it is during feeding, the horse should be fed alone, and only experienced people should be allowed to enter his stall to feed him. If girthing up is the problem, others should be cautioned not to be near his head and he should be securely tied so he can't reach his handler (see Saddling: Problems While Being Cinched or Girthed Up, page 131).

○ If he remains aggressive, find an expert to help you. Seriously aggressive horses need professional help to guide them into more acceptable behavior. If possible, watch the trainer with other horses and see what methods he uses. If they tend to involve primarily force or punishment, look for someone else. However, if your horse is the rare one who has no respect for humans, he may need a certain amount of very firm treatment to change his mind. Round pen training may be a good approach with this horse, because it sets the human up as part of the horse's herd, but as the dominant member. This is easy for the horse to understand and adapt to without provoking resentment. However, being in a round pen with a truly aggressive horse can be dangerous and should be left to experts.

WHAT NOT TO DO ABOUT IT

⋒ Don't punish! This is easy to say, but hard to do. If the horse has actually grabbed you and hurt you, it is almost impossible to keep yourself from hitting back. That is another, and equally important, reason why you need to be very careful to avoid situations where the horse might bite while you are working on curing the problem. The horse is biting because he expects to be hurt, so if you punish you are only telling him that he needs to bite sooner and harder the next time. If you keep the horse at a public facility, you may run into a serious problem with other people who don't get it. Many people have been brought up to believe that the way you teach horses is to punish them when they do something wrong, and will insist that if the horse tries to bite, *not* punishing is "spoiling him." You need to protect the horse from these people while you are dealing with the trust issue. You may have to move his stall or install a feeding system that doesn't require anyone to enter the stall to feed him, if that is his problem. But do whatever you have to, to keep him from being made worse. If you decide the horse has a respect issue, rather than a fear issue, you are still better off not punishing him at first.

TALKING HORSES

Aggressive behavior is sometimes passed on by a mare to her foal. This is a very important reason why broodmares should be well socialized and the foals accustomed to handling from birth. If you buy a young horse from the breeder you may have the opportunity to meet the mare, which will be of help in predicting the temperament of the young horse.

BLANKETS: FEAR OF BLANKETING

Louise is very active in showing year-round. Since she lives in a fairly cold climate, she doesn't want her horse, Max, growing a heavy winter coat, both for reasons of appearance in the show ring and because it takes a long time to cool him down after riding. However, Max is very frightened of being blanketed, and just as frightened when the blankets are removed. Louise managed to keep him blanketed last winter, but he seemed to get worse, not better, as the season progressed. She isn't looking forward to the cold weather this year, because she's afraid she may not be able to blanket him at all.

WHAT YOUR HORSE WANTS YOU TO KNOW

⋒ *I feel trapped.* A horse's instinct, as a prey animal, is to fight anything that seems to be trying to hold on to him. The size of the blanket, and the confining straps are very scary if the horse has never worked out his relationship to people. He continues to think of them as predators, thus the blanket is perceived as a trap.

∩ *Ouch, that stings!* Some blanket fabrics, and also, for some reason, certain horses' coats, seem to generate a lot of static electricity. When the blanket is pulled off the horse gets a shock. He soon learns to anticipate it and become very uncomfortable.

WHAT TO DO ABOUT IT

∩ This is an advance and retreat situation (page 27). You begin with something comparatively small, such as a large towel. Allow the horse to touch it and smell it, then rub his body with it, starting at his shoulder. If he pulls away, stop, wait a few seconds and come back again. You can either wipe it across him quickly and remove it or place it on him for a second, holding it still, then removing it. You have to find the amount of contact that causes the minimum reaction, then stay at that level until he accepts it before moving on to more contact. Be sure to go over all the places the blanket will touch, especially around his hindquarters, but be especially careful in that area, not proceeding as long as there is any flinching, which could precede a kick. Using the same technique, introduce him to a soft rope around his middle, in the area where the surcingles will fall. This does not need to be at all tight, but the horse should accept contact all the way around. Surcingles that are too loose invite the horse to catch a foot in them when lying down or getting up. If you plan to use leg straps, the horse must learn to accept those as well by having a soft rope brought around his upper hind leg, then dropped away, until he will allow it to lie there. Once the horse accepts the towel and the ropes, use a light blanket or sheet and repeat the process. Allow plenty of time—usually at least several days of practice—for the horse to get accustomed to the blanket, and give him lots of smiles and praise when he accepts it.

∩ Removing the blankets in too much of a hurry is often the cause of big problems. Static electricity is one of those problems. One solution to that is to have a 100 percent cotton sheet as the bottom layer, since it doesn't hold static electricity as well as other fabrics do. Spraying the blanket with an anti-static spray is very helpful, especially if the blankets are removed and put back on every day, so the spray can be reapplied.

∩ Another action that can get everyone in a lot of trouble is forgetting to undo a surcingle. This is particularly likely to happen if the horse is wearing two or more blankets. One of the surcingles either gets forgotten completely, or doesn't fully disengage, or gets caught in the fabric. As the blanket is pulled off over the horse's hindquarters, the surcingle catches around his flanks, becoming a flank strap of the sort that is used on rodeo bucking horses—with the same results. A bucking horse can be very dangerous both to himself and the handler, especially if they are in a stall or other tightly confined space. The way to avoid this problem is to take the fronts of the unfastened blankets by one side and swing them out away from the horse before trying to remove them. A fastened surcingle will show itself immediately, and without scaring the horse. Leg straps can also be forgotten, but most horses don't seem to mind having them slide down their legs as much as they do the surcingles.

∩   Some horses are more comfortable if the blanket is not slid down over the hindquarters during removal. The usual method after undoing all fastenings is to fold the front half of the blanket back over the back of the blanket, then slide the folded blanket back and off. For a horse who is bothered by this, you can try folding the blanket in thirds, folding the front third back over the middle, then the back third forward over the middle, and pulling the folded blanket off down the horse's side. However, if the blanket is contoured around the back, trying to fold it forward can be almost as disturbing to a sensitive horse, so experiment carefully.

WHAT NOT TO DO ABOUT IT

∩   Hurrying, or tying or holding the horse tightly in an effort to get him to stand still are all ineffective and potentially dangerous. The horse already feels trapped and threatened, and further restriction may lead to kicking or pulling back on the ties. Punishing him for moving will only remind him that, after all, you are a predator. Maybe this is the time you are going to eat him!

TALKING HORSES

A blanket is most dangerous to horse and handler when it is not fully fastened. If the horse starts moving when the surcingles are fastened and the front is not, the blanket can slide back around his flanks in the same way as when a surcingle gets caught. This can result in violent and dangerous bucking and kicking, which can injure anyone in the vicinity. However, if the horse gets loose with the front fastened and the surcingles undone, and moves off at speed, the blanket will eventually slip around in front of him like a bib. Once this happens the movement of his front legs is restricted so that he cannot stop except by falling, and can injure or even kill himself. The safest answer is that when the horse is confined, always fasten the chest straps first and undo them last. However, if the horse is in a field or other place where he could get loose, fasten the surcingles first and undo them last.

BRIDLING: FUSSES ABOUT HIS EARS

Even though Jim is a fairly tall man, he still has difficulty bridling his new horse, Boomer. Boomer opens his mouth to the bit willingly enough, but as soon as Jim's hand gets near his ears to slip the headstall over them, he starts to flip his head and flatten his ears, raising his head as high as he can and twisting it away. Because Jim is tall, he is able to get the bridle on eventually, but each time is a little bit more difficult than the time before. Jim can tell that Boomer is thinking seriously about rearing to get away. He needs to find an approach that will give Boomer confidence, instead of scaring him more.

WHAT YOUR HORSE WANTS YOU TO KNOW

⋂ *I'm afraid you're going to hurt my ears.* Most horses are initially sensitive about their ears, or "ear-shy," and need help to overcome this fear.

⋂ *I don't know you very well, so I am not willing to let you handle a sensitive area.* The horse has not learned to trust humans as a group. It is possible that he is more manageable with someone he knows well, but it is doing a disservice to both him and any future handlers to leave him with this distrust.

WHAT TO DO ABOUT IT

⋂ Depending on how long your horse has been doing this, it may be weeks or months before he is really comfortable about having his ears handled. See Ear-Shyness, Overcoming, on page 59 for the technique that will help him accept this.

⋂ Besides overcoming the specific ear-shy problem, you should consider one of the programs that deals with relationships (pages 26–35). Not only will the horse be helped, but your knowledge and understanding will be increased greatly as well, making you a more capable equestrian and thus better able to help your horse with any future problems.

⋂ If you can ride your horse in a Parelli or similar halter or a hackamore (which doesn't have to be pulled over his ears) during his training to overcome the ear-shyness, his training will progress faster. You should definitely try not to use the type of headstall that has a hole for only one ear, since it is impossible to put on without handling the ear.

⋂ Plan to put on and remove his stable halter by unbuckling the crownpiece rather than using the throat latch snap.

WHAT NOT TO DO ABOUT IT

⋂ Any attempt to restrain your horse for bridling, especially by holding his ears, will only exacerbate the problem by arousing his prey-predator instincts.

⋂ Hurrying the process by trying to get him to accept more hand-to-ear contact than he is ready for will create worry and fear, rather than trust.

TALKING HORSES

If you ride with an ordinary bridle, while you are waiting for your horse to develop enough trust to let you handle his ears, it would be nice if you didn't have to keep upsetting him when you put on the bridle. There is a solution, but it takes a little practice and you may need to borrow a spare hand until you get the knack. You begin by unfastening the bridle where the cheekpiece joins the crownpiece. If the bridle has a caveson (noseband), unless you really need it you should remove it altogether. You can then slide the browband either off completely, or at least off the left side of the crownpiece. Holding the left cheekpiece in your left hand, place your right arm over your horse's neck not too far from his withers. Then reach down and take the crownpiece in your right hand so that you are holding the bridle under your horse's neck, with your right arm on top of his neck, as though you were putting on a halter. Holding the bridle up with your right hand, slide your left hand down and put the bit into your horse's mouth, then slide your left hand up the cheekpiece (this is where you might need that extra hand, so you don't drop the bit out of your horse's mouth). Now bring the crownpiece across the horse's neck, just behind his ears but without touching them. If the browband is still on the bridle, hold the cheekpiece and crownpiece together in your right hand for a moment while you bring the browband around with your left hand. Again, you may need an extra hand here. Slip the browband over the crownpiece, then buckle the cheekpiece and fasten the rest of the bridle as usual. This is a good deal harder to explain than it is to do!

BRIDLING: RAISES OR THROWS HEAD WHEN REMOVING

Marian has just come home from a pleasant trail ride on Mike, who has given her his usual well-behaved ride. She removes his saddle, picks up the halter and prepares to remove the bridle. After unfastening the throat latch and caveson, she reaches up to take the bridle off over his ears. As soon as her hand touches the crownpiece, Mike begins to twist and shake his head, sometimes so violently that he knocks her off balance.

She finally gets it off over his ears, but then he throws his nose up so that the bit doesn't drop out of his mouth. Now the bridle is swinging around as well, but fortunately Marian still has the reins fairly high up on his neck, so she is able to control his head long enough to get him to drop it and relax his jaw so the bit falls out of his mouth. This whole scene, which goes on more or less in the same way each time they finish a ride, bewilders Marian, because Mike doesn't mind in the least having his bridle put *on*. Nor does he show any signs of ear- or head-shyness at any other time.

This is a rather extreme example—most horses don't show a combination of problems like this—but fussiness about having the bridle or halter removed is quite common. Many people just live with it, but if you have ever been hit in the face with a horse's head, you know that head-throwing of any sort is to be avoided or cured as soon as possible!

WHAT YOUR HORSE WANTS YOU TO KNOW

∩ *You are hurting my ears!* Or *I'm afraid you're going to hurt my ears!* The horse has a muscle at the base of his ear, a little smaller than a ping-pong ball, that prevents the bridle from falling forward over his head. Many people remove the bridle by putting their hand between the horse's ears and pulling straight forward. The bridle catches on the muscle on each side, just like it's supposed to. When the handler forces it off, it hurts! The horse shakes his head in anticipation of the discomfort, trying to get it over with or at least ease the pressure by moving his head around.

∩ *When you pulled the bridle off, the bit jabbed me in the mouth! I want out of this!* The combined discomfort of the pull on the backs of the ears and the pull on the mouth is *really* upsetting, and the horse throws his head in protest. (If you forgot to undo the caveson or the curb chain, the horse will find it very difficult to open his mouth even if he doesn't throw his head up.) The dangling bridle only adds to the confusion and discomfort.

∩ *The bit also banged on my teeth suddenly when the bridle dropped.* This makes some horses tense their jaws, so their mouths don't open and they can't let go of the bit.

WHAT TO DO ABOUT IT

∩ Any time you remove the bridle or halter over the horse's head, you *must* remove it one ear at a time. First unfasten the throat latch, and caveson or noseband and curb chain, if you have them. Then stand just *behind* the horse's head, on the left side, facing forward. Rest your right hand on his neck as high up as you can reach comfortably. If he understands the head dropping command (page 14) you can ask him to drop his head. Then slide your left thumb under the crownpiece below the horse's left ear. Lift the crownpiece slightly and slip it off over the horse's left ear *only*. Then, if you are tall enough, reach across the horse's poll, still with your left hand, and slip the crownpiece up and over the horse's right ear. To keep the horse from raising his head and getting the bit caught, keep your left forearm gently against his nose and slide it down slowly, holding the bit up a little until the horse opens his mouth and drops it, when you can let your hand and the bridle slide down the rest of the way. If you aren't tall enough to reach across his poll, hold the bridle up while you walk around the horse's head until you can reach behind his right ear with your right thumb, then slip the bridle the rest of the way off as I've just described, using your right rather than your left hand.

◠ Once you can do this fairly well, you can start asking the horse not to fuss about it, since you are no longer hurting him. It may take awhile to convince him, so be prepared to be patient. (This is another place where the clicker works well.) Begin removing the bridle as described, but as soon as your horse starts to shake his head, just freeze your hand where it is. When he stops shaking his head, remove the bridle a little further or click and treat. Continue until the bridle is free of both ears. At this point you should have your forearm across his nose, so if he has raised his head, just keep your arm there without any pressure and wait until he starts to drop, when you can slide your hand down his nose a little. Try to get his nose down before you remove your hand altogether. Do *not* slide your hand all the way down before he drops the bit. If he has a very tense jaw, it will help him to open his mouth if you make a point of relaxing your own jaw, opening your mouth and shaking your jaw to loosen it. If his head is up, it is also important to keep your face vertical and look up with your eyes only. If you tip your head back to see him, you are telling the horse to lift his head even more.

◠ Over a period of time, once he becomes aware that you will not hurt him, the horse should keep his head low and still while you remove the bridle. Safer for you and a nicer finish to the ride for him.

WHAT NOT TO DO ABOUT IT

◠ Don't try to hold the horse's head still with your body, hands or arms. In the first place, you aren't strong enough, and in the second, you will only make him feel that he is trapped and needs to fight you.

◠ Don't be in a hurry. Finish your ride 10 minutes early, if need be, to allow plenty of time to take the bridle off as slowly as necessary.

TALKING HORSES

Even though halters don't fit as tightly as bridles, because they are often made of wider, stiffer materials they can still hurt the horse's ears during removal. They should be removed the same way as the bridle. If that seems like too much effort, consider this: Every time you do something rapidly and carelessly that makes the horse uncomfortable, you're telling him that you don't think it's worth your time to be careful of his feelings. That attitude does not build trust, and it may come back to haunt you some time when you want the horse to do something unusual or difficult. Since he already knows you don't care if you hurt him, why should he take a chance on doing something that looks scary, just on your say-so?

BRIDLING: WON'T OPEN HIS MOUTH

Ann has finished grooming and saddling Cooper, in readiness for a trail ride with some friends, who are already mounted and waiting. All she has to do is put on the bridle, but the thought of it makes her tense and annoyed. Cooper won't open his mouth to take the bit. Ann always wins eventually, but she hates the struggle, and so does Cooper. She wishes she could figure out a way to make bridling easier for both of them.

WHAT YOUR HORSE WANTS YOU TO KNOW

∩ *My jaw is **really** tense, and when you try to get me to open my mouth, I feel even tenser!* Horses can suffer from TMJ—temporal-mandibular joint dysfunction—just like people. That means the jaw hinge and the muscles that surround it are very tight, and opening the mouth wide is difficult. That could be one cause, and it could be made worse if Ann, or someone before her, had the habit of yanking the bit up quickly as soon as Cooper opened his mouth a little.

WHAT TO DO ABOUT IT

∩ The best exercise to start with is some friendly game (page 30) or Tteam mouth work, involving playing with the horse's mouth and lips, and putting your fingers into his mouth (at the bars, where there are no teeth to accidentally bite you!). The horse should be played with until he willingly allows your fingers in his mouth and on his tongue, and opens his mouth to accommodate them. If he seems to have a lot of trouble with this and you have a good equine chiropractor in your area, you might explore having his jaw adjusted. This has other benefits as well, since a tense jaw creates tension in the whole body, adding unnecessary stress. A good equine dentist might also be able to solve the problem.

∩ When you are putting the bridle on, use your right hand to hold the bridle, placing your forearm across the front of the horse's head, rather than bringing it around behind or under his jaw. This suggests to the horse that he should drop his head and relax his jaw. If you are tall, you can rest your right forearm on the horse's poll; if not, you can rest it above the horse's left temple. Hold the bit in your left hand. Be sure the bit is held up against the place where the teeth meet, so that when the horse opens his mouth the bit can slip in easily, rather than rattling around on the outside. I like to put my left thumb in the left upper corner of the horse's mouth, keeping the bit in place with my fingers, but some horses are more comfortable if you control the bit with your thumb and insert your fingers in the right side of the mouth. Some people like to use the left hand in front, holding the bridle, and the right hand for the bit, though I think this gives you a little less control. Whichever way you do it, keep a soft, lifting pressure with your upper hand. This keeps the bit from sliding out of place while you're waiting for the horse to open his mouth, and also enables you to bring the bit smoothly upward when he does. If he opens his mouth, allows the bit in a little way, then clamps down again, just wait quietly, then ask him to open again, using your thumb or fingers.

∩ It is very helpful for the horse if you mimic what you want him to do. That is, drop your head and open your mouth a little, making soft yawning, relaxing motions. Praise when you feel the least bit of yielding, and be ready with a small, manageable treat when the bit is in place.

∩ Sometimes rubbing a little molasses on the bit will encourage the horse to want to lick and open his mouth.

∩ If you feel the horse is resistant rather than tense, you can ask by inserting your thumb as usual, then escalate to pressing on his gum with your thumbnail. Just be sure to ask with the least amount of pressure first, so that the horse learns there is an easy signal to respond to, rather than waiting until he is made uncomfortable.

WHAT NOT TO DO ABOUT IT

∩ Don't be in a hurry, either when you are starting the bridling process or when the horse starts to open his mouth. If the horse feels you will give him as much time as he needs, he is more likely to be able to relax his jaw.

∩ Don't try to force his mouth open. Your hands should be gentle and massaging, not prying. Even if you are using your thumbnail, it is only to create a little discomfort so he wants to open his mouth himself.

CLIPPING, RESISTANCE TO

We were visiting another stable one day to look at a horse who had been advertised for sale. As we waited for the horse to be brought out, I watched a young groom standing in the grooming stall clipping a horse. The horse's ears were back, his tail was swishing back and forth and he was fidgeting in a rather annoyed way. Since he was obviously a mature animal and this was a show stable, I was rather surprised, because most show horses in our area are accustomed to being clipped and usually take it quite calmly. However, when I watched more closely, I could see the source of the problem. The groom was holding the clippers so that the points of the blades dug into the horse's skin at every stroke!

This was an unusual case and the horse had good cause to be unhappy, but many horses are uncomfortable and fidgety even about being clipped correctly, especially in the head area.

WHAT YOUR HORSE WANTS YOU TO KNOW

∩ *I don't understand what you're doing!* The horse feels the odd vibration, hears the loud noise and feels the tug of the hair being removed. If he doesn't have a good feeling of trust, all these elements can be very disturbing.

∩ *The noise **really** hurts my ears.* In the head and ear area, that loud noise can be very painful to the horse's sensitive hearing.

WHAT TO DO ABOUT IT

∩ Anything as unusual as clipping needs to be approached especially carefully. First, the clippers should be run at a distance, preferably when the horse is in his stall, so he doesn't associate it with something being done to him. When he is comfortable with the sound, the clippers should be turned off, the horse brought out and held or ground tied, not crosstied. He should be encouraged to look at and smell the clippers first, then, still not running, they should be held flat and run over his body so he can feel that they don't hurt. If the horse has sensitive areas, pay particular attention to them. Then take the clippers a few feet away and start them up so that the horse gets used to the sound again. When he seems comfortable, bring the running clippers over and, holding them in your hand, roll your hand over and lay it against the horse's shoulder so he can feel the vibration through your hand, which he trusts. Then lay the running clippers flat against him, in different places on his body and legs. Finally, run the clippers with the hair, then against the hair on his shoulder and begin to clip. Clip the body and neck first, and try to leave the legs and head for another day. Plenty of treats will help to make this a pleasant experience.

∩ If at all possible, use a pair of smaller, quieter clippers for the head and ears. For one thing, it is much easier to get into all the little angles and corners. But more important, there is less vibration and *much* less noise. If you have to use full-size clippers, try to stuff cotton in the horse's ears to deaden the noise.

∩ Some horses just never get comfortable with the clippers around their ears, no matter how much you work with them to desensitize them. For these horses, if they must be clipped, the twitch (page 19) is the humane way to go. The endorphins it releases help the horse deal with his tension. Sometimes, once the horse has been twitched a few times, he loses his tension enough so that he no longer needs its help when his ears are clipped.

WHAT NOT TO DO ABOUT IT

∩ Never tie a horse when you are going to be doing something to him that he might find threatening. If no one is available to hold him, you can hang the lead rope over your arm. Being allowed to move around gives the horse psychological support while he adjusts to the new experience.

∩ Don't make the horse stand too long the first time. Often you have to take things very slowly, so you may only want to do half the body, then put the horse back in the stall for a little R&R. You can continue later on that day or the next day. If you wait much longer than that, the initial cutting will start to grow out and the clip will look uneven.

TALKING HORSES

Sometimes the trouble is in the bit itself, either in its size or shape, or in the material it is made of. There are a number of books and web sites with information on bits and bitting that are worth looking into.

COLD WEATHER BEHAVIOR

Caroline enjoys riding Buck three seasons of the year, but when the weather gets really cold his manners get so bad that riding him becomes a chore, and scary as well. He spooks at the least little thing, and is prone to take off bucking whenever she asks for an increase in speed. He is also very reluctant to stop once he gets going, and in the arena he doesn't want to stay on the rail or go into the corners.

WHAT YOUR HORSE WANTS YOU TO KNOW

∩ *I'm cold!* Some horses deal better with cold weather than others, but all horses, like any athlete, function better when they are warm. People in the United States who can afford it take their horses south in the winter, especially if they are showing or if the owners wish the training to continue at a steady rate, because the cold interferes with the horse's functioning so much that it is difficult to maintain even the status quo, especially with younger horses.

∩ *I need to run and buck to get warm.* Problems with cold weather riding are more common in stabled horses than in horses who live outside, providing the latter grow plenty of fur and are protected from the worst of the weather. They still need ways of keeping warm, such as other horses to huddle with, space and adequate footing to run and play in and micro-climates formed by the lay of the land or vegetation.

WHAT TO DO ABOUT IT

∩ Focus on getting the horse fairly warm and loosened up before you ride. One of the problems is that a cold horse finds it difficult to carry the rider without strain, mostly because cold, tight muscles make it hard to get his hind legs underneath him well enough to compensate for the additional weight in front. The best way is free-longeing—encouraging the horse to run freely in a moderately large area where he can work out his own tensions with bucking and running. With practice, horses get very efficient at loosening themselves up in a minimum amount of time, usually about 5 or 10 minutes at the most. Longeing on a line is a less desirable option, because it is hard for the horse to really loosen himself up on the small circle, and harder still for the handler to allow him to play safely. Thus, what frequently happens is the horse just has to trot or canter around until his muscles loosen up, but this also makes him fitter, so that the next day he takes a little longer to loosen up, and so on until you end up longeing more than you ride.

∩ Horses who are kept in stalls almost always need some sort of blanketing, unless they grow a very good coat and the stable is very tight and warm. Many stable managers believe keeping doors and windows closed leads to respiratory problems in horses, so their barns are quite cold and a horse standing alone in his stall has trouble staying comfortably warm. After a very cold night you may come in and find horses bucking and running around in their stalls in an effort to get warm. A horse kept in these conditions should wear enough blankets that when you slip your hand under them he feels slightly warm to the touch.

∩ When a horse comes from a warm barn where he was blanketed into the cold outdoors, unless he will trot away quietly right away he will soon get chilly and uncomfortable, no matter how warmly he was dressed before. Many people therefore ride in quarter-sheets, which are short blankets that cover the horse's hindquarters. However, these are primarily intended for race horses, who will be galloping and will be ridden a comparatively short time. Cold is felt primarily on the horse's neck and shoulders, which is why he has a mane. It's also why you put your towel around the same area if you come out of a swimming pool on a cool day. You can find short blankets that come further forward and can make a big difference in the horse's attitude. Sometimes warming the horse up in a neck sweat will be even better. It's sort of like wearing a big, warm scarf.

WHAT NOT TO DO ABOUT IT

∩ Don't have the same expectations of your horse in the cold weather as you do when it's warmer. Your horse's reactions will be much slower, especially when it comes to stopping, which requires more collection and thus more flexibility than other work. Expect to spend at least 30 to 40 minutes just getting your horse loose enough to do the things that are easy for him. Don't expect to make great strides in training in the very cold weather, either. However, you can do a lot of confirming of good habits, so your horse becomes more consistent in the things he already knows.

⋂ Don't make the mistake of not dressing warmly enough yourself, especially your legs and feet. Cold muscles are tense muscles, so you ride less well and your tension carries over to the horse, making it harder for him to relax even when he is warm. You are also more likely to fall if he acts up, and more likely to get hurt if you do fall.

TALKING HORSES

At my stable, I had a number of novice riders who were doing mostly slow work. In the winter they just put their saddles or bareback pads right over the blankets. The stable was warm and the arena was cold, but the horses behaved perfectly all winter long because they were always nice and warm!

DOCTORING: APPLYING EYE OINTMENTS

Connie's horse, Jock, got some hayseed under his eyelid, which finally had to be removed by the veterinarian. There was, fortunately, no damage to the eye itself, but he needs to have ointment put in the eye several times a day. The vet put it in with no trouble when she was demonstrating to Connie, but Jock was still partially sedated at the time. Now, when Connie tries to apply the ointment herself, Jock flings his head around and the ointment goes everywhere except where it belongs. Connie is also afraid she might poke Jock's eye with the tube.

WHAT YOUR HORSE WANTS YOU TO KNOW

⋂ *Poke your finger in my eye? You've got to be kidding!* No horse likes having his eyes fooled with, any more than you would. And if the eye has been hurting for awhile and is sensitive, he is even more reluctant.

WHAT TO DO ABOUT IT

⋂ Spend a few minutes with the clicker (page 27) and some treats, getting the horse to lower his head (page 14) and allow you to bring your hand near his eye. Use advance and retreat (page 27), if necessary. Try to get him to allow you to cup your hand over the eye, rather than actually touch it.

⋂ When you are ready to apply the ointment, first be sure the halter is fairly snugly fitted to his head. A flat halter is better than a rope one for this. Then, if it is his left eye, stand facing the left side of his head and slide your right hand under the cheek piece of the halter. This will stabilize your hand so that if he moves his head, your hand will go with it. Hold the ointment tube in your right hand, with the point of the applicator near the front corner of his eye. Keep the applicator *parallel* with his eye, *not* pointing in toward it.

○ Now rest your left wrist on the side of the horse's nose and place your left thumb against the horse's lower eyelid near the front corner and roll it downward. At the same time, use your index finger in the little groove of the upper eyelid, also near the front, and push it upward. The horse will try to scrunch his lids together, but do the best you can. Praise him for holding still, and remain gentle and smiling even if he fusses. Hold the applicator flat, close to the membrane inside the lower lid, in the corner of the eye. Then draw it along the inside of the lower lid, squeezing out ointment as it moves, laying a thin line. Take the tube away, let go of the eyelids with your left hand, and use your left thumb to gently rub the lower lid and spread the ointment.

○ If it is the right eye that needs treatment, do everything with the other hand. Since both hands have to do something intricate, being left- or right-handed doesn't make much difference. Being ambidextrous would help.

○ Follow-up treatment of eyes after an injury is extremely important, so if the horse is *very* reluctant, use a twitch on him (page 19). It will reduce his fears, as well as making it easier to keep his head still. If you use the twitch quietly and correctly, he will soon find that the eye treatment is not painful and will stand without the twitch.

WHAT NOT TO DO ABOUT IT

○ Don't worry if you don't apply the ointment perfectly. The vet makes it look easy, but she has had a lot of practice. As long as you get a good part of it on the eye, it will be fine.

○ Needless to say, don't hurry or get angry if the horse is fussy.

DOCTORING: DRENCHING

Drenching means to dose a horse with some sort of liquid medicine. The usual technique is to use a plastic turkey baster, which is about 10 inches long and has a narrow mouth at one end and a rubber bulb at the other end that you squeeze and release to draw liquid up into it, then squeeze to force the liquid out again.

So, your horse needs medicating and you have the liquid in the turkey baster. You put it in the horse's mouth, he throws his head and swings it around and if you squirted any liquid into his mouth you discover that drenching is also what tends to happen to the person who is trying to give the medicine, because most of the liquid splashes on anyone in the vicinity!

WHAT YOUR HORSE WANTS YOU TO KNOW

∩ *What are you doing?! What the heck is that? It sure feels funny in my mouth and I don't like it!* Horses are always a bit wary of new experiences, especially if they involve invading personal space.

WHAT TO DO ABOUT IT

∩ The horse should be accustomed to having your hands in his mouth and not be bothered by them. Use the Tteam (page 34) mouth work. Lots of horses like having their gums rubbed and their tongues played with; in fact, some of them will stick their tongues out for you to rub them! Don't wait until your horse needs medication to get him accustomed to having his mouth played with. If he has head-shy issues (page 78), deal with those first, then spend a few minutes as often as you can getting him accustomed to your hands in and around his mouth. Use advance and retreat (page 27) so you don't come across as threatening or invasive. Do be very careful, though, because the horse can hurt you quite unintentionally if your fingers are in the wrong place at the wrong time.

∩ Once he is accustomed to letting you put things in his mouth, it isn't too hard to introduce the baster or what ever applicator you use, just to get him used to it. If you fill it with something tasty like apple juice, you'll have him begging for more!

∩ Because of the length of the horse's head, you need to squirt the liquid well back. It is easier and safer to hold the baster on the outside of his teeth, because if you try to get it inside the teeth and he bites down on it, he could hurt himself. You'll want to raise his head, squirt the liquid in, then gently hold his mouth closed as best you can while he uses his tongue to work the liquid back to his throat. Don't hold his mouth so tightly that he can't work his tongue. He will spill a lot of the liquid, but some of it will get down his throat.

∩ He needs to learn to raise his head when you lift up on it, and horses are just as reluctant to raise their heads when you want them to as they are to lower them! Use the same techniques to teach head raising as you do to teach head lowering (page 14). He must also learn to accept your hands holding his mouth shut, without fighting. Getting hit in the face by a thrashing horse's head is no joke. You can practice all these actions in separate steps, just for a minute here and a minute there when you're grooming or untacking.

WHAT NOT TO DO ABOUT IT

∩ Don't hurry and don't try to get too forceful. If you have never had a chance to practice the steps I've just outlined, take your time and let the horse figure out that you're not trying to kill him. Smiles, praise and treats work wonders.

DOCTORING: FEAR OF SHOTS

It's that time of year again. No, not tax time—time for Jeff, Sally's equine friend, to get his annual flu and other shots. It always seems to be a traumatic time because Jeff makes a big fuss, dances around the barn with his head up and, more often than Sally thinks he should, has a very sore neck the next day.

Since most of the other horses in the barn seem to accept the shots with fairly calm resignation, Sally doesn't think the shots are being given roughly. She just thinks life would be a lot easier for everyone if Jeff could learn to be more relaxed about his shots. She also knows that situations do arise where a horse has to be given a shot every day for several days, and she might have to give them herself, which she would find very difficult as things are now.

WHAT YOUR HORSE WANTS YOU TO KNOW

⋂ *It's gonna hurt. I know it's gonna hurt!* Perhaps when he was a youngster Jeff was injected clumsily, or someone made too much of a fuss or held him too tightly and scared him. Whatever the cause, when the veterinarian approaches with the needle, Jeff gets tense and then, of course, it hurts much more than it should.

⋂ *I need to move around to relieve some of my tension.* Prey animals depend on movement to save them, so in any situation where they feel threatened, being made to hold still increases the threat.

WHAT TO DO ABOUT IT

⋂ In this situation, you need to do two things: First, you must build the horse's trust, and second, you need to desensitize him, especially in the neck area. Trust is mostly a matter of the horse accepting your authority, so that if you tell him it's all right, he accepts your authority rather than trying to take over and manage a situation that he really doesn't understand. Tteam leading (page 34) and Parelli games (page 29) would probably be the way to go.

⋂ To desensitize the horse, first get him to the point where he is comfortable being touched and stroked everywhere on both sides of his neck. Then gradually accustom him to being lightly slapped and punched, which is what most vets do just prior to giving a shot. Slapping works well when giving shots to the average horse, since it desensitizes him and he doesn't notice the prick of the needle. However, if the horse has learned to expect that the needle will hurt, slapping just warns him the hurt is coming up, so he tenses. If the horse finds that nearly all the time the slap is followed by a rub, rather than a needle, he will begin to relax about it, so when he does get the needle it will be less painful.

⋂ Teaching him to keep his head down during the desensitizing training will help with neck relaxation. Also, the lowered head creates a more trusting, accepting attitude.

∩　Clicking and treating when he stands quietly for the slapping will help him have more pleasant associations with the procedure.

∩　When the shot is actually given, stand on the opposite side and firmly pinch the skin in front of the horse's shoulder, which will redirect his attention.

∩　Try to be very grounded and have soft eyes (page 9), so your appearance as a predator is minimized. In addition, your relaxed body will help the horse relax.

WHAT NOT TO DO ABOUT IT

∩　As always, any action like yanking or shouting is only going to create more tension, as will trying to *force* the horse to stand perfectly still.

∩　Many owners make the mistake of patting and cajoling the horse when he is making the biggest fuss. This makes him think that making a fuss is not only acceptable, but desirable. Any sort of fussing should be treated very objectively, with the treats saved for when he starts to offer a more acceptable response.

DOCTORING: SOAKING A LEG OR A FOOT

Brian's horse, Easy Rider, has an injury, and the vet says Easy needs to have his lower leg soaked for 10 minutes twice a day. Brian gets a pail and fills it with moderately hot water, as directed, and puts it, and Easy, on the aisle. He thinks about crosstying Easy, but wisely decides against it because he hasn't tried this before and isn't sure what Easy will do. Instead, he has a friend hold the horse. Then Brian picks up the injured leg and tries to place it in the bucket. Easy starts to put his foot down, but the bucket isn't quite in the right place, so his foot comes down partly on the side of the bucket. He jerks his foot up, knocks the bucket over and scares himself. After several more tries, Brian finally gives up and uses a clean towel as a compress to soak the leg. Since he is going to be doing this for several more days at least, he would like to get Easy to stand in the bucket on his own.

WHAT YOUR HORSE WANTS YOU TO KNOW

∩　*Oooh, that feels weird. I don't like to put my feet in or on anything funny.* Horses instinctively reject stepping on anything that feels strange. This goes back to prehistoric horses, who had toes rather than hooves, and whose only way of escaping predators was to run. If they stepped on something that injured a foot, their life expectancy was considerably shortened!

WHAT TO DO ABOUT IT

Ω Depending on which area has to be soaked, you may be able to use a shallower, wider container that won't tip as easily. Rubber feed tubs are best, although of course they need to be thoroughly scoured out. For an injury on the bottom of a hoof, you can use a tub that is about four inches deep. For injuries up to the top of the pastern, use an eight-inch-deep tub. For the fetlock/cannon/tendon area, you need an ordinary full-size rubber water bucket. The rubber is preferable to plastic because it is more flexible and quieter if the horse bangs against it. If possible, remove the handle altogether. If not, tie the handle down securely so the horse can't get a foot through it if the bucket turns over. You can, of course, also use the bucket when the injury is to the lower leg, but shallower tubs are easier, if you have one available.

First introduce the horse to the empty bucket or tub. Let him see it, then rub it on his body, using advance and retreat (page 27) if he is unsure about it. Finally, rub it around the leg to be treated.

Then, with the horse either being held or groundtied (not crosstied), place him so he is standing squarely on all four feet. Pick up the bad leg and hold it up briefly, making sure you have it higher than the height of the bucket. Then take the hoof in your hand and gently move it in a downward spiral until it is on the ground. Some horses have trouble balancing when you do this and will pull the foot out of your hand and stamp it on the ground, but try it several times to see if you can get him more relaxed about it.

Now introduce the bucket, still empty. Lift the foot up, place the bucket so the center of it is where the hoof was, and lower the foot into it, using the spiral technique. As soon as the foot touches the bottom of the bucket, praise him or click and treat (page 27). If you have someone holding him, she should have a treat at the ready and praise or click and treat as soon as the horse's foot is down. If she holds the treat so the horse has to turn his head slightly toward the bucket to eat it, that will help keep the foot down. If he takes his foot out again right away, give him a minute, then quietly put it back in and repeat the same drill, encouraging him to put weight on it. Your holder can help by turning his head and pressing gently on his opposite shoulder to encourage him to put weight on the leg.

Continue until he starts to understand that he gets a treat when he puts his foot down, and starts to wait for the treat. Then withhold the praise and treat for a little longer, gradually increasing the time until he keeps his foot in the bucket for a minute or so. Once he stays there (whether he figures it out right off or takes several trials to get the idea), wait a minute or so, praise and treat again, then ask him to lift his foot and take the bucket away. Wait a little while, then repeat, leaving the foot in the bucket longer each time.

When he will stand in the empty bucket, you can either put warm water in the bucket and put his foot in, or put the foot in the bucket first, then add water gradually.

⋒   Sometimes the horse is pretty relaxed about the whole thing and just pulls his foot out of the bucket after a few minutes, out of apparent boredom. In that case, stand on his other side and when you see him starting to shift his weight, ask him to pick up the foot that is not in the bucket, which will prevent him from lifting the other one. Hold it up a minute, praise and treat, then slowly put it down and praise and treat again. After awhile he should get the idea that you don't want him to lift his foot out of the bucket.

WHAT NOT TO DO ABOUT IT

⋒   Don't try to force him to hold his foot in the bucket if he seems frightened.

⋒   Don't tie him unless and until you're sure he won't be frightened if he knocks the bucket over.

DOCTORING: TREATING WOUNDS

Darlene's new two-year-old, Stoney, comes in from the field limping. She looks the horse over and discovers a puffy swelling on one leg. When she starts to inspect it more closely to see whether there is heat in it and what the cause might be, he tries to pull away, running backward and sideways to escape her touch. She tries to soothe him but he wants no part of her, and continues to refuse to allow her to touch or treat him.

WHAT YOUR HORSE WANTS YOU TO KNOW

⋒   *That hurts. I'm afraid.* Horses who have not had careful and thorough handling as babies don't understand that humans can be there to help, even though they may look like predators.

WHAT TO DO ABOUT IT

⋒   Use some Parelli friendly game (page 30) to get the horse to stand to your touch in the general area of the wound. Then use advance and retreat approach (page 27) to the sensitive area, putting your hand first on his body, then gradually working downward. If experienced help is available, have someone hold the horse. If the horse understands the clicker concept (page 27), the person holding the horse can handle the clicker and treats, rewarding each time the horse accepts your touch without moving.

⋒   When he accepts your hand near the injury, start with some Tteam circles (page 34) with your fingertips, going no closer than he can accept. The Tteam will relieve some of his discomfort and help him relax.

∩ Finally, if the injury is a wound and it appears to be infected, take a warm, moist compress and use the same advance and retreat to get him to allow the treatment. Work around the wound carefully, gradually moving toward the center. Often the compress feels good and the horse becomes more willing to accept it. Be effusive with praise throughout, when appropriate.

∩ If the wound is extremely painful and sensitive and you think you can apply the twitch (page 19) without too much difficulty, its use, and the endorphins released, will make the horse more comfortable during treatment.

WHAT NOT TO DO ABOUT IT

∩ Don't get loud and aggressive, but don't be *too* sympathetic either. If you start acting as though you think the horse has every right to overreact, you won't be helping him. Try to save your praise and attention for the moments when he is being brave. There's a delicate balance here that you have to find.

TALKING HORSES

A note on when to call the vet about a wound: If the injury is one that you would go to a doctor for, if it were on you, then call the vet for your horse. If the wound looks as though it might develop into something serious if not treated, and you are unable to get the horse to accept treatment from you, an experienced vet will probably have better luck. If necessary, he can tranquilize the horse.

Most important, especially in the case of puncture wounds, is the need for a tetanus shot.

EAR-SHYNESS, OVERCOMING

Juliet bought Cremorna knowing that she had been badly abused. Juliet spent a long time gaining Cremorna's trust, and the mare will now accept almost all normal handling. But she still is unwilling to have her ears touched. Juliet cannot put the bridle on normally and she is concerned that if Cremorna should develop any physical problem in her ear area, it will be very difficult to treat.

WHAT YOUR HORSE WANTS YOU TO KNOW

∩ *I'm afraid to have my ears touched.* Some horses have never been desensitized about having their ears handled. In addition, if the horse has a history of being abused, it is likely that someone has treated her roughly, perhaps twisting her ear to make her stand for clipping or doctoring.

⋒ *I don't understand why you need to touch my ears.* Most horses will cheerfully rub their ears against the fence or another horse if they itch, indicating that the ears themselves are not sensitive, but an ear-shy horse doesn't want *you* to touch them. This shows that she doesn't relate to humans well enough yet to accept something merely because you want it.

WHAT TO DO ABOUT IT

⋒ Using approach and retreat (page 27), begin by placing your hand on the horse's neck at a point where she is comfortable. Then quickly brush your hand up over her ear as though you were brushing a fly off of it. Wait a few seconds and do it again. Don't make a big issue of it, and don't worry if she shakes her head at first. Make a few more passes, then do something else for awhile. Over time she will shake her head and pull away less as she realizes you aren't hurting her. Then you can start slowing the movement so that your hand rests on her ear for longer and longer periods.

⋒ Stay relaxed and grounded. When you are approaching the ear with your hand, look off into space and smile a little, as though you were thinking of something else, rather than watching the horse like a hawk and frowning in concentration.

⋒ Once she will let your hand rest on her ear, you can use the same method to gently squeeze the ear a little, just for a second, or rub it or massage the tip. Eventually you could introduce some Tteam ear work, which she will find soothing, and which has other useful applications, such as acupressure for colic.

⋒ As the horse becomes more accepting, introduce some clicker training (page 27), rewarding the horse for longer periods of acceptance or allowing more contact, until eventually you are able to handle the ear normally.

⋒ Be sure you work both ears, from the front as well as from both sides if you can reach. During retraining, try to use a bridling and haltering technique that does not involve pulling them over the horse's ears.

⋒ Consider investigating a relationship program in depth (pages 26–35) to build greater trust between you and your horse.

WHAT NOT TO DO ABOUT IT

⋒ Any sort of restraint or force will only strengthen the horse's fear that you intend to hurt her.

⋒ When you start the retraining program, don't set any time limits that might make you, and thus the horse, feel pressured.

FEEDING PROBLEMS: BOLTING HIS GRAIN

When Jessie puts Cody's grain in his manger, the horse goes after it like a starving crocodile, banging the bucket and inhaling the grain as fast as he can. Fortunately, he doesn't get a great deal of grain at a time, but Jessie is concerned that he might develop colic because he doesn't seem to chew at all!

WHAT YOUR HORSE WANTS YOU TO KNOW

∩ *I have to eat really quickly, before someone takes it away from me.* If a horse is fed with other horses and is low horse in the pecking order, the other horses will try to take his grain away, sometimes not even bothering to finish their own before they move in on his. Before long, the horse learns that any grain he doesn't eat immediately, he will never see again. This defensive behavior stays with him even after the cause is removed.

WHAT TO DO ABOUT IT

∩ The usual way to deal with this is to put some moderately large, round rocks, slightly larger than your fist, in the feed manger. The horse has to eat around the rocks, which forces him to slow down.

∩ Some people put the horse's salt brick in the manger, which has the same effect. However, sometimes the salt breaks up or leaves a residue in the manger so the grain gets too salty, and the horse may not eat as much. This is especially true of the colored salt bricks, which contain other minerals.

∩ If the horse isn't getting any supplements or other fine substances in his grain, the grain can be poured over his hay ration, assuming that the ground underneath is reasonably clean and dry. He will have an entertaining and busy time finding every single speck of grain!

WHAT NOT TO DO ABOUT IT

∩ It is probably best not to feed him in the same space as another horse, unless he is the dominant one. Even then, he may gobble his grain so he can get the other horse's. Horses are great believers in doing unto others, but doing it first!

FEEDING PROBLEMS: MAKING NOISE WHILE WAITING

Gerry is in the feed room preparing the grain for her two horses. When she brings the pails into the stable, both horses immediately start to paw. Joey stands at his door and paws so that he bangs on the door, while Sukey prefers to stand in front of her manger and dig a hole, apparently with the intention of reaching China. The behavior stops as soon as they have their grain, but it is destructive as well as very annoying. Gerry shouts at them, or runs over to their stalls and threatens them, but while this may stop them briefly, they start again as soon as she steps away. She enjoys spending time with them and likes the feeding routine, but is getting rather frustrated with this behavior.

WHAT YOUR HORSE WANTS YOU TO KNOW

∩ *Pay attention to me! Me first, me first!* The horses are perfectly well aware that they are annoying Gerry when they paw, but they want attention any way they can get it. This is especially true when food is involved!

∩ *This is sooo exciting. I haven't had so much fun all day.* Horses who spend a lot of time in stalls or small paddocks get rather bored. Feeding is one of the highlights of the day, so it is greeted with much anticipation.

WHAT TO DO ABOUT IT

∩ This is a fairly simple problem. You want the horse to stop pawing, so you must mark and reward—that is, positively reinforce—the behavior you want and not the behavior you don't want. You can use the same methods if the horse bangs on his feed bucket or does any other annoying, attention-getting conduct.

∩ When the horse paws, simply stop wherever you are in the feeding process. You may even turn around and leave the stable for a moment. It doesn't make any difference whether all the horses paw, or only one. When the pawing starts, the feeding stops.

　　When the pawing stops, you start feeding again. As soon as it starts up again—which it will—handle it the same way. The first day or two feeding will take longer than usual, but once the horses figure out that silence is golden and noise means no supper, quiet will quickly become the rule at mealtime.

∩ You have to be very consistent, especially in the beginning, so be sure to allow yourself enough feeding time so that you are not tempted to ignore the pawing "just this once." If you do, you are liable to find yourself right back at square one, although the second round of training the horses will figure it out a little faster. But they will also figure out that they can make *you* give in if they are persistent, so you have to be more determined than they are.

WHAT NOT TO DO ABOUT IT

∩ Don't waste your energy yelling at your horse for pawing. As Gerry found out, it only works for a brief moment.

∩ Don't try to punish him by going to the stall and hitting him. When you reach the stall the horse will, of course, stop pawing, so you will then be punishing him for stopping.

FEEDING PROBLEMS: PICKY EATER

James is a fairly big horse, but Margie finds it hard to keep weight on him. She feeds large amounts of both hay and grain, but half the time the hay is strewn around the stall and some of the grain is still left in the manger when the next mealtime arrives. Since she works him quite hard, she worries that he may suffer nutritional deficiencies or lose even more weight, especially when the show season starts.

WHAT YOUR HORSE WANTS YOU TO KNOW

∩ *Yuck! That is soooo much! It makes me sick just to look at it.* Horses can suffer from the same psychological disorder as small children. If you give them a big plate full of food, which they feel they have to eat, it's a real turnoff. After they have spread it around the stall, it doesn't taste too good, either.

WHAT TO DO ABOUT IT

∩ Of course, you should have him checked by the veterinarian to make sure there isn't a problem, especially with his teeth. And if a horse who usually eats well suddenly stops eating, suspect colic or some other serious problem and call the vet immediately.

∩ If his health and his teeth are good, then you just need to restore his appetite. This treatment may take a few days, or a few weeks, but I have never known it to fail. You may want to cut back a little on the horse's work schedule, and you wouldn't want to make changes in feeding at any especially stressful time in the horse's life.

Clean any waste hay out of the stall. Then, rather than feeding the horse all you want him to eat, give him just a small flake of hay and perhaps half a quart of grain for breakfast, whatever he will finish fairly promptly. Wait several hours, then give him another small flake of hay. As long as he keeps eating it up, you can do this four or five times during the day. If he doesn't eat it all, take the leftovers out and next time give him a smaller amount. Give another small helping of grain around midday.

At night, as well as another small ration of grain, give him one flake of hay, then put several more in a haynet and tie it up in his stall. This will give him more to eat during the night, but it won't get scattered around, which seems to contribute to lack of appetite.

Once he starts acting a bit hungry when you offer him hay, increase the amount of hay, but not the grain. Unless the horse is in very poor health or has a problem with his mouth, high-quality hay is what puts the weight on. When he is eating as much hay as he needs, (which is usually around 15 or 20 pounds a day) and his weight is good, if his energy level is low you can increase his grain, as long as his appetite remains good.

WHAT NOT TO DO ABOUT IT

◖ Don't increase his grain in an effort to put weight on. Grain gives energy, so horses who do work that requires high energy may need larger quantities of grain. But for most horses four quarts a day is ample, and it's too much for many horses. More grain than he needs tends to make the horse hyper and spoil his appetite, so he often loses weight rather than gaining.

TALKING HORSES

Haynets can be dangerous if they're not hung properly. As the hay is eaten, the net collapses and hangs down where the horse can get a foot caught in it. Use a hanging ring at least five feet off the ground. After putting the hay in the net, draw the string up tight around the mouth, then thread it through the ring. Now take the string down to the bottom of the net and thread it through the little circle where the netting comes together at the bottom. Take the string up and thread it through the ring again, pulling it tight so that the bottom of the net is also pulled up to the ring. Fasten it securely with a quick-release knot (page 188.)

FEEDING PROBLEMS: THROWING GRAIN OUT OF THE MANGER

When feed is put into his manger, Jingles buries his nose in it and swings his muzzle from side to side, throwing grain in all directions. Later he will nose around on the ground and pick much of it up, but it is certainly a wasteful way to eat.

WHAT YOUR HORSE WANTS YOU TO KNOW

⋒ This one is a mystery. Whether the horse thinks there is something better at the bottom of the manger, or simply likes to play with his food, is unknown. It really becomes a problem if you are trying to feed the horse medication or a powdery supplement with his grain.

WHAT TO DO ABOUT IT

⋒ Putting rocks in the manger, as you would for bolting (page 61) works equally well for this problem. However, you also need to use either a deep bucket or a manger with a fairly large lip. Otherwise, the horse will throw the rocks out as well. Be sure the bucket or manger is solidly fastened to the wall, so he can't fling it around, either.

⋒ The hay method for bolting works well here too. Even though the grain still ends up on the ground, at least it is in one place.

WHAT NOT TO DO ABOUT IT

⋒ Any sort of punishment would, of course, be pointless.

FEET, REFUSING TO HOLD UP

Jack has finished grooming Mariah, all except for her feet. Mariah will allow him to pick out her front feet without difficulty, but when he tries to do her hind feet she will only hold them up for a few seconds, and then tries to pull away. Jack is fairly strong, so he can hold on through the first few pulls, sometimes long enough to finish cleaning the hoof, but she usually gets her foot away before he is ready to let it go. If he hasn't finished, she will pick it up again, but then they go through the same routine. It makes what should be an easy task rather lengthy and demanding. Besides, Jack worries about how he would handle it if she required some sort of treatment for which she had to hold up the foot longer.

WHAT YOUR HORSE WANTS YOU TO KNOW

⋒ *I'm afraid I'm going to lose my balance.* Horses who are not introduced carefully to standing on three legs often get tense about it. Being tense makes the balancing even more difficult, so the horse gets more unsure and feels compelled to get all four feet on the ground.

⋒ *Hey, take it easy. I don't bend that way!* Sometimes a horse finds it difficult to hold her leg in a position from which her handler can easily pick out the hoof. She may have muscular or neurological problems, or the handler may simply be holding the leg in an awkward way.

∩ *I'm scared it's going to hurt.* Occasionally, a horse has had her feet treated with a medication that was painful. This is particularly true in the case of thrush, a fungal disease that destroys soft tissue in the clefts of the hoof, eventually eating its way down to sensitive areas. Medications used for thrush are often cauterizing in their effect, based on the concept that thrush originates in the hard outer layer of the hoof, which is not sensitive to pain. However, if the thrush is deep and the medication reaches the sensitive tissue, treatment can be extremely painful. Once a horse has been subjected to this a few times, she becomes very reluctant to hold her foot up, especially if you have to dig deep to clean the clefts.

WHAT TO DO ABOUT IT

∩ Work the horse on exercises to help her balance, such as backing and stepping sideways with front and hind legs (see porcupine game, page 30).

∩ Use the method described on page 67 to teach the horse to lift her foot and hold it by herself. Then use the clicker to teach her to hold it for extended periods, first rewarding for a few seconds, then gradually withholding the click for longer and longer intervals. When the horse will hold her foot up for a reasonable length of time by herself, begin holding it in your hand. Then add the action of cleaning, shortening the time period in the beginning if it seems necessary.

∩ When you first take hold of the foot, allow a little movement in case the horse needs to adjust her balance in the beginning. With her hind legs especially, be sure to stand well under the horse with your own leg, so that you are not pulling the leg too far away from her body for comfort.

∩ If the horse is not seriously upset about holding her foot up, when working with the hind leg place the hoof so that it rests on the inside of your knee. Thus, if you are working on the left hind, you are facing the horse's tail with your knees bent, and the hoof is resting on the right (inside) of your left knee. In this position the horse has to push you out of the way to put her foot down, which requires a pretty big effort. It is also a very solid position for her foot, which makes her feel more secure.

∩ If the horse seems to be having a problem relaxing her leg after picking it up, use Tteam (page 34) exercises to improve her balance and freedom of movement. Be lavish with praise, or click and treat when she improves in any of these exercises.

∩ If previous painful treatment seems to be the cause of the problem, use an advance and retreat (page 27) approach. After picking the foot up, at first just put it down again without attempting to clean it at all. Then progress very gradually through brushing the superficial dirt off with your fingers to using the hoofpick gently, just on the sole, to eventually complete cleaning. Clicking and treating, or just praise and treats, will teach the horse the desirability of holding her foot up and also take her mind off the feared pain.

WHAT NOT TO DO ABOUT IT

◠ Don't try to hang on to the foot. The horse has to learn to hold it for you, rather than making you struggle to hang on to it. If she pulls it away, just let it go without comment, then ask her to give it to you again.

◠ Be careful not to grab too tightly with your hand on the wall of the hoof. If the horse has sharp clinches (turned-under horseshoe nail ends), they can rip your fingers if she pulls away suddenly.

◠ Don't punish her for pulling away. As soon as you do so, you become a predator and the horse wants to have all four feet on the ground so she can escape.

◠ Don't get too involved in trying to calm her fears, to the point where she thinks that pulling away is desirable. Just be as businesslike as possible, and quietly but firmly start again.

FEET, REFUSING TO PICK UP

Bear is a big horse and very solid, so when he decides he isn't going to give Al his foot to be cleaned, it can be quite a struggle for Al to pick it up. Once the foot is off the ground, Bear is good about letting Al clean it, but when he puts it back down again it's there to stay, and Bear is in no hurry to give the next foot. The farrier has been complaining that he wishes Al would spend some time to get Bear a little better trained about it.

WHAT YOUR HORSE WANTS YOU TO KNOW

◠ *I'm afraid if I give you my foot I'll lose my balance.* It takes some practice and skill for the horse to balance himself on three legs. Most horses learn it fairly easily, but if the horse has a conformation weakness or has been handled awkwardly, he may become tense about it.

◠ *Give me one good reason why I should give you my foot.* A big part of developing a good relationship with a horse is so that he will want to please you. If no one has made an effort to build a relationship of mutual trust and caring, the horse has no reason to be cooperative. If, in addition, his early training in a particular skill has been abusive or nonexistent, when he grows big enough to resist he may well do so.

◠ *When you get really pushy I feel threatened and I want to keep my feet solidly on the ground in case I need to get away.* Horses are naturally very protective of their feet, since they need them to run with—their first response to danger. Any sort of aggressiveness awakens the horse's prey instincts, especially if there is already a relationship problem. Even though you might never have been abusive to him, if the horse seems to be lacking trust you have to make an extra effort to gain it.

WHAT TO DO ABOUT IT

◠ Before the horse can pick up a foot, he must be standing so that he can take the weight off that foot. Always begin work on the feet by moving the horse around as necessary until he is standing reasonably squarely on all four legs. (Tip: whichever foot he moved last will be the easiest to pick up.) If he is still seems awkward about picking up his feet, use exercises that involve moving backward and sideward to develop his coordination. Parelli games (page 29) and Tteam mazes (page 34) are both helpful. Backing is particularly important with a horse who has trouble picking up his front feet, because he has to learn to shift his weight off them in order to back.

◠ Especially with a large horse, he must *give* you the foot willingly. There are several signals that will usually cause the horse to reflexively pick up his foot. Parelli recommends pinching the chestnut on the front leg or the cap of the hock on the hind leg. Another way is to pinch the tendon on the back of the leg just below and behind the knee or hock. The most commonly used method is to pinch the tendon just above the fetlock joint, but this is the least desirable, simply because it is more work for you to bend over so far, and leaves you in a very bent-over position when you have the hoof. If the horse has developed a resistance to all the normal methods, you can press with a blunt hoofpick in the soft back of the heel, just above the ground. If he is really resistant you may have to begin by leading his head off to one side to force a step, praising or using the clicker (page 27) as soon as the foot starts to leave the ground.

◠ Which method you use is not really important. The important thing is to notice the slightest impulse on the horse's part to lift the foot and reward him with praise, smiles and treats. This is an excellent place to use the clicker, because you can mark the lifting movement so clearly that the horse quickly understands what is wanted. Once he is lifting the foot easily, you can shape the behavior by withholding the click for a tiny bit longer, until he will wait for you to take the foot in your hand. The important thing is that the horse is in control of holding up his own foot, so not only is it easier for you, but less threatening for him.

WHAT NOT TO DO ABOUT IT

◠ Impatience, anger or hurrying will all create tension in both you and the horse, making him less willing to listen.

TALKING HORSES

I had a pony mare once named Delight who was sometimes very tense about her feet. She would start to panic and try to rear if she happened to be feeling nervous that day. I found that if I was careful to breathe and stay very grounded, especially being sure to keep my toes relaxed, it would allay her nervousness and she would allow me to work on her without a fight.

Feet: Refusing to Stand for the Farrier

Liz has spent a lot of time giving her colt, Willie, careful ground training, including teaching him to pick up his feet and hold them up for her. But when the farrier comes to work on him, Willie is very fidgety and fussy, pulling his feet away and generally making trimming and shoeing very difficult. Liz is at a loss to explain this.

WHAT YOUR HORSE WANTS YOU TO KNOW

∩ *I'm not comfortable with this person handling my feet.* It may be that another shoer was impatient with the horse, or perhaps it's something this one is doing. Or it may be that while the horse is comfortable with having his feet picked up, the additional activities involved in shoeing are threatening.

WHAT TO DO ABOUT IT

∩ First, observe the farrier very carefully. Just because he went to farrier school, or even has been shoeing for years, doesn't necessarily mean he is good at handling horses. If your horse is accustomed to intelligent and sympathetic treatment, he will be less than accepting of the "stand up there, you!" school of handling that is still sometimes found.

Questions to ask yourself as you observe:

Does the farrier make sure the horse is standing squarely before he picks up a foot? If the horse is out of balance to begin with, picking up a foot is only going to make him more insecure.

Does the farrier follow the movements of the horse's leg as the horse moves it to adjust his balance? A good farrier can do this without letting go.

If the horse pulls away, does he get angry or does he just quietly pick the foot up again and go on? There is a fine line between babying a horse so he never learns to accept being shod, and bullying him into it. Ask your farrier if he will work with you on the problem. If he doesn't seem interested, follow your gut feelings and, if necessary, ask around to see if there are other competent farriers. You certainly don't want to sacrifice correct foot balance and shoeing for a sympathetic attitude, but look for both.

∩ You should have a hoof rasp and a shoe puller in your toolbox anyway, in case you need them. Use the rasp and a hammer on his hooves to accustom the horse to those actions.

∩ Do some Tteam leg exercises to improve his flexibility and balance.
   With each leg, pick it up and then, instead of putting it straight down or
   allowing the horse to put it down, hold the leg with one hand on the fetlock or pastern and one on the hoof, and move it in slowly descending
   circles to the ground. The circles should be small at first and centered
   over the point where his foot was when you picked it up.
       You may find that the horse will tense up and try to pull the foot
   away. This is from lack of balance. First, try to stay very centered and
   grounded yourself. If he pulls his foot away and puts it down, quietly
   pick it up again and, as you circle it down, try to feel tension forming and
   shake the foot as you would your own in a shakeout (page 8) to release it.
   Eventually you should be able to circle the foot down until the toe is
   touching, let go and have the horse remain like that for a few seconds
   before putting the foot all the way down. If the horse has a lot of difficulty with this exercise, it is a sure sign that he is having trouble with his
   balance when he has to hold the foot up for long periods. Continuing to
   work on it will help, as will any exercises that ask him to manipulate his
   feet in unusual ways. Backing, stepping sideways, walking over rails and
   through mazes all are exercises to increase his balance skills.
       When he can place his foot back in the same spot without losing
   balance, try very gently stretching it out in front, behind, and a little off
   to the sides, and asking him to place it on the ground in those positions.
   This increases his flexibility as well as his balance.

WHAT NOT TO DO ABOUT IT

∩ Don't tie or crosstie a horse who is having problems balancing. Be there
   to hold him yourself, or see that someone experienced does so.

∩ Don't use a farrier who gets rough with your horse.

∩ When working with the horse yourself, don't get too aggressive about
   holding on to the hoof. If he is really losing his balance, you will only
   make him more tense and less able to balance.

GATES, PROBLEMS WITH ARENA

When Erica is finished with her ride on Jerry, she dismounts in the arena and
takes him to the gate to get back to the stable. As she approaches the gate, he
balks for a brief time, then races through it, almost knocking her down in the
process. She pulls him up sharply, but the same thing happens every time she
brings him through this gate. Erica is very confused by this behavior, because
Jerry only does it when he is going out of the arena, not coming in from turnout.
She has noticed that when he's being ridden, he tends to rush past the gate, unlike
her previous horse, who tended to get rather sticky as he neared it.

WHAT YOUR HORSE WANTS YOU TO KNOW

◠ *Something bad is going to happen to me here.* A horse who shows consistent fear in a limited situation is remembering a bad experience. Horses, being herd animals, will always try to return to the herd when they feel threatened. So a horse being ridden in an arena, and perhaps having more demanded of him than he is ready for, will instinctively run to the gate in an effort to return to his herd. This can develop into a very bad habit, especially if the horse feels really threatened by the work situation. He may try to crash through the gate or jump it. Some trainers in this situation will hold the horse at the gate and punish him severely, in an effort to make him afraid of the gate, and thus less likely to try to run through it. This is too abstract a concept for the horse, who simply comes to believe that gates are a place where horses get beaten. Since he doesn't understand why, he panics whenever he is near the gate.

◠ *If I go through quickly, maybe I can avoid trouble.* When the horse has to go through the gate, he reverts to his basic instincts. Running away is the horse's natural solution to almost any problem, even when it doesn't work.

WHAT TO DO ABOUT IT

◠ This problem has two parts: the horse's original fear and discomfort that caused him to want to leave in the first place, and his fear of being punished at the gate. Improve the relationship, especially in the arena. Do some groundwork in the ring, but make it fun, not work. Parelli, clicker and Tteam (pages 27 and 34) all offer games you can play with your horse to help him learn to enjoy being in the arena with you.

◠ To help with his fear of the gate, use the techniques described in Stall Problems: Fear of Doorways (page 139). In addition, because it is *you* the horse is really afraid of in this case, spend time near the gate just patting, scratching or playing the friendly game (page 30)—whatever it takes to make the horse realize that no matter what other people did, *you* are not going to punish him for being near the gate.

WHAT NOT TO DO ABOUT IT

◠ Don't punish or pull the horse up sharply. Any punishment, or feelings of annoyance or anger on your part, will only reinforce his belief that when he goes near the gate, he will be hurt. He doesn't know why, or how to avoid punishment except by avoiding the gate.

◠ Don't allow him to rush forward and then pull him up. This is extremely confusing, since one minute you're saying, "Go ahead, do your thing," and the next you're saying, "Stop what you're doing!"

TALKING HORSES

Sometimes, if the horse has developed an escape reflex in a frightening situation, he can be completely unaware of what he did between the time he started and the time it was over. Think of times when something really scary happened to you—say, your horse spooked really badly. You find yourself staring down at his neck with a deathlike grip on the reins and his sides, with no recollection of how you got there! That's why any sort of correction doesn't work. The horse doesn't remember what he did once that flight reflex took over. You have to work on solving the problem at a point before he "loses it."

GRAZING IN HAND PROBLEMS

Martha likes to graze her horse, Foxy, on the lush green grass that grows around the stable area. The field where Foxy spends most of his time isn't all that big, so the grass gets eaten down. Foxy loves grazing on the better grass, of course, but he seems to crave it so much that he drags Martha around, sometimes trotting away to what he thinks is a better place, with her trailing behind and shouting at him to whoa. He never actually tries to get away from her, but he doesn't listen to her requests either. When she wants to take him in, it takes her quite a while to get him to bring his head up and keep it up.

WHAT YOUR HORSE WANTS YOU TO KNOW

- *I really crave this delicious stuff.* Grass has essential enzymes in it that horses need and that aren't found in hay, so naturally horses try to get as much of it as they can. There is also the occasional horse who has serious nutritional deficiencies and has real trouble restraining himself.

- *Eating grass is a lot better than going back to my stall or that boring field.* The horse has no incentive to leave the grass once he gets there.

- *I don't have to pay any attention to you if I don't want to.* The horse has your number and he knows it. He's learned that he can use his strength and there's nothing a mere human can do about it.

WHAT TO DO ABOUT IT

- The main problem that needs to be dealt with here is the lack of respect or desire to please you. Using whichever training system (page 26) you feel most suits you and your horse, begin a consistent program to teach him to respond to your commands without resistance, whatever the circumstances. Once you have achieved a measure of respect and obedience in the arena or round pen, you can bring the horse back to the grass and ask for the same behavior.

⋒ Positioning your body correctly relative to the horse's head makes all the difference in who controls whom. When holding your horse, imagine he is carrying a long stick in his mouth that sticks out several feet on each side. As long as you are in front of that stick, your leverage will be such that you can keep him from easily pulling away from you. As he turns his head to graze, the imaginary stick turns as well, so you have to keep moving to keep ahead of the stick. Read Leading: Won't Go When Asked (page 91) and Leading, Breaking Away While (page 83) to learn more about how to keep the horse from pulling away.

⋒ To get him to bring his head up when you are ready to leave, have a tasty treat ready to give him the moment he lifts his head. Then give a firm but brief upward tug on the lead rope. Wait a couple of seconds and repeat, a little firmer and a little quicker. If you get no response, stand almost in front of him and start tapping on his nose with your toe—not hard enough to hurt, but enough to annoy him. Imagine trying to get someone to move out of your way in a crowded room. Just keep bothering him and eventually he will lift his head. The moment he does, praise, offer him the treat, then immediately ask him to lead off. If he comes willingly, you can give him another treat on the way home.

⋒ If you are taking him back to his stall, it's also a good idea to have something tasty waiting in his manger. If he is accustomed to expecting that, he will have a greater incentive to return.

⋒ If you think the horse's cravings are extreme, you should explore nutritional supplements, both with your veterinarian and with reputable sources of information about horse nutrition, of which there are many on the Internet (see Appendix A for some suggestions). If you feel he needs more good grazing, once you have him listening to you you can make a point of giving him an adequate grazing period—say, 20 minutes—as frequently as possible.

WHAT NOT TO DO ABOUT IT

⋒ Don't try to control him or pick up his head by pulling. He can outpull you any time, and you may annoy him into trying to break away entirely.

TALKING HORSES

Eventually, if something isn't done, the horse's behavior can become more dangerous, either to you or to him. All of the training systems mentioned in the Introduction begin with the premise that the horse has to want to please you. This is most necessary when there are temptations that override what control you have. That means you must begin some consistent training so that the horse responds to your commands without resistance. It isn't all that hard, but it does take time and persistence.

GROOMING, FUSSING OR FIDGETING DURING

When Susan arrives at the barn to ride, her Thoroughbred horse, Jamie, is standing peacefully in his stall with his head down. He comes to the door and politely takes the carrot she offers him. She then slips on his halter and lead and brings him out to be groomed, as she does every time she rides. And, as he does every time she grooms him, as soon as she starts to work he puts his ears back, walks around on the crossties as much as possible, flips his head up and down, swishes his tail violently and, in general, turns into a perpetual motion machine. No amount of firmly or even loudly voiced "whoas" or slaps when he moves has any effect on his behavior. Susan's previous horse, an older Quarter Horse, always stood quietly while being groomed, as do all the other horses in the stable. Susan feels Jamie is becoming spoiled and disobedient.

Not only is this situation aggravating for Susan, it is also potentially dangerous for both of them. If Jamie becomes more upset he may accidentally step on Susan's foot or even unintentionally kick her. Their ride will also be unfavorably affected by the tension created during the grooming.

WHAT YOUR HORSE WANTS YOU TO KNOW

⋒ *Ouch! That hurts!* We have a tendency to assume horses are all alike in certain ways, and one is their degree of sensitivity. But some horses have more sensitive skin than normal, and Thoroughbreds are most likely to be so sensitive. Since Susan's previous horse didn't mind, or even liked being groomed vigorously, it hasn't occurred to her that Jamie is trying to tell her that he does not! The head throwing expresses tension and discomfort.

⋒ *I want to get away!* Jamie has learned not to try to break away when tied, so he does the next best thing: He moves around as much as he can to get away from the brushing. If your horse is not as well trained, he might pull back on the crossties until he either breaks them or falls down.

⋒ *If you don't stop I'm going to kick!* The violently swishing tail is the horse's warning that he is ready to try to drive you out of his space. Unless you become very aggressive he probably won't actually do so, but he is letting you know that he is feeling really threatened.

WHAT TO DO ABOUT IT

⋒ Begin by putting down all the grooming tools and just placing your hand quietly on the horse's shoulder near his withers. Be sure you are solidly grounded and breathing, and that your arm and hand are soft and relaxed. At first, don't pat or stroke the horse; simply let your hand lie there. This says to him, "When I touch you, it isn't going to hurt and I'm not going to invade your space more than you can accept."

∩ If he continues to move around, keep your hand on his shoulder and follow him quietly, making no attempt to force him to stand still. Wait for a moment when he stands still, even for a few seconds, and praise him. Quietly remove your hand, back away for a minute and repeat. If even that is too much, start by swiping your hand quietly but quickly across his shoulder, then wait and repeat. Gradually slow your movement until your hand rests on him.

∩ Within a few minutes he should figure out that you aren't going to hurt him. Then start gently "grooming" him all over with your hand, stroking with the lie of the hair in a brushing motion. If he seems especially sensitive in some places, back off, then quietly approach them again (advance and retreat, page 27) When he accepts this, use a circular currying motion with the flat of your hand on the areas you would normally curry.

∩ Carefully try different grooming tools to see what he will accept without discomfort. Rubber grooming mittens with little pimples, or even a dampened towel, will work for the most sensitive horses, as will very soft finishing brushes. Once he discovers that grooming does not hurt, and even feels good, much of his sensitivity will go away. Then you can eventually go back to more normal grooming tools, although probably always used with care.

∩ If he seems very flinchy, you may want to spend some time on the friendly game (page 30), or use Tteam to get him more relaxed about being touched. Working on these exercises every day when you groom will help with his sensitivity, and also your mutual bonding.

WHAT NOT TO DO ABOUT IT

∩ Don't try to groom your horse in a hurry. Hurry creates tension. This is especially true if you're late, and angry because you're late. The horse senses your anger and thinks it's directed at him, so he interprets your fast moves as aggressive ones.

∩ Don't yell at him or slap him for moving. He will associate grooming with punishment, making him even more reactive. If he moves, quietly move him back, then praise him. When he stands quietly for longer than usual, tell him how good he is.

∩ Don't let your body position become tense in an effort to be ready to move out of his way. He will pick up on this as a flight signal and be even more likely to move.

TALKING HORSES

Scratching is like the mutual grooming horses give one another if they are good friends. Besides telling your horse that your touch can be pleasant, it changes your relationship to buddies, rather than master and slave.

Mutual grooming can become very mutual, with the horse scratching your back as you scratch his. This is fine with an older horse. With a young horse, you need to be careful that he doesn't try to escalate it into a rougher game.

Look for little places, such as just behind the shoulder near the withers or at the base of the neck, that are "itchy spots"—places where the horse likes to be scratched. Start scratching gently, just the way you like your own back scratched. If the horse seems to like a little more pressure, go ahead. Eventually this becomes a loving little game that you play together. It also can be fun to watch as the horse works his body to get you to scratch in just the right place.

HALTERING, RESISTANCE TO

Danny is a very pleasant, obedient horse once his halter is on, but he is not as easy to halter as he should be. Elizabeth would prefer to turn him out with his halter off, for safety reasons, but even though he will walk up to her, especially if she has grain, when she starts to put on the halter he flips his head around and generally makes things more difficult than she would like.

WHAT YOUR HORSE WANTS YOU TO KNOW

⋒ *I'm afraid of being trapped and restricted.* Unless it is approached carefully, putting a halter on a horse is very much a predator type of action—think lion grabbing horse by nose and pulling him down—so a horse can easily develop fears about it.

⋒ *I want to be with you, but not if I have to let you put the halter on.* Because Danny will walk up to Elizabeth, and because he is pleasant as soon as the halter is on, he is saying that it isn't Elizabeth herself, but the action of putting on the halter, that is upsetting.

WHAT TO DO ABOUT IT

⋒ If the horse is taught to put the halter on himself—that is, to voluntarily put his nose into the halter rather than having it pulled up around him—and to voluntarily drop his head to allow it to be fastened, the choice then becomes his and he no longer feels threatened by the halter. This should be worked on in the stall, where he has no thoughts of escaping.

⋂ The first thing to teach the horse is to drop his head when asked to do so—something he needs to know for other reasons anyway (page 14). Once he will drop his head easily, use a halter with the crownpiece unfastened. If possible, put your right arm over his neck as in bridling an ear-shy horse (page 59). If this is not possible, slip it under his neck, then reach up with your hand to ask him to lower his head. Hold the halter nose up with your left hand so that when he drops his head, the halter will be there. You can make it even easier and more desirable by holding a treat in the palm of your left hand, so he has to put his nose into the halter to get the treat. Hold the halter as still as possible with your right hand, so that he's the one doing the moving, not you.

⋂ If he swings his nose off to the side to avoid the halter, use the tapping technique (Parelli "bothering," page 12) on the side of his nose to get him to bring it back toward the halter. Remember to stop tapping, smile, praise or click and treat at the slightest move in the right direction. If you are patient, persistent and quick to reward correct reactions, he will soon learn to put his nose in the halter by himself. Then all you have to do is fasten the crownpiece.

⋂ Using advance and retreat (page 27) is also helpful. Slip the halter over his nose, then immediately slip it off. Repeat this a number of times so that he stops thinking you are going to hang on to him.

⋂ Once he has learned to consistently put his nose in a halter with the crownpiece undone, you can ask him to do the same with the crownpiece closed and the throatlatch unsnapped. Hold the halter crownpiece in your right hand, with your forearm either over his poll or over his left temple and the halter nose in your left hand. Ask for a head drop, rewarding and praising as before.

⋂ When he drops his nose into the halter, let go of the nosepiece with your left hand and bring it up so it's holding the crownpiece, lifting it up if necessary to bring the nosepiece to the correct level (see Appendix B). Now, use your right hand to gently guide first his left ear, then his right, as you bring the crownpiece over his poll. If you can't reach across, do just the left ear, then walk around to do the right one.

WHAT NOT TO DO ABOUT IT

⋂ Don't try to pull the halter up in a hurry "before he can get away." He is much faster than you are, and will only become less willing to approach.

⋂ Don't chase him with the halter. Have a lead line attached to the halter and quietly put that around his neck first.

⋂ Don't try to sneak up on him and pretend you don't have the halter with you. It won't take him long to figure that one out!

⋂ When asking him to lower his head, don't think about pulling or pressing it downward. That will only make him fight you. Just apply enough pressure to make him a little uncomfortable (page 16).

⋂ When using the closed crownpiece, don't try to pull the halter over both ears at once. It's uncomfortable for him and, while it may not hurt him, it won't raise you in his estimation, either.

HEAD-SHYNESS, OVERCOMING

Every time Sue tries to do anything around Jake's head, from brushing to bridling, he puts his head up as high as he can reach, swings it around or pulls it away. She has to keep a halter on him all the time or she would never get near him. His head-shyness is the same psychological problem as ear-shyness (Ear-Shyness, Overcoming, page 59), but a great deal worse because it involves the whole head.

WHAT YOUR HORSE WANTS YOU TO KNOW

⋂ *I don't trust you around my head.* Rough or ignorant treatment is always the cause of sensitivity on the horse's body. A horse who has been handled in this way for any length of time will need special attention to get over it.

⋂ *I'm afraid you're going to attack me.* The prey-predator aspect of the horse-human relationship always predominates in the horse's mind unless someone takes the time to help him work past it.

WHAT TO DO ABOUT IT

⋂ Try to stay very grounded as you work around the horse. The tenser you appear to him, the harder it will be for him to relax and accept you.

⋂ As with ear-shyness, use approach and retreat (page 27) to overcome the horse's initial fears. You can probably work from both the neck and the muzzle toward the more sensitive areas.

⋂ The psychology of the Parelli friendly game (page 30), with its casual approach, rather than a more intense "training" attitude, will help both you and the horse to be more relaxed as you work on this problem.

⋂ Clicker training (page 27) often works well in fear situations. Try to mark the instant the horse shows less fear or is less reactive.

⋂ The bonding aspect of Tteam (page 34) is very soothing to both horse and handler.

⋂ Work on the head drop (page 14), starting as far down the neck as necessary and praising the horse's slightest move toward yielding.

⋂ Considering how deep-seated this fear is, it's surprising that it can be completely eliminated. But it can, and doesn't take as long as you might think. Still, it takes time and requires patience.

WHAT NOT TO DO ABOUT IT

⋒ Avoid confrontations as much as possible during the retraining period, since each one will set the training back. Use a padded halter with a releasing device that you can safely leave on, and if possible, just attach some reins to it to ride with. If you need to use a bridle, use the bridling technique described on page 23.

⋒ Try to keep restraints to a minimum. The more the horse thinks you're trying to hold on to him, the more threatened he feels. Especially, *never* try to grab an ear to hold him.

⋒ Don't be in a hurry. It took time for the horse to develop this fear, and it will take time to eliminate it.

TALKING HORSES

To many horses, placing and keeping your hand on their nose challenges their dominance. Even though this is handled in very much the same way, with approach and retreat, it has nothing to do with fear. Rather, it has to do with lack of respect. As such, it is much easier to cure. If you are politely persistent while not attempting to challenge the horse by asking for too much submission all at once, and remember to thank and praise him when he yields and accepts your hand even slightly, he will soon give you the respect you deserve.

KICKING AT OTHER HORSES

Jan enjoys riding with her friends and, although she likes trail riding too, she likes working on her own skills in the arena, and on those of her horse, Gerry. Unfortunately, while Gerry is very talented and athletic, he is not very well socialized and will kick at other horses if they get too close. When there are more than one or two people in the arena this can make things difficult for Jan, because she has to put in so much thought and planning to avoid the others. She also has to be careful in the stable if other horses want to pass when Gerry is on the crossties. Things are better on the trail, because Gerry doesn't mind being at the end of the group. But it is a problem that needs some serious attention.

WHAT YOUR HORSE WANTS YOU TO KNOW

⋒ *I am scared of these other horses and need to defend myself.* Many horses have very poorly developed social skills with other horses, although they may have learned to get along well with humans.

⋒ *I don't know what else to do.* If the horse perceives a situation as threatening and he can't run away, he may see kicking as his only option.

WHAT TO DO ABOUT IT

∩ Even though this problem occurs while riding, like so many problems it is best dealt with on the ground. Using any or all of the four methods described in the Introduction, begin by building his trust and confidence in you. If he can think of you as his protector, he is less likely to feel threatened by other horses.

∩ To work on this problem, you need the help of other riders and horses. In the arena, back the horse into a corner and ask the other riders to stay fairly far away at first. Watch the horse's reactions closely. If he ignores the other horses, invite them to ride a little closer, until he becomes aware of them but doesn't seem too threatened. Turn his head very slightly away from an approaching horse, so the situation doesn't feel so confrontational, and ask other riders *not* to ride directly at him. If he responds with ears back or attempts to swing on them, restrain him but otherwise ignore the behavior. As they continue to ride by—sort of advance-retreat under saddle—he should eventually start to accept them better. Look for either ignoring or at least passive response, and praise or click and treat (page 27) all desirable behavior.

∩ Once he is fairly accepting from the corner of the arena, put him in the middle, making sure that no one approaches him too closely from behind. Be prepared to turn him quickly in a small circle if he looks like he's thinking of kicking.

∩ If you have been doing Parelli games (page 29), play the games with him to keep his focus on you and his mind off the other horses.

∩ Place the horse facing straight across the ring and invite other riders to come in and halt parallel to him, as though they were lining up in the show ring. At first they should line up about 15 feet (five meters) away and only stay for 30 seconds or so before moving off. Then they should gradually decrease the distance and increase the length of time, as you observe the horse's responses and praise or click and treat when he seems to be accepting their presence fairly comfortably.

∩ If other riders in your stable are using Parelli, ask if you can do some group Parelli seven games. By keeping him busy with other horses who are paying little or no attention to him, you are teaching him that he can safely ignore them.

∩ When you go back to riding in a group, reintroduce him to the group step by step, just as you did on the ground.

∩ In the stable once you feel he is ready for it, when other horses want to pass by, lead him over close to the wall and parallel to it. Then stand by his shoulder and turn his head toward the other horse as he passes. This position prevents him from swinging his hindquarters out. Once the other horse passes, even if your horse's ears go back, when they have come forward again praise or treat him.

WHAT NOT TO DO ABOUT IT

∩ Don't completely isolate him from the other horses. This will only make him more nervous when he has to be with them.

∩ When riding, avoid situations where he approaches another horse head on, or where another horse rides close by when he is on the rail. The first is confrontational, the second makes him feel trapped—either of which might cause him to kick in what he sees as self-defense.

∩ Don't try to force him to accept the close presence of other horses until he is really comfortable with them at a distance. That means that, at the beginning of the training, when you are in the stable he should be put into a stall when other horses are passing, rather than forced to let them into his space before he is ready.

TALKING HORSES

Horses are often removed from the natural life of the herd at an early age, put into training and physically isolated in stalls. If they do run with other horses, it may be only others of the same age, rather than older horses who can teach them their social skills. Under these circumstances, it is not surprising that some horses lack good herd manners. It is more surprising, and a credit to the general good nature of the species, that there are comparatively few such horses.

KICKING AT PEOPLE

Marylou's horse, James, has one habit she doesn't like at all. When she opens the door of his stall, if he has his tail toward her and she tries to walk in, he lifts his hind leg at her in a threatening way. He has never actually kicked her, but she has never pushed the issue, either. He usually moves over on his own after a minute or two, so she can walk in and get him. Her friend Mimi's horse, Chiquita, doesn't kick under those circumstances, but does tend to kick when Mimi goes to tighten the girth. Both women realize that kicking can be dangerous, but since punishment hasn't accomplished much, they aren't sure what to do next.

WHAT YOUR HORSE WANTS YOU TO KNOW

∩ *I feel threatened.* The horse who kicks in the stall may have been punished in the stall, or may feel he has to defend his space or his food. The horse who kicks at the girth has almost surely been girthed painfully tight.

∩ *I feel trapped.* Kicking is essentially defensive rather than aggressive behavior. The horse uses it when he can't run away.

WHAT TO DO ABOUT IT

∩ Safety first. Don't enter the stall unless you are sure the horse will allow you to approach his head.

∩ In the stall, choose a time when the horse does not have food in front of him. If the horse turns his tail as you come to the door, try using approach and retreat (page 27). Some horses just don't want you pushing into their space uninvited. Smile and praise at the least indication of polite acceptance of your presence. Then begin by asking the horse to turn and face you while you are still outside the stall. If one is available, use a breast chain or stall guard with the door open. Shake grain in a bucket or, if he recognizes the sound, bite on a carrot or apple as you would to feed him. When he starts to turn around, or even turn an ear, smile and praise. However, if he comes toward you in a threatening manner, quickly step back out of reach and wait until his attitude changes and his ears come forward before approaching and offering a treat. Advance and retreat as often as necessary until he makes the connection between bad attitude—no treat, good attitude—treat.

∩ If he does not respond to treats, stand outside the stall, behind the door-post, and tap him on the side of his hindquarter to ask him to move, using a stick if necessary to reach him safely. Use the "dingo" method (page 14), looking carefully for any response. Try not to cause pain, which would only make him aggressive. You only want to make him uncomfortable. Imagine asking someone to move over in a crowded room. Be very patient but persistent, and very quick with praise at the slightest "try" on his part.

∩ If the horse is very hostile, use feeding time as a way to get to him. Start with the hay. Bring it to the stall door, put up the breast chain if there is one, and wait for him to turn and face you. If he does so politely (that is, fairly slowly with his ears forward), smile, praise and give him the hay. If he is at all rude or aggressive, step back out of reach and wait. When his ears come forward, praise and step forward again with the hay, but be ready to step back if he becomes aggressive again—as many horses do when food is nearby. Continue until he waits politely for you to drop the hay.

∩ Repeat using grain, but do not attempt to place grain in a manger on the far side of the stall at first—you could be in danger as you leave the stall. Use a substantial bucket or a shallow feeder. When he gives you the proper behavior, place the grain near the door. If you use a bucket, tie it or clip it to whatever you can find within reach, because you don't want the bucket with its handle rolling around in the stall. A shallow rubber feeder can simply be placed on the floor of the stall.

⋒ Out of the stall, use any of the training methods in the Introduction to teach the horse to face you and come to you and, more important, to build trust, since this is mostly a trust issue.

⋒ Aggressiveness about moving over may be caused by clumsy handling. Read Stall Problems: Crowding (page 137).

⋒ For kicking during girthing, see Saddling: Problems While Being Cinched or Girthed Up (page 131).

WHAT NOT TO DO ABOUT IT

⋒ Don't escalate the problem with punishment. The horse has already shown that he feels threatened. On the other hand, walking away from the stall entirely tells him that kicking works.

⋒ When actually entering the stall with any horse who has his tail to you, *don't* touch him on the hindquarters first. Get his attention so you're sure he knows you're there. Speak or click and look for a response from his ears or head to show that he heard. Then, if there is room, walk quietly past his hindquarters to his head.

⋒ Don't try to shove your way through a small space.

LEADING, BREAKING AWAY WHILE

Martha's pony, Sylvester, is very gentle and pleasant to ride, but she would like to be able to spend more time with him on the ground, grazing him, playing with him and just generally enjoying his company. Unfortunately, she learned not long after she got him that when he gets tired of being with her, he spins around and breaks away from her and will not allow himself to be caught. Several grown-ups have tried to break him of the habit, with no success.

This can be a very tricky problem to deal with. One of the secrets to basic horse training is never allow the horse to find out he can win by using strength. Once he learns that, he just gets smarter and smarter about using it.

WHAT YOUR HORSE WANTS YOU TO KNOW

⋒ *I know I can get away with this. I can outsmart you and outpull you. And then I can go do what I want.* Ponies are very smart, and perhaps they need to be to survive among larger animals. Because they are small, ponies are frequently given to children to train before they have become confirmed in good manners. The child's lack of experience leads to mistakes in handling, which may either annoy the pony or simply teach him ways to take charge and be disrespectful.

🜚 *I'm stronger than you.* If the horse can get *you* to pull, he can use his strength to pull away.

🜚 *Once I'm free, I know that if I allow myself to be caught I'll be punished.* No question that trying to catch an animal who won't allow you to catch him is frustrating and infuriating, and the horse senses your annoyance. No way is he going to let you near him when you're feeling like that!

WHAT TO DO ABOUT IT

🜚 The best place to start is probably with clicker training (page 27). Clicker is best here because it quickly changes the horse's attitude about control. Rather than feeling he has to control the situation by getting away from the handler, he finds he can control things in a way that is more to his advantage (all those treats) by trying to please his handler. Besides teaching him to give to pressure on the lead rope, you can teach him to follow a target when being led.

🜚 To teach him to give to pressure, work with the horse in the stall or other small confined area, so that breaking away is of no advantage to him. Use an extra long lead rope so he can swing all the way around without making you pull, which would give him the advantage. Begin by pulling the lead rope gently and smoothly to one side, standing by or a little in front of his head, not behind it (see Grazing in Hand Problems, page 72). If he pulls away, let the rope run through your hand without resisting (wear gloves to avoid rope burns), catch him again if he actually breaks away and try again, using less pressure or combing the rope (page 33). Look for the slightest tendency to yield instead of resist, then release the pressure and click, praise and treat. Continue asking for yielding, at first accepting any effort, then gradually withholding the click and reward until he yields more with his head, and then with his feet, still to a very soft pressure.

🜚 In addition to the clicker, another technique used to teach the horse to face you when you drive his hindquarters away would be the Parelli driving game (page 32). The original bad habit almost surely developed from his handler trying to drag the horse around by the head. This is very predatory behavior and creates resistance very quickly. If, instead of trying to pull the head toward you, you chase the back end away, it has the same effect physically and is psychologically much more effective.

🜚 If the horse seems to have an aggressive attitude, some round pen training (page 34) might well be effective in changing it. Round pen work teaches the horse that comfort comes from facing you and allowing you into his space. It also shows him that you can control his movement even when you aren't holding on to him, thus making breaking away a less desirable option. Get him moving around, then ask him to stop and turn away from the gate each time he approaches it, until he gets a little tired. Watch for him to start looking toward you, and praise him when he does so. When he comes to you submissively, ask him to walk quietly behind you to the gate. Thus, he learns that you will allow him freedom, provided he accepts it on your terms, not his.

∩ Playing other Parelli, Tteam and clicker games will improve the horse's attitude toward you and his desire to please, but be prepared to wait quite awhile for the horse to completely get over his aggressive behavior.

∩ The horse breaks away by turning his head very quickly away from you, which then puts him in a position to use his whole body to push against the rope and overpower you. Tteam leading (page 34) will help you to position your body correctly to make this more difficult for him.

∩ While you are retraining, try to avoid situations that give the horse the advantage. You may have to exercise a little ingenuity to do this. Tack him in the stall and mount him as soon as possible, keeping him in an area where he is restricted by doors or gates.

∩ As a temporary restraint, you can lead the horse using a longe line and longeing surcingle as a sort of block-and-tackle to give you a physical advantage. Fasten the longe line to the side ring of the halter, then run it back through one of the upper rings on the surcingle, then either back through the halter side ring again if it will run freely, or through a snaffle bit ring and back to your right hand. (The bit must have full cheeks to keep it from pulling through the horse's mouth.) Attach a regular lead line to the center ring on the back of the halter that you use for normal leading. Staying ahead of the horse (page 88), lead him with that line, held very lightly in your left hand. When he starts to spin away, let that line go and use both hands to pull very quickly on the longe line. Since it is doubled, you will have to pull twice as far to have an effect on the horse. You want to make contact before he gets his head turned the other way. If you are reasonably well coordinated (and since the horse won't be expecting you to have all that extra power), you will be able to bring his head right back to you. Immediately make much of him, give him treats and allow him to stand with you and find out what a nice place that can be. This procedure will give you temporary control over the situation, but is too clumsy and time consuming to be used all the time. Also, if it is used improperly, a smart horse will learn to overcome it, so the important thing to work on is his attitude using the other methods.

∩ For catching the horse once he is loose, see Turnout: Refusing to Be Caught, page 172.

WHAT NOT TO DO ABOUT IT

∩ Don't drag on the lead line. This is predatory and invites the horse to fight the line.

∩ If the horse does get away, when you finally get him back don't let him see your anger or frustration. Instead, praise him for allowing you to catch him.

LEADING, RUNNING OVER HANDLER WHILE

Gerry's young gelding, Skitch, is not at all aggressive, but he is rather playful—not surprising in a gelding of that age. When Gerry leads him, Skitch slides in directly behind him, then nibbles on the back of his coat. However, if something sudden happens behind them, Skitch jumps forward, and since Gerry is right in front of him he bumps into Gerry hard. It's not much of a problem for Gerry, who is big and athletic, but it would be dangerous for a smaller or less agile person.

WHAT YOUR HORSE WANTS YOU TO KNOW

◯ *Hey buddy, let's play!* Skitch is at a playful age, but many older horses like to play games too. You don't want to discourage that, but you do want to set some safety rules.

◯ *If you insist on being in front, I'll just get back here and tease you.* In Leading, Rushing Ahead While (page 87) we discussed teaching the horse to stay behind your head, making you the "lead horse." But some horses, prevented from walking past you, will get directly behind you, so close that, were you another horse, you couldn't kick out effectively. They then try to establish some control from that position.

◯ *Oops. Well, you don't really mind, do you?* Horses don't understand things like relative size. They assume all mature animals can look after themselves, and if you don't like being bumped, you can always kick, right? Horses have to be taught to respect others' space, and the younger they learn this, the better.

WHAT TO DO ABOUT IT

◯ Teach him to walk beside you rather than directly behind. Psychologically this is more effective because he can't do much to annoy you from that position, so he tends to give up and accept you as leader. This is comparatively easy to teach, once he has learned not to run past you (page 88). Rather than holding the stick where you can swing it across in front of him, hold it in your left hand so you can reach behind you and tap him. Use the four-step Parelli technique (page 29), ending with a sharp tap on his left shoulder. You shouldn't have to turn your head very far to do this; a quick glance tells you where he is. When he moves over a little, praise him, wait, then ask for more movement. As with most of these dominance game behaviors, you have to be both persistent and consistent until the new behavior is set.

∩ You may want to gain a little respect before you try to lead the horse at all. Many people like to run quickly through the Parelli seven games (page 29) to get the horse to be attentive before beginning to work with him. You don't necessarily need to do that, but you could use one of the games that asks the horse to move out of your space, such as the porcupine or driving games, combined with some friendly game so that you don't just come across as bossy!

∩ If your horse tries to nibble on you no matter where he is, see Nipping (page 105).

WHAT NOT TO DO ABOUT IT

∩ Don't get careless, especially with a young horse. Many people who have a good relationship with their horses assume the horse would never hurt them. They probably wouldn't do so on purpose, but horses don't know their own strength.

∩ Don't get so aggressive with the stick that you make the horse angry— usually the result of the handler not noticing the initial try and thus confusing and frustrating the horse.

LEADING, RUSHING AHEAD WHILE

When Mary Kate leads Josh out to the field or to graze, he pushes past her and walks rapidly ahead, dragging her with him, even though she tries to block him with her body. He doesn't attempt to get away from her, but she really can't stop him until they get to where he wants to go. He ignores tugs on the rope and just bulls along.

WHAT YOUR HORSE WANTS YOU TO KNOW

∩ *I'm the boss.* In horse herd dynamics, the lead horse is the one in charge. Horses try to establish a higher place in the pecking order by pushing past as many other horses as they can.

∩ *I don't mind including you in my herd.* On the plus side, a horse who doesn't try to get away has a good bond with his handler and some innate respect for humans, even if he doesn't have the best manners.

WHAT TO DO ABOUT IT

∩ Start by teaching the horse to drop his head on command (page 14). This is an act of respect and submission, and puts the horse in a frame of mind to accept your leadership.

∩ Then, using any combination of Tteam, Parelli or clicker training (described in the Introduction) you are comfortable with, teach the horse that he must walk with his head just behind your shoulder and about half an arm's length away. Use a Parelli halter or an ordinary flat halter with a chain attached in the Tteam fashion, if desired (page 34). Carry a carrot stick, a Tteam wand or a dressage whip. Begin the training in the stable aisle or the arena, where there is nothing to tempt the horse to push past you.

Stand a little in front and to one side of the horse's head, facing him. Play the friendly game with your stick, touching him and moving it around his head. If he knows the driving game (page 32), use the stick to ask him to back a step or two. Then ask for a head drop. Now, holding the lead in your right hand about eight inches from the halter and the stick in your left hand, out of the horse's way, turn to face the direction in which you want to walk.

If the horse doesn't start right up, start walking, giving a little cluck or a soft pull on the lead to tell him it's all right to come along. (If you're using the chain, keep the pull *very* short and soft, or the chain will stop him instead.) Then, using mostly peripheral vision, watch carefully for the slightest attempt to move his head past your shoulder. Horses are often very sneaky about it! When you see him trying to move past you, pull back firmly on the line with your hand and take a firm step *ahead* at the same time. This takes practice, as your tendency will be to step back in order to pull, which puts the horse where he wanted to be. Only pull on the line until you feel resistance, then quickly release and *smoothly* pull again if necessary. **The horse can only pull on you if you don't release**.

If he keeps trying to get past you, swing the stick up and down in front of his face as energetically as necessary to get his attention. The moment you see or feel him backing off, stop any aggressive actions, praise him and perhaps stop him and give a treat or click and treat. *Be sure when you stop him that you stay in front of him until he is fully stopped.* Then you can turn and face him. If his head has come up, ask him to drop it again. Then proceed as before. This needs to be practiced in a confined area until the horse is consistently staying behind you, before you can dependably lead him in tempting circumstances.

∩ If he is still showing a tendency to rush past, use a quick turn to the left. By turning him, you will change your relative positions so that you are still in front. Praise him as soon as he is behind you again. Complete a circle and then proceed in the original direction. You may do a number of circles in the beginning, but if you are patient and light with your hand, not draggy, the horse will tire of the game.

∩ If the horse is very disrespectful, use the porcupine or yo-yo game (pages 30 and 33) to work him in the round pen (page 34) to remind him that he must pay attention and respect your space.

WHAT NOT TO DO ABOUT IT

∩ Don't try to block the horse by getting behind his head, in front of his
shoulder. He may be well mannered enough not to actually run over you,
but you won't be teaching him anything better.

∩ Don't use a heavy pull on the rope to slow him down. It only teaches
him to pull back. And, since it is predatory in nature, it makes him irri-
tated and perhaps frightened.

LEADING, SPOOKING WHILE

Eloise's horse, Toddy, walks out of the stable peacefully enough, but when a gust
of wind makes something rattle his head comes up and he jumps forward, just
missing Eloise. She brings him around her and proceeds on her way, but something else soon sets him off again. Getting him from here to there nearly always
becomes a project. He seems to be positively looking for trouble!

Spookiness—fear of small, unimportant things resulting in sudden and violent movement—is a natural and essential part of a prey animal's makeup. The
stalking lion touches a branch, making the leaves rattle. A predator casts a
shadow where no shadow usually appears. The prey animal who pays no attention to these small things pretty quickly ends up as someone's lunch. But the
prey animal can't spend his whole life on edge, so he learns to depend on the
herd for protection. In the herd the lead horse, usually a mare, is the one who
determines whether something should be treated as dangerous.

In human-horse relationships, the horse first perceives us as predators,
which of course we are. After we have overcome that problem through kindness
and training, then, if the horse is to be a safe, dependable mount, he must learn
to accept his human as "lead horse." The horse *wants* to be able to turn to someone in authority, just as children want their parents to take over in situations that
are scary or beyond their control. This training, accomplished first on the
ground, can then be transferred to the ridden horse. You ride what you lead!

WHAT YOUR HORSE WANTS YOU TO KNOW

∩ *I'm scared.* He really is genuinely frightened, if only temporarily.

∩ *I want to get away.* Flight, generally toward the safety of the herd, is the
horse's immediate instinct. The fact that someone is in the way is
momentarily irrelevant.

∩ *I need someone to help me.* The safety of large prey animals lies in the
protection of the herd, either through mutual defense or the confusion of
many animals running in different directions.

WHAT TO DO ABOUT IT

∩ Spooking can never be completely overcome, any more than you could learn not to jump at a totally unexpected sound. But the horse can learn not to react violently and to trust your judgment in unusual situations. The Parelli friendly game (page 30), where the horse is gradually introduced to more and more difficult situations, works well for most horses and handlers to overcome spooking.

∩ If you have a round pen (page 34), that can also be a useful approach to teaching the horse to "spook in place"—that is, to look or even startle at the scary situation but keep his feet on the ground. Start with something that is mildly scary, such as waving a towel around. If the horse runs, continue to wave the towel until he slows down or stops, at which point you stop waving it. You can shape the behavior by gradually asking him to accept having the towel flapped right at or over him, and by using different and gradually more scary moves. It's the same principle as the friendly game, except that you use a round pen instead of a line. You can add a click and treat (page 27) to either method.

∩ Tteam leading (page 34) is essential to getting the horse to accept his handler as "lead horse." Once the horse is leading properly, take him for walks. When he shows signs of being unsure, such as raising his head, let him stop and check out the situation. Ask him to drop his head (page 14), which helps him turn to you for support. If he seems very unsure, you can ask him or allow him to turn *slowly* and walk away 50 feet or so, turn back around and stand and look, then approach the difficult place again. As the horse gains confidence that he will be allowed some input, but at the same time realizes he can and should depend on your judgment, his spookiness will gradually diminish. Tteam also has many exercises to deal with spooking.

∩ Some horses try to deal with a frightening situation by speeding up, ready to either wheel or race by if the "bear" actually does jump out at them. Ask the horse to stop every time he speeds up, even a little, leaving the line loose as long as he stands. Don't allow him to walk on on his own, but insist that he wait quietly for a command to move forward. In this way he learns to stop, look and listen (to you), rather than panic and run.

∩ You can add clicks and treats (page 27) to any of the above techniques, as he shows willingness to stand quietly and accept your authority.

∩ Startling is a reflex, not a planned action on the part of the horse. Therefore, you must allow enough time for the startling/spinning/shying/bolting reflex to be replaced by a less threatening reaction, such as pausing and glancing at the offending object or, eventually, ignoring it altogether.

∩ You can't possibly introduce the horse ahead of time to everything new and startling that will come up in his life. What you can do is to create a conditioned reflex to turn to you in moments of fear, rather than to panic on his own.

WHAT NOT TO DO ABOUT IT

∩ Don't punish the horse for startling. This can lead to the horse startling, then going right into some sort of violent behavior to avoid the punishment for something he can't help.

∩ Don't get into effusive patting and "It's okay, boy," which leads the horse to believe that spooking is desirable behavior. Treat the spooking objectively and save the praise for moments of courage.

TALKING HORSES

Horses tend to be more jumpy when they are already physically tense. Hence, spookiness occurs most often in cold weather, or with horses who are not sufficiently loosened up after standing in the stall, or who have been confined in the stall for several days. This is because at some level the horse realizes his body is not reacting at peak efficiency. Thus, if a predator should happen along the horse might be nabbed before he can react, so he overreacts to compensate.

LEADING: WON'T GO WHEN ASKED

Alice brings Gus out of the stable door and turns to lead him to the outdoor ring about 100 feet away. As soon as he realizes the ring is their destination, Gus stops. Alice clucks and tugs, and, very reluctantly, a step at a time, Gus walks to the ring for his ride.

Balking—refusing to go—when being led is a tiring and aggravating behavior. Some horses do this when they find they are not allowed to be the leader, as another way of maintaining control. It can also develop during early training when the horse responds as best he can to a tug or a tap, and instead of being rewarded is treated as though he had not responded. Eventually he gets frustrated and figures, "Why bother?" It is a vice that may show up under saddle as well, and while not as dangerous as many other riding disobediences, it is probably the most frustrating.

WHAT YOUR HORSE WANTS YOU TO KNOW

∩ *I'm bigger than you and I know it, and I don't really have to come if I don't want to!* This is somewhat the same attitude as the horse who breaks away (see Leading, Breaking Away While, page 83), but more of a passive-aggressive behavior.

∩ *I'll get there eventually, but I'm going to make you work for it.* The horse is pulling your chain and he knows it. This is typical of horse games.

WHAT TO DO ABOUT IT

∩ Successful leading begins with good technique on the part of the leader. Most people don't make their meaning clear to the horse, or they ask in such a way that they threaten him. Stand a little in front of the horse's head, usually on the left side—although both you and he should learn to lead from both sides. Look in the direction you wish to go, at a point about 15 feet in front of the horse, not at the horse himself (which would make him think you wanted to talk to him, or perhaps confront him). With a little slack in the rope, breathe out and start to move forward, taking a very small step. If you don't feel him coming immediately, give a soft, *brief* tug on the rope, much as you would tug on someone's sleeve to get their attention. Add a little cluck as well, if the horse doesn't seem to be responding. Try to keep your leading arm and hand very relaxed, as though you were leading a toddler by the hand. If the horse is ordinarily willing, this should be sufficient to get him to follow.

∩ If you are still having trouble, sometimes the simplest way works the best. When you feel him begin to stop, quickly turn him in a circle using the lightest of tugs on the line, then walk off in the original direction *with the line slack.* You can use another soft, smooth tug or two, just to tell him you want him to keep going, but leave the line fairly loose. Most of the time it's the handler's heavy, unremitting pressure on the line that causes the initial balk.

∩ If the horse has developed the habit of balking, you will have to do some retraining. Since balking is not uncommon behavior, virtually all training systems have a way of dealing with it. I like using the Tteam "dingo" (page 14) because it is easy to adapt to a riding situation. Using the Parelli four steps of pressure (page 30) and clicker techniques (page 27), will help improve the horse's attitude. The Parelli circling game is another way of teaching the horse to keep going, although it may be a bit trickier to learn.

WHAT NOT TO DO ABOUT IT

∩ Don't try to drag the horse with the lead line, and especially don't haul on the line when he starts to move. He may stop again, but just ask him to start as before. Dragging on the line when he is moving is punishing him for doing what you wanted.

∩ Never use a chain, or anything else, across the nose of a horse you are trying to get to go forward. The pull across his nose makes him stop.

∩ Don't hit him painfully hard to get him to go. Horses who balk tend to be the kind of horses who just "shut down" when things get too unpleasant. Hitting him will only make the balking worse.

LEG WRAPS, FUSSING ABOUT

Colleen is going to ship her horse, George, to a show about a two-hour trailer ride away. This is the first time she has shipped him anywhere since she bought him a few months ago. She knows most people in her barn wrap their horses' legs or put shipping boots on them to protect them during the ride. Since she already has a set of wraps, she decides to use them. She has never wrapped George before, but he stands fairly calmly while she puts them on, although when she leads him out to the trailer he picks his feet up in an exaggerated way. Colleen knows that many horses do this when the bandages are first put on, but quickly relax afterward. It's rather a hot day, so Colleen hopes the horses will be comfortable during their ride. The trailer leaves, and Colleen follows a little while later with her tack and clothing.

She arrives at the show grounds at about the same time as the trailer. When they unload George he seems rather frazzled and upset, and the driver says he was either kicking or pawing quite a bit during the latter part of the ride. His bandages are still on, but look rather disturbed and rucked up around his legs. George is very fidgety, and even with someone to hold him she has trouble getting them off. However, once they're off he seems more comfortable and starts to settle down. Colleen is relieved, because she really didn't want to have to compete on a horse who was so obviously upset and uncomfortable.

WHAT YOUR HORSE WANTS YOU TO KNOW

⌒ *Those things around my legs were hot and uncomfortable and itched like crazy! I wish I could have gotten them off. I sure tried!* When I first started shipping horses regularly, the van driver, who had shipped horses all up and down the East Coast for years, taught me a simple rule: "If the horse is accustomed to wearing wraps much of the time—what are known as standing wraps, for horses whose legs undergo a great deal of stress—then ship him wrapped. If he isn't, don't wrap him." He had observed that horses who weren't used to being in wraps very often would get themselves in more trouble fussing about the wraps than they would have if they wore nothing. I have followed that rule faithfully and never had a horse hurt worse than an occasional little nick. I also stood and watched while a person taking a young horse out of my barn in something of a hurry insisted on wrapping him, and the horse kicked the trailer half to pieces before it was out of the driveway!

WHAT TO DO ABOUT IT

⌒ Colleen would have been better off not wrapping George for that rather long trip on a hot day when he wasn't accustomed to it. But he still should get used to wearing wraps, because he may need them. If the weather is not too hot, it can be very helpful and restful to the horse to be wrapped for the homeward trip, after he has been working hard most of the day and his legs are tired. (You should probably cool the legs off first with a hose or sponge.) The support of the wraps takes some of the strain off his tendons and may prevent stocking up (soft swelling in the lower leg). And, of course, there are many leg injuries that require the horse to be wrapped 24/7. In those cases, however, the horse usually isn't traveling, so he has a chance to get used to the wraps in a less stressful situation.

Ω Most horses who are handled regularly have no trouble allowing their legs to be wrapped, but it is still a good idea to become quick and efficient at putting them on and removing them. It takes practice to get them snug enough so they don't slip and are evenly distributed over the leg. If you aren't sure about how to wrap correctly, get some experienced help or read a book (you'll find some suggestions in Appendix A), since badly applied wraps are much worse than none.

WHAT NOT TO DO ABOUT IT

Ω If you are planning to wrap the horse for shipping, don't try to do it in a hurry. Allow enough time to wrap him, and enough time for him to stand in his stall and get used to having them on. Then lead him around for a few minutes, if needed, until he seems comfortable.

Ω Don't wrap a horse unnecessarily. Some people think it looks cool and professional to wrap their horse every time they ride, but supporting the horse's legs all the time tends to weaken them, and also leaves you nothing to fall back on when he *does* have an especially stressful day.

LONGEING: HORSE WON'T START

Lucia would like to teach Rusty to longe, but he doesn't seem to get the idea at all. When she tries to get him to move out on a circle, he just turns and faces her. If she swings the longe whip at him, he backs up. A couple of times he has started to run at her a little aggressively. Both of them are frustrated by the whole thing and Lucia doesn't know what to do about it.

WHAT YOUR HORSE WANTS YOU TO KNOW

Ω *What do you want? You're telling me to turn and face you, and I'm doing it, and then you tell me that's wrong! Grrrrr.* Your eyes, center, line and whip all have to work together. If any one of them is wrong, the horse becomes confused. You also need to understand the horse's natural responses to those signals.

WHAT TO DO ABOUT IT

⋒ If you are already familiar with Parelli (page 29), the driving and yo-yo games, which lead you to the circling game, will set the horse up for longeing.

⋒ Free-longeing in a round pen or small enclosure, using your center (page 10) to guide the horse, will also teach him the rudiments and teach you how to use your center to direct him, without the additional complication of the longe line.

⋒ If you can't do any of the above, try this: Begin with the Parelli friendly game (page 30) to familiarize the horse with the whip you will be using. Then use Tteam dingo (page 14) to teach him to step forward to a whip signal. Since longe whips are generally whippier than a carrot stick or wand, be careful not to hurt him when you signal. Remember, you want him to *respond* to the whip, not flee from it.

⋒ Now place the horse against the wall or fence, facing the way you want him to go. Left hand around (turning left) is easier for most horses. Stand opposite the base of his withers, which is a little behind his center. Face the direction you want him to go and try to keep looking in that direction, glancing at him with soft eyes (page 9) when necessary. Hold the longe line loosely in your left hand. Hold the whip in your right hand, parallel to the horse's body. Hold it sort of near the middle, wherever it will balance comfortably. The handle should be pointing toward the horse's head and the tip toward his tail. Coil the lash up around the whip or your fingers.

⋒ To ask the horse to move, gesture with the tip of your whip, aiming *behind* his hindquarters or above his croup. At the same time, look in the direction you want him to go and reach out with your left hand in the same direction. But don't pull hard on the line, just hold it more or less in front of him. Cluck and begin walking in place as further encouragement. If the horse starts to turn toward you, swing the handle of the whip toward his muzzle. Continue to work back and forth with the whip until he starts to move forward. If he doesn't move at all, use the dingo tap on top of his croup. If the whip seems to be annoying him, go back to the friendly game for a few minutes, then try again. Don't use the whip hard enough to hurt, just enough to bother him.

⋒ Once he starts to move, let the line out a little bit and walk along beside him, always staying slightly behind his center so you are sending him forward. Gradually let the line out, continuing to hold your position behind his center facing forward, and keeping your eyes forward on the point where you want him to look—about 15 feet away, on the ground. If he slows down, use the whip *horizontally* behind him to keep him going. If he looks as if he is going to turn toward you, swing the whip toward his head and neck. If he stops and turns to face you, take him back to the fence and start again.

⋒ When the horse "disobeys," rather than getting annoyed, try to figure out what *you* are doing that has confused him.

⋂ The first time, only work him in the easy (left) direction, so that he understands fairly well what you want him to do. The next time, if he seems to have the easy direction figured out, you can ask him to go the other way, using the same method as before.

WHAT NOT TO DO ABOUT IT

⋂ Don't aim the whip toward the *side* of his hindquarters. The horse interprets this as a signal to turn his hindquarters away and face you.

⋂ If the horse is facing you, don't wave the whip up and down in front of him. It may make him rear, or if he is annoyed and frustrated, rear and strike.

LONGEING, PULLING AWAY WHILE

On cold days, Janet would like to be able to longe Lex for a few minutes before riding, just to loosen him up and make things a little easier for him. However, Lex apparently had some bad experiences before she bought him. He will go around once or twice, then swing his head hard to the outside, pull the line out of her hand and bolt away. She has tried bringing the line around her back to give her extra purchase, but although she can sometimes hold him this way, he continues to fight her.

WHAT YOUR HORSE WANTS YOU TO KNOW

⋂ *Hey, you're making me lose my balance!* The continuous, unilateral pull of the longe line puts a strain on the horse, causing him to want to lean away from the pressure. Think of carrying something heavy in one hand. To balance yourself, you have to lean *away from* the pressure. To make matters worse, pulling the horse's head to the inside, especially before he has been warmed up, throws his hindquarters to the outside. The horse needs to have his inside hind leg on the same track as his foreleg in order to balance comfortably, and he will resist pressure that interferes with that.

WHAT TO DO ABOUT IT

⋂ If at all possible, free-longe the horse, rather than line-longeing him, at least for a while. Besides avoiding the issue while you do some reschooling, free-longeing is a better way to let the horse loosen up, because he can release his tensions in whatever way works best for him.

⋂ To retrain, begin working in a somewhat confined area, so that having the horse break away is not a big deal. Wear gloves, so you can hold the line more lightly and still have control of it and so that if the horse does pull away, your hands won't get burned. Before starting, go through the five steps (page 7), so you are well centered and grounded.

○ Eventually, you would like the horse to longe without turning his head away and to be able to make a circle while you stay in one place. However, neither of these things is easy, or even possible, for a horse who is not well balanced, whether from lack of warmup or lack of skill. Therefore, you need to listen to what the horse is telling you with the line. If he pulls on it, he isn't saying, "I'm going to pull away." He is simply saying he needs a little more freedom for his head in order to balance. Keep the line slightly loose, easing it or moving as necessary when the horse makes it tight.

○ To bring the horse around the circle, ease the line, then give a gentle, smooth pull as his inside front leg comes off the ground. This will cause that leg to step toward the center, and the rest of the horse will follow. Then ease the pull as that foot comes down, which will allow him to rebalance and place his hind leg where it needs to be.

○ If the horse is carrying his head to the outside, reach out ahead of him with your hand or move farther ahead of him, so the line is leading him rather than pulling inward or back (see Grazing in Hand Problems, page 72). Try to keep looking in the direction you want him to go, so you "lead" him with your eyes. At the same time, reach out with the whip to a point behind his tail, so he understands that he should keep going. You may have to adjust your position quite a bit at first, until you both understand what to do.

○ If there is a particular place where he usually pulls away, as he approaches that place but *before* he starts to pull, let the line go slack so he can't grab it, step over so you are more behind him, look in the direction you want him to go and gently chase him forward with the whip and your voice. Praise effusively if he gets past the spot safely, even allowing him to stop for a treat a little farther on.

○ If he starts to really pull away, let the line run out quickly so there is nothing for him to pull against. Move toward and in front of him as much as you can, give a smooth pull on the line and release the instant you feel resistance. If he has turned too far to recover, simply let the line fall, without anger, let him go and stand quietly for a moment so he realizes you aren't going to chase him. Let him stop, then go up to him in a pleasant, positive way. (See Turnout: Refusing to Be Caught, page 171.)

○ Using side-reigns helps the horse to balance on the longe, but you must have the knowledge and experience to adjust them properly or you may do more harm than good.

WHAT NOT TO DO ABOUT IT

○ Don't try to use more strength, or fix the line around your body, to get him to come around. You will only frighten him more and create more

resistance. Even if you win, you will have destroyed his confidence in
both you and longeing.

LONGEING: TURNING TO FACE YOU

When Barbara is longeing Jayjay, every once in awhile, for no apparent reason,
he will stop and turn around to face her. But when she does ask him to stop, he
turns in and walks toward her, instead of staying out on the rail. She feels he is
being disobedient, but she isn't sure why or quite what to do about it.

WHAT YOUR HORSE WANTS YOU TO KNOW

⋂ *You rang, madam?* If you swing the longe whip toward the side of the
   horse's hindquarters or step toward them or even focus on them with
   your eye, the horse interprets this as a signal to move them away, which
   brings his head toward you. This is one of the steps in gaining respect
   and submission from a horse (see pages 4 and 5), so it should not be
   treated as disobedience. The same thing happens when you ask the horse
   to stop. When he stops, he turns toward you, in effect saying, "Yes,
   ma'am. Now what would you like me to do?"

WHAT TO DO ABOUT IT

⋂ When using the whip, if you want the horse to go forward, swing it horizontally so that it comes up *behind* him. If you want him to stay out,
   point the whip toward the junction of his neck and head and use it vertically. Alternatively, to keep the horse out you can hit the longe line with
   the whip, or flip the line up and down a couple of times as in the yo-yo
   game (page 33).

⋂ In the early stages of longeing, accept the horse turning toward you. That
   is, don't punish him for it. If you didn't want him to stop, simply turn him
   and start him up again (page 94). If he stops in the same place every time,
   send him forward as he approaches that place.

⋂ When he is more experienced, he will be ready to learn to stay on the
   circle when he stops. Begin by having him moving fairly slowly. Then
   walk across the circle so that you are close to the perimeter, well in front
   of him, as you use your voice to ask for a halt. When he stops, walk
   toward him along the circle, smiling and using soft eyes, stop so you are
   facing the side of his head and praise. Then start him again. Do this a
   number of times over several longeing sessions, so he gets accustomed
   to stopping on the circle.

⋂ Next, don't walk quite so close to the perimeter as you ask for the halt.
   Rather than looking at him, look in the direction you want him to be

looking when he stops, using soft eyes so you can see him as well. If he starts to turn in, gesture with your whip toward his muzzle to discourage him. When he stands on the circle, approach him and praise.

○ If he turns in any direction, walk over to him and quietly turn him to face the correct way, then praise him, again standing facing the side of his head.

○ Whether he stops correctly on his own or needs to be placed, once he is standing quietly, back away toward the center of the circle a step at a time. Look firmly at his head to convey that you don't want him to move. Encourage or discourage with your voice—"whoooaaa" or "gooooood"—as you move.

○ When you reach the center, praise and ask him to move forward, being sure not to point the whip at his hindquarters. With a little patience and practice, you can teach him to stop on the circle, then wait for your next command.

WHAT NOT TO DO ABOUT IT

○ Don't get annoyed with him. He thinks he's doing what you want.

○ Don't try to chase him out by swinging the whip in his face from in front. You may teach him to rear instead!

MANE PULLING, RESISTANCE TO

Mary is getting Jackson ready for the show season, and she shows in a discipline that requires a short, thin mane. So she starts to work on Jackson's mane, which has been somewhat neglected since the previous season. She takes the pulling comb and starts pulling out the longer hairs, but almost immediately he starts fussing and tossing his head. "I don't understand it!" Mary says to her friend Elizabeth, who is nearby. "Everyone knows that it doesn't hurt them to pull their manes. Why is he making such a fuss? What a brat!"

While it is true that horses are far less sensitive to having hair pulled out of their manes than we are about hairs pulled out of our heads, they do not totally lack nerves in that area. It makes sense for them to have limited sensitivity, since the mane can get caught in brush or branches, but if there were no feeling at all the horse might get so careless that he lost large amounts of hair, and thus some important winter protection.

If only a few of the longest hairs are pulled out every time the horse is groomed, the mane stays tidy and the horse never gets upset. However, what often happens is that the mane is neglected for a long period. Then along comes someone in a hurry—perhaps a horse dealer who wants the horse to look nice for a prospective buyer—who only has a little while to clean him up. Rather than pulling out just a few hairs, he puts a little muscle into it and starts pulling the hair out in clumps. When the horse starts to fuss, he is restrained in whatever way will work until the mane is pulled the way the dealer wants it. After a few days the horse heals and nobody is the wiser, until the next person goes to pull the mane. The horse remembers the previous, very painful experience and does whatever he thinks he must to prevent it happening again.

WHAT YOUR HORSE WANTS YOU TO KNOW

◠ *I don't care **what** you were told. That hurts!!* Even if you are pulling carefully, once the horse has been hurt, his tension about mane pulling makes him far more sensitive.

◠ *I'm not letting you pull any more hair out if I can help it.* Horses can get pretty violent about mane pulling, sometimes requiring a tranquilizer to sedate them enough to get the job done. And people go right on saying that it doesn't hurt! Helloooooooo!

WHAT TO DO ABOUT IT

◠ If the horse has a naturally thin mane anyway, you can use the correct method of just pulling a few hairs every day. This is a sort of approach and retreat (page 27), and you can use clicker methods (page 27) and treats when he stands quietly. Stay near the withers for awhile, which is easier for the horse to accept, then gradually move up toward the ears.

◠ The correct method for pulling the mane is to grasp one or two long hairs in the fingers of your left hand. Then, using either the fingers of your right hand or a pulling comb held in your right hand, scrape the other surrounding hairs up toward the top of the neck until most of the length of the hairs you want to pull is exposed. Then, with your left hand, wrap those two long hairs around your right fingers (wearing a glove is a good idea) or around the first couple of teeth of the comb. Pull sharply down on both hands simultaneously and the hair will be pulled out, not broken off.

A horse who is accustomed to this and expects it to hurt, thinking you're going to pull out a handful instead of only a few hairs, may begin to tense up as soon as he feels you starting to scrape the hairs upward. If this is the case, do just this part, using approach and retreat but *not* pulling the hair out, until he gets over most of his fear. Then you can pull out just one or two hairs and he will eventually realize that it doesn't hurt, particularly if lots of treats are forthcoming when he stands still.

◠ If the horse's mane is very thick, long or coarse, the method of choice is the trim kit, which consists of barber's thinning scissors and a comb knife. Besides being painless, it is much faster. Many people think you can't get a natural look when you do this and that the mane will not be suitable for braiding. That will only occur if you use poor technique. After all, most women have their hair cut at the hairdressers—as opposed to having it pulled out!—and a good haircut can look as though the hair grew that way. The trim kit is also a good way to shorten the mane while the horse is still fearful of normal pulling, or to deal with a mane that has gotten way out of hand.

∩ To keep the mane looking natural, use the thinning scissors (be sure they have teeth on both blades, not just one) at the base of the mane first, as close to the neck as you can. Insert the scissors parallel to the top of the neck and snip no more than twice, move up the neck about an inch and repeat. Continue up the whole neck. Comb out the loose hair and repeat, but only once. If the mane is still very thick, cut down through the length of the mane, holding the thinning scissors at constantly changing angles so that the hairs are cut at all different lengths, and snipping only once in each place. After going up the whole mane and combing out the loose hair, you may repeat if necessary, but only once.

∩ Then take the comb knife, which looks like a straight razor with teeth, and use it *exactly* as the pulling comb is used when doing normal pulling, except that you hold the hair up against the cutting edge of the comb instead of wrapping the hair around it, pulling up with your left hand as you pull down with your right to cut. The big mistake is to use the comb knife to cut a straight line at the desired length. For the mane to look natural, the hairs must be different lengths with only the longest hairs approximately the same length.

∩ The first time you try the trim kit, work on the lowest six inches, down near the withers, until you learn the technique.

∩ A very nervous horse may still be frightened of the scraping and pulling at first, even though the hair is actually being cut, not pulled out. Use the advance and retreat technique (page 27) to help him work through it.

∩ If the horse has been seriously traumatized, you may want to use either the twitch (page 19) or a mild tranquilizer, either medical, homeopathic or herbal, while using one of the methods I've described. This will reduce some of his fear and enable him to realize that it no longer hurts. After one or two sessions he should no longer need such help.

∩ If the horse has a nicely shaped neck and a very wide mane path, so that the mane is extremely thick, consider roaching the mane—that is, clipping it completely off. On such horses this often gives a crisper, neater, more finished look than you can get by trying to create attractive braids. Don't clip right at the withers where the saddle pad goes—pressure on the clipped area may cause ingrown hairs and soreness. If you are very skilled, another option is to roach most of the mane longitudinally, leaving about half an inch of mane path with the hair long enough to braid (always on the *right* side).

WHAT NOT TO DO ABOUT IT

∩ Don't wait until the last moment before deciding your horse's mane needs pulling. This is not fair to the horse and will only cause further trouble.

⋒ Don't be impatient if the horse still makes a fuss even when you *know* you are no longer hurting him. The horse needs plenty of time to find out it doesn't really hurt. Just remember how you feel in the dentist's chair!

MOUNTING, MOVING DURING

Jacqueline has Brody all tacked and ready to ride. Since she is rather small and he is quite tall, she likes to use the mounting block. She leads him to the mounting block and halts him, then circles around to climb on the block. As soon as she starts to put a foot in the stirrup, he walks away. She brings him back and tries again. Eventually, by holding him fairly tight and talking very firmly, she is able to get her foot in the stirrup and mount, although he walks away again while she is swinging her leg over.

WHAT YOUR HORSE WANTS YOU TO KNOW

⋒ *Being mounted frightens me. It makes me think of lions jumping on my back.* When the horse is learning to be mounted, the trainer must take "the time it takes" to get him really comfortable about it, since it is a very predatory action.

⋒ *I'm afraid of losing my balance.* If the horse is mounted clumsily, it is difficult for him to keep his balance. Loss of balance is one of the things that really scares a horse, since, in his wild state, if he loses his balance and falls he may be eaten.

⋒ *I'm afraid you're going to pull the girth up too tight.* Some people make a practice of bringing the horse to the mounting block and then pulling up the girth extremely tight to compensate for either their own lack of mounting ability or the horse's lack of withers to hold the saddle in place.

⋒ *Being ridden is not fun for me.* A horse who has been ridden in either a very demanding or an abusive way eventually figures out that the ride starts with mounting, and he wants no part of it!

WHAT TO DO ABOUT IT

⋒ First the horse should be desensitized, especially in his back and croup area, where he will be touched during mounting. Even though he has been mounted many times before, he may still have issues that were never dealt with. The horse can be either crosstied or groundtied or held, depending on what he is accustomed to. Include this work as part of his grooming session. Standing first on the ground, and later on a small portable stool, stroke the horse all over his back and croup, using both a caressing touch and a quick sweep, as though you were swinging a leg over. From the stool, reach across and stroke the opposite side, and lean or half-lie across his back. Make a game of it, not a stern lesson, the same way you would play cuddling or touching games with a baby. Use a lot of breathing and grounding to help the horse relax. Take as much time with this as the horse needs. Several weeks or several months spent getting the horse to where he enjoys having you mount, as opposed to being tense and afraid, will affect your whole future together.

∩ Once the horse is comfortable with having you stroke and lean on his back, he can be reintroduced to the mounting block. Clicker principles (page 27) work very well in this situation. If he is really nervous, begin by leading him all the way around the block at a fair distance, then bringing him as close to the block as he can handle. When he stands still, praise or click and treat. Gradually bring him closer, clicking and treating as he shows more willingness and courage. Once he will stand beside the block, let him stay briefly, then take him away and bring him back several times, clicking and treating each time he comes up and stands next to the block. When he is doing that well, delay the click and treat about 10 seconds, so he begins to get the idea that he should stand and wait. Increase the time little by little until he will stand calmly as long as you want.

∩ Next, instead of standing by his head, move toward the block so you can climb up on it, but don't do so. Click and treat if he doesn't move. If he moves, calmly reposition him but don't give him a treat. Instead, make your move again, perhaps moving only one small step. Once he will allow you to move from his head toward the block, gradually increase the number of steps until he will let you stand on the block. Don't ask him to stand and wait with you on the block at this point. As long as he doesn't move when you get on the block, that's worth the treat. Only when he will let you walk from his head to the block without moving, and has done so consistently, should you then ask him to wait a longer time with you in mounting position.

∩ Now continue the process through leaning over, patting the saddle, stroking his croup, reaching across and patting his opposite shoulder, picking up the stirrups with your hand and dropping them again and whatever else you can think of to challenge him a little. If he walks away, don't stop him. Just bring him around and back into place again and pick up where you left off, or a step or two before. Treat and praise often. Finally, place yourself in mounting position (see below); place your foot in the stirrup and take it out; stand in the stirrup and step down again; stand in the stirrup and swing your right leg over, then back, and step off; and finally mount all the way and reach down to give him a treat from the saddle.

∩ This sounds like it might be tedious, but if you don't try to hurry or do it all in one sitting, it gets to be a game with the horse trying to see how high a score he can get. Fun for you both!

∩ If you want your horse to be happy standing for mounting, you have to learn to mount in a way that is pleasant and easy for him. The technique most English riders are taught involves standing in front of the horse's shoulder facing the rear. Then the rider either tries to haul herself up from that position or hops around awkwardly until she is facing the horse's side or perhaps more forward, pulling the horse off balance and probably poking him with her toe in the process. She then drags herself up his side, which is very hard for him to cope with, and collapses onto the saddle with a thump.

∩ Here is a mounting technique that is the least physically demanding for both rider and horse. It may take a little practice to change your mounting habits, especially where you place your hands, but your horse will thank you.

Place your horse so the cantle of the saddle is opposite the middle of the block. To help him balance, before you start to mount rock the saddle from side to side, using the pommel or horn, until he takes a little sideward step, placing his front feet further apart. This gives him a wider stance, which is more secure.

Now stand about opposite the cantle, facing the horse's head, so that you can just reach the pommel with your right hand without bending over. Take the reins in your right hand, snug but not tight, and position your hand so you are holding the pommel or horn. Reach down with your left hand and turn the stirrup so the outside of it is now facing the rear, and put your foot in so the back of the ball of your foot is resting on the back of the stirrup. Place your left hand on the mane, picking up the left rein and turning the horse's head a little to the left at the same time, if you like. Some horses find it easier to balance you this way.

Now you are ready to mount. Push off with your right foot and straighten your left knee *and your left hip*, so you are standing *straight up* in your left stirrup for a split second before bending both hips slightly so that your center (navel) is over the center of the horse and you are balanced between your foot and your hands. If the saddle tends to turn because the horse has flat withers, you can move your right hand to the off-side so you are pressing down on that side, rather than on the middle of the saddle. Now swing your right leg over, still keeping your upper body as upright as possible, and sit down gently, picking up the off-side stirrup as you do so.

∩ Because you are mounting *along* the horse's long axis, rather than *across* his short axis, and staying behind his center of gravity throughout the mount, it is much easier for him. Because you are not trying to turn 180 degrees in the air, it is much easier for you.

WHAT NOT TO DO ABOUT IT

∩ Don't yank on the bit to make the horse stand. This may work for the moment, but it only makes him more unhappy about being mounted, and doesn't get to the cause of the problem.

⋂ Don't dig or kick him with your toe while mounting and then expect him to stand!

⋂ Don't position yourself so that during mounting you pull the horse off balance either frontward or sideways. He will have to move to regain his balance. Another advantage of mounting from the rear is that the horse cannot be pulled off balance to the rear. He has those hind legs to hold him up.

⋂ Don't tighten the girth immediately before mounting. Instead, tighten it ahead of time in small increments with short walks in between.

⋂ Don't tighten the girth extremely tight in an effort to compensate for flat withers that don't keep the saddle in place.

TALKING HORSES

You can use all the same techniques to teach to horse to stand for mounting from the ground. When mounting from the ground, stand a little more toward the horse's hindquarters, so that you can get your foot in the stirrup more easily. Once you master this technique you can mount any horse from the ground, provided his saddle will stay on and you don't have the lower the stirrup so far down that you can't get your leg over the horse once you're standing in the stirrup.

NIPPING

(*Also see* Biting People)

Julie is holding her horse, Mitch, while she chats with her friend Ann. Mitch is standing fairly close and occasionally butts her lightly with his nose. She pushes his head away and continues to chat. Mitch then reaches out and grabs her sleeve with his teeth, giving it a good yank before letting go and jumping back, away from the reprisal he expects. This is generally the extent of his play, although he occasionally makes a mistake and grabs a little flesh. He seems to know this and to be apologetic, or at least ashamed of his mistake.

WHAT YOUR HORSE WANTS YOU TO KNOW

⋂ *Gotcha last!* Nipping is usually part of a game, especially with male horses. It is different from biting in that it is not intended to cause serious damage. Geldings turned out together will often spend long periods grabbing at one another with their teeth. If they are wearing halters the game is even more fun, because you can drag the other guy around if you get a good grip on his halter.

⋂ *Careful! Don't go there!* Nipping may be a warning that you are treading
on ground that the horse considers threatening. The most common time for
a horse to nip a person in this way is during girthing or cinching.

⋂ *I feel very tense and need a way to work off my tension.* Some horses are
compulsive nippers, just as some people smoke or bite their nails. These
horses tend to be much more mouthy in situations where they feel insecure. They tend to grab at objects such as lead ropes, rather than just at
living beings, showing that it is a mouth compulsion rather than simply a
desire to play games.

WHAT TO DO ABOUT IT

⋂ The same techniques you used to deal with the respect issue in Personal
Space: Mugging for Treats (page 124) also work for ordinary nipping.
The horse needs to learn respect and stop treating you like a pasture
buddy. He is still trying to establish dominance over you; pasture nipping is very much like the "I'm the king of the castle" game you played
as a child. Persistence is the goal here. Every time the horse starts to
push into your space he is invited out of it again, until he realizes you
just aren't going to play.

⋂ Use arm blocks (a Parelli technique) so the horse bumps his own nose or
head when he swings it to nip. This discourages him without being confrontational.

⋂ An *occasional* very stern scolding and body blocking, chasing back with
the lead line or otherwise energetically driving the horse out of your
space, may be necessary. However, if you find you are using an aggressive manner with him most of the time, you need to rethink the problem,
since you are not attacking the cause but only treating the symptom, and
only temporarily.

⋂ Compulsive nipping occurs when the horse feels insecure, and developing respect will help here too, because having you as his herd leader will
make him feel more protected and secure.

⋂ Structured fun like the Parelli games, clicker training or Tteam work
(described in the Introduction) occupies the horse and releases some of
his tension constructively. As he learns how to play the games and is
made to feel successful, he also feels more secure. If the horse is a gelding and doesn't get to spend time in the herd, games with you will also
satisfy, to some extent, his need to play.

⋂ Working with his mouth, as described in Tteam and Parelli training (see
Biting People, page 38), often works very well with a nippy, mouthy
horse. It releases much of the tension and also puts you in more control
of his mouth.

WHAT NOT TO DO ABOUT IT

⋂ Don't punish a horse who is nipping from nervousness or compulsive mouthiness. He really can't help it and may not even realize he is doing it, so punishment is unfair and he won't associate it with the behavior. Compulsive *biting*, as opposed to nipping, is the result of punishing a compulsive nipper, and is very difficult to cure.

PANICKING AGAINST CROSSTIES

Bill has Archie standing crosstied on the aisle where he boards. It is a fairly busy spot, with horses and people going to and fro as Bill prepares to groom and tack up, and since it is raining outside it seems busier than usual. Suddenly the outside door opens and a woman steps through carrying an open umbrella. Archie is standing only a few feet from the door, so the umbrella is almost in his face. Startled, he steps back a couple of steps and reaches the end of the crossties. When he feels them tighten, he panics and pulls back. The woman with the umbrella realizes her mistake and quickly leaves, but it is too late. Archie continues to fight and pull back, feet slipping wildly, until suddenly one of the ties lets go and he comes crashing to the floor. He scrambles to his feet and stands stunned for a moment, allowing Bill to get the other crosstie unfastened so that nothing further happens. Both Bill and Archie are shaken, although except for a few scratches neither is hurt.

WHAT YOUR HORSE WANTS YOU TO KNOW

⋂ *I have to get away, I have to get away!* This is the old predator-prey thing again. If a horse is restrained by the head, he immediately thinks of a predator trying to drag him down so he can be finished off.

WHAT TO DO ABOUT IT

⋂ As in all panic situations, your safety and the safety of any bystanders is paramount. In this situation not only is the horse's mind out of control, but also his body, especially if the floor is slippery. He is almost bound to fall, and if the crossties or whatever they are fastened to break, the fall will be sudden, uncontrolled and violent. Anyone in the way risks serious injury. The horse, of course, is at risk as well, but you may not be able to do anything to help.

⋂ Try to stay as calm and grounded (page 7) as you can. If the horse senses you are also panicked, it only increases his fear, since he then believes his "herd" is being attacked too.

∩ If you happen to be behind the horse when he starts to pull back, you may be able to get him to go forward again by using a voice command or perhaps flapping a coat or something similar that will catch his eye and get him moving away. Under no circumstances should you get any closer than eight or 10 feet—that is, the length of his body. If both crossties, or his halter, break suddenly, he may go right up and over backward, and could easily land on you if you are too close.

∩ If he responds to your signals to go forward, the movement will probably be equally panicky and sudden, in which case he will hit the crossties again, this time going forward. Horses don't fight pressure from this direction, but if he hits them suddenly his feet may go out from underneath him and he might flip onto his back. If he gets trapped and is struggling in that position, if you can safely reach his head and sit firmly on it he will stop struggling at least long enough for you to untie him so that he can get up. Again, think of your own safety, and get help if you can.

∩ An ounce of prevention—that is, teaching the horse to give to pressure—would have been well worth it. Once the horse has "learned" to pull back, he will continue to do so at the slightest provocation, since he now believes some kind of predator is concealed inside the crossties, just waiting to get him. You should begin a retraining program as soon as possible. Now that the horse has had a bad experience, the retraining will take more time.

∩ Retraining begins with the Parelli yo-yo game (page 33) or something similar. With the horse standing about a horse length away, facing you and attached to the rope you are holding, ask him to come toward you. At first you use a technique called combing the rope (page 33). The combing action creates a slight tension without any feeling of restriction, so it is very nonthreatening.

Continue combing the rope, crouching down in an inviting way and smiling to encourage the horse to come to you, praising *and releasing the pull* when you get the slightest effort. It will also help to use the clicker (page 27) when you get a response.

When the horse gives and comes consistently to a combing action, switch to using a very light but steady pull. Again, the most important thing is to release the pressure the instant the horse moves toward it. If at any time he starts to pull back against it, walk with him so the rope doesn't get any tighter but doesn't get any looser either. As long as you stay directly in front of him, you can walk forward faster than he can walk backward. Keep your eyes soft (page 9), so he doesn't think you're attacking him,

When the horse is very consistent about giving to the steady pull, the next step is to put him in a confined space such a stall, where he can't back too far, and run the rope from his head through a ring or around the stall bars and back to your hand. This looks to the horse more like he is tied. Go back to using the combing to get him to walk up to the ring, and when he is comfortable with that, switch to a steady pull.

Thereafter you can gradually introduce more difficult situations and a somewhat stronger pull, until the horse is thoroughly conditioned to step *toward* a pull, rather than pulling away from it. Give him lots of time before you actually try to tie him, though. It takes just as long or longer to break a habit as it did to develop it.

⋂ A second, associated method is called *dallying*. For this you need a long rope and a solid round post or vertical strut in a stall partition. A heavy ring bolted to a solid support would also work. Take the horse into the stall, wearing a rope halter so there is just narrow pressure on the crown. Begin by taking the rope from the halter jaw ring, threading it around the post and back to your hand. Put light pressure on the rope. If the horse pulls back, allow the rope to follow him without a fight, letting go if necessary. If your rope is long enough, the horse will back into the wall before you run out of line. If he gets loose, bring him quietly back and start again. Look carefully for any signs of acceptance or yielding, and praise accordingly. Be prepared to repeat this lesson many, many times until the horse realizes he is not being hurt and you aren't going to give up. As the horse becomes more comfortable, take a turn around the post so there is greater resistance, but you can still ease the rope if necessary. When he is really solid in the stall, move him to a larger area, such as a paddock.

⋂ Crossties are different from a single tie because they leave the horse totally exposed from the front, so he feels very threatened by anything coming toward him that he doesn't fully understand. If he has any tendency to spook at all, he may find himself pulling back before he knows it. Therefore, you should spend a lot of time with any horse "sacking him out." This is a variation of the friendly game (page 30), found in all the training systems, where you use advance and retreat with scary things like tarpaulins and plastic bags and anything else you can think of. You allow the horse to look at the object and smell it first, and then attempt to touch his body with it. The horse will probably move away, especially if the object is very strange or the horse is inexperienced. The important thing is not to push the envelope too much, so that the horse gets too frightened to think or decides you're trying to hurt him. Instead, be very passive but persistent about continuing to present the object, until the horse accepts it touching him all over without him moving. It is not possible to introduce the horse to every possible scary situation in the world, but if you introduce him to a great variety of them he is most likely to assume that most new things are okay, rather than the reverse.

⋂ The Tteam game called Taming the Tiger helps to overcome the fear of crossties. Begin by establishing a comfortable feeling with the horse, using whatever method you like, so that he is not afraid of you. This can take five minutes or a month, but is essential if the horse is going to accept being tied in your presence.

Now place the horse in the corner of a paddock, standing with his right side close to one fence and his tail near the other. There should be either a large, heavy ring or a smooth metal fence, so that you can pass a rope around it and the rope will slide freely. The horse's tail should be close enough to the corner that he can't back more than a couple of feet. You will need a flat, stable halter, a 20-foot length of light but strong rope (⅜-inch soft braided line is easy to handle) and a lead shank fitted with either a 30-inch chain and snap or a 30-by-¼-inch soft line and snap. Run the long rope from the right ring on the horse's halter nose through the ring or around the fence, back through the ring on the back of the halter, and into your left hand as you stand on the horse's left side. Fasten the 30-inch chain or line to the halter as described on page 17, and also hold its attached lead line in your left hand, with your finger between the two lines to keep them separated. This is going to take a little dexterity, because you will have to pull or release twice as much line on his right side as the chain lead to keep them equal. Carry a wand or the equivalent in your right hand.

Work with the horse, stroking, patting or Tteaming him, until he is standing quietly. Be well grounded yourself. Then, standing slightly in front and to one side of him, gradually apply some pressure on the two lines. If he steps forward, immediately release the pressure and praise him. Then back him up to where he was and repeat a few times, perhaps applying the pressure a little more quickly, though still not roughly. If you have previously introduced him to some scary things, such as tarps and plastic bags, have an assistant wave or flap them in front of him to see if he backs up into the pressure you are holding on the lines. Again, if he responds to the pressure by stepping forward, lots of smiles and praise.

If at any time he starts to back and continues to back against the pressure, ease the lines just enough so that the pressure doesn't increase and let him back into the fence. Still keeping the pressure on the lines, reach back with the stick and use dingo (page 14) to ask him to come forward again. As soon as he starts to give to the pressure, release it and praise.

The horse *has* to find out that the way to escape the pressure is not by fighting it, but by moving toward it, which is against all his instincts.

∩ Using ties with elastic inserts will prevent the horse from feeling threatened by them, provided he doesn't pull back so suddenly and so far that he reaches the end of the stretch. This is a useful in-between step while you are retraining.

∩ Another safe way to tie him is to use little loops of knitting yarn to attach the snaps to the halter. If the horse pulls back the yarn will break, but so easily that the horse won't have any reason to panic. Since you know he won't hurt himself, this little trick has the added virtue of ensuring you will be much calmer, which he will sense. Best not to use these in a situation where he can get completely away, or he may learn to break them for the fun of it (see Tying: Won't Tie, page 176).

⋂   If you use quick-release snaps on the crossties, install them so that the releasing snaps are at the wall, where you can safely reach them. Be sure to get the kind that have an easy-to-open snap at the halter end. Sometimes you want to undo the snap at his head in a hurry to avoid a problem, and some snaps are very awkward to get undone. True, the horse can't undo them either, but that isn't always a good thing.

WHAT NOT TO DO ABOUT IT

⋂   Don't go for his head when he starts to pull. If you reach for his head to try to unfasten him, you will only panic him further—and are in a very dangerous position if he suddenly leaps forward, which horses sometimes do. This is why you want the release snaps to be at the wall, not at his head!

⋂   Most so-called quick-release knots will only release quickly if the horse has not yet pulled on them. Once they are pulled tight, they jam and are not much easier to undo than any other knot. There are some knots in Appendix B that do work in any situation. The sampan knot (page 188) is probably the best. Another knot you can always get undone (although not necessarily instantly) is a bowline with the last turn made by tucking a loop through, so you can pull the end and undo it (page 189). A bowline can be worked back and forth to loosen it if it is jammed by a sudden, hard pull, which is not true of the ordinary quick-release knot.

⋂   Don't raise your voice. Shouting will frighten him still more. If you use your voice at all, use it calmly and firmly. It may be necessary to speak loudly if he is clattering around, but it should be a carrying voice, not a shriek. Hard to do when you are frightened yourself!

PANICKING: STEPPING ON THE LEAD ROPE OR REINS

Sukey is grazing Rocky and has turned away to talk to someone in the parking lot. Suddenly she hears a commotion behind her and turns to see that Rocky has put his foot on his lead rope. Before she can react, he flings his head up, the snap lets go and he bolts away. In a moment he stops, turns and looks, as much as to say, "Wow! What was that?"

WHAT YOUR HORSE WANTS YOU TO KNOW

⋂   *A vicious but invisible animal has grabbed me by the halter. Help!!* This is one of the more common annoyances that occur with horses. The handler gets a little careless and the horse puts his foot on his lead rope or his reins. If he has never learned about this, all he knows is that he can't see what has hold of him, so he panics and tries to break free. All too often it is an expensive bridle that breaks!

WHAT TO DO ABOUT IT

∩   Turn the horse loose alone in a safe space—round pen, arena or field— where there is nothing to get tangled in. Put him in a strong halter and attach a soft rope to the back ring using a bowline (page 189). The remaining rope should be about three feet long. Do not leave a loop at the knot that the horse could get a foot caught in.

     He will walk around and graze, and inevitably he will step on the rope. But when he throws his head up he won't be able to get away. Eventually, in the course of having a fit, he will move his foot and the rope will come free. He will be somewhat upset, but after a few minutes he'll forget about it and step on it again. After awhile he will start to figure out that there's no one there to eat him, and that if he moves the foot with the funny lump under it the pull will go away. Keep an eye on him, but don't say anything unless you see him step on the rope and quietly lift his foot off of it. Then you can tell him how smart he is!

     A horse who has learned this is much safer, so it is well worth teaching him. When he understands the principle, you can put him out with a longer rope so he learns to deal with that as well. This, and the friendly game, can be used to train him to be safely staked out.

∩   Use the same methods recommended in Panicking Against Crossties (page 107) to teach him about giving to pressure.

∩   Also play the friendly game (page 30) with ropes and the savvy string, wrapping them gently around his legs and eventually applying some pressure so that he learns not to fight those sorts of things, either. This protects him if he puts his leg through a looped rope.

WHAT NOT TO DO ABOUT IT

∩   Don't get too careless before he is trained. He can hurt himself and will certainly break equipment.

PANICKING WHEN CAUGHT IN SOMETHING

Margie was leading Star down the rather narrow aisle of the stable where she boards the horse. As they turned the corner to go into the arena, he caught a hind foot in a piece of baling twine. (Someone had pulled it off a bale without breaking it, then carelessly left it hanging on a hook so that the loop lay in the aisle.) As Star felt the loop catch his foot, he leaped forward then kicked violently, banging the wall and frightening himself still further. Fortunately, because it was only baling twine, the loop quickly broke and Star suffered nothing more serious than an abrasion. But Margie realizes that had it been baling wire or even ordinary rope, there could have been serious consequences.

WHAT YOUR HORSE WANTS YOU TO KNOW

∩ *I'm being attacked!* Being caught anywhere arouses the horse's prey instincts. He feels a predator is trying to bring him down.

∩ *I've got to get free immediately.* Since he feels his life is at stake, he is desperate to get away.

WHAT TO DO ABOUT IT

∩ If you find yourself and your horse in this situation, the first thing to realize is that the horse is panicking and doesn't know what he is doing. This makes him very dangerous, so you must look out for your own safety first. Keep a steady, gentle hold on the lead, if possible, and try to stay calm and grounded. Talk to him quietly. As in the panicking situation described in Panicking When Left Alone (page 114), look for moments when the horse stops fighting, even for a second, and praise effusively. If he is accustomed to the clicker, the sound of it may help restore some of his self-control. Meanwhile, try to figure out a safe way to unfasten whatever he is caught in, without getting within range of his legs if he should start to fight again—which he may well do when you try to free him. If you can't see a safe solution, call for help, if possible from an experienced horse person.

∩ The best solution to problems like this is to prepare your horse to deal with them. The Parelli games (page 29) teach the horse to accept all sorts of things that would frighten an untrained horse. Horses who have received preventive training will, if caught, stand for hours waiting to be rescued, whereas an untrained horse will often fight until he is seriously injured or even dies. You can combine the Parelli work with clicker training (page 27) and often get even faster and more reliable results.

∩ Until your horse is trained, and just as a general rule of sensible behavior, look around your stable and surrounding area. Are there things a curious horse could get caught in or on? Often people will leave wheelbarrows, pitchforks and the like where a horse can knock them over, and where two horses playing, and thus distracted, might easily get in trouble.

WHAT NOT TO DO ABOUT IT

∩ Don't pull hard on the lead rope or bridle in an attempt to control the horse. That is the action of a predator and may make him fight harder.

⋂ Don't raise your voice, which people tend to do when frightened. Seeing your horse in danger is very frightening to you as well!

TALKING HORSES

Along with your first aid kit, you should have a small group of tools available. These should include a sharp knife (for cutting rope,) wire cutters, shoe pullers and cinch lifters (and get your shoer to show you how to use them), a pinch bar to pry boards apart, and a hammer, screwdriver, wrench and pliers to make small repairs before they lead to accidents.

PANICKING WHEN LEFT ALONE

Nancy has two horses at her small stable: her horse, SuzyQ, and her husband Jim's horse, Mac. As long as they both ride at the same time, all is well, but they both have jobs that require occasional weekends and trips. If the person who stays home wants to go for a ride, the horse who is not being ridden gets very upset, especially SuzyQ. From the moment she suspects Mac is going without her, she races up and down the fence line screaming loudly and seemingly with no consideration for her own safety. If left in her stall, she alternates between rearing, pawing and racing around the stall. Luckily, the stalls have full-height doors, or she would probably attempt to climb out. She seems to keep up the behavior most of the time Mac is gone, because when Jim returns she is nearly always sweating. He ends up having to walk her, which he does not enjoy. If Mac is left alone he whinnies a few times, but then resigns himself to the inevitable and goes back to grazing. Jim and Nancy wish SuzyQ could learn to do the same.

WHAT YOUR HORSE WANTS YOU TO KNOW

⋂ *There is no one here to protect me.* Mares especially have trouble adapting to being alone, since in nature a mare is virtually always part of a stallion's herd. The young males, by contrast, are driven out of the herd as soon as they are sexually mature and able to look after themselves. They usually find other males to bond with until they are mature enough to challenge another stallion for his herd, or at least to steal a few mares for themselves. But as a rule they are not quite as dependent on company as mares.

⋂ *I am totally unable to deal with this!* Panic by its very nature is self-perpetuating. The more out-of-control the horse is, the more frightened she feels. Fear is, itself, very frightening.

WHAT TO DO ABOUT IT

∩ Keep your own safety in mind any time you are working with a frightened horse. No matter how fond she is of you normally, when she is truly panicky she can run right over you and not even know it.

∩ Clicker training (page 27) can be used very effectively in a situation like this. In any situation where the horse is exhibiting panicky behavior, there will be moments when the behavior stops, however briefly. The running horse stops to turn around or catch her breath; the horse who is pawing excitedly will rest her foot on the ground momentarily, if only to change feet. Fear also occurs in waves; that is, it increases and decreases in intensity from moment to moment. By marking each time the horse stops the panicky behavior, and especially by marking with a jackpot when the horse shows some measure of self-control as the fear decreases for a moment, you help her learn how to control her behavior. It works the same as biofeedback does for humans. Since the horse finds the panic itself disturbing, she is usually very happy to continue to develop more self-control, once she learns how. It is very helpful to the horse's self-control if you focus on grounding yourself as much as you can. If the horse's behavior gets you upset and your body shows it, it will be that much harder for the horse to regain control of herself.

∩ Parelli games (page 29) can also be used, especially once the horse has her initial panic under control. The games give the horse something else to focus on, as well as increasing her trust that her human can look after her. As the horse becomes calmer and more submissive, praise or clicks and treats can be added to give the horse more incentive to control her behavior.

∩ A peek-a-boo game can be introduced. This is just another form of advance and retreat (page 27). It requires two people. At first the other horse is taken a short distance away, not even out of sight, and brought back. This is done a number of times, so the nervous horse begins to understand that her friend will return quickly each time. She is also praised and treated for any signs of self-control. Excitable behavior is ignored. Next, the other horse is taken out of sight and returned, using the same procedures as before. Then the other horse is taken out of sight and the handler of the nervous horse looks for a break in her behavior, just as we saw in the earlier clicker training. When the horse shows the beginning of a break, she is clicked, but then the treat is that *the friend comes back in view*. The behavior is then shaped so that the horse is asked to maintain self-control for longer and longer periods with her friend out of view. Eventually she should be able to stay under control more or less indefinitely. Here the horse learns that she will get her friend back sooner if she maintains self-control.

WHAT NOT TO DO ABOUT IT

◠ Don't make a fuss over the horse when she is panicking, such as excessive patting or giving treats. This tends to encourage the very behavior you're trying to eliminate.

◠ Don't yell at the horse for pawing or banging the stall. The horse would rather be yelled at than get no attention.

PAWING: DANGEROUS STRIKING

A new horse has just come into Marty's stable, on trial from a dealer, and he has a nasty little cut on his forearm, probably from a kick. The cut has obviously been neglected for a few days, is swollen and looks infected. It is hardly life-threatening, but Marty wants to clean it up and put some ointment on it right away, before it develops into something serious. Her assistant, Pam, holds the horse while Marty prepares to clean the wound with warm water. The horse seems very insecure and fidgety, so Marty cautions Pam not to stand directly in front of him, and positions herself very carefully out of reach of his hooves. Sure enough, when she places the warm compress on the wound the horse rocks back and strikes out sharply with his foot. He misses both of them, but his intent is clear. Marty wants to treat the wound, but she doesn't want to get either herself or Pam hurt in the process.

WHAT YOUR HORSE WANTS YOU TO KNOW

◠ *Get away from me or I'll make you sorry.* Serious striking is one of the few truly aggressive things a horse does. If he really means business, the horse goes up on his hind legs and attacks with both front feet, not just one. When a horse has had a lot of unsympathetic handling, he assumes anything that hurts is intentional, so he immediately defends himself. In this case, because the danger is from in front, he uses his front foot to retaliate.

WHAT TO DO ABOUT IT

◠ Besides the obvious safety issue, the important thing is to gain the horse's confidence as soon as possible. Clicker training (page 27) would probably be most effective. If you are really unsure of the horse's reactions, give the treats from a shallow bucket rather than using your hand. Put the horse in a stall with a double door if available, because with the bottom door closed there is no risk of his striking if he still feels threatened. If you use a breast chain or stall guard, stand to one side as much as possible. Use a simple target to teach the horse the rules of the clicker game, until he makes the connection between the targeting, the click and the treat. Don't worry about a little mugging at this point, as long as it is friendly.

⋒ When he seems to be relating better to you and is fairly relaxed and interested in the game, bring him back out of the stall and prepare to work on the wound again (as in Doctoring: Treating Wounds, page 58). Use the clicker to reward him for standing and submitting. This is a little tricky to read, so unless you are fairly sure of yourself, it's best not to take any risks. You need to be very confident and grounded, calm and smiling in order to succeed—all of which are difficult if you are too unsure of yourself. If the cause of the striking is something less immediate than a wound that needs treating, you could put off this second step until the next day, giving the horse further time to think about the clicker and understand it.

WHAT NOT TO DO ABOUT IT

⋒ Don't endanger yourself or others with a horse who is being truly aggressive. If the clicker, which is the least threatening technique you can use, doesn't work, leave the wound alone until you can get professional help, perhaps having the horse tranquilized so he can be worked on safely.

⋒ Don't respond with aggression to a horse who has already decided to hurt you. You can't be sure he'll back down, and if he doesn't it could have serious consequences.

PAWING FOR TREATS

Beth always brings treats to the stable when she comes to ride Max. He is quite polite about taking them, so she doesn't feel she is teaching him bad habits. However, if she happens to meet a friend on the way into the stable and stops to chat, Max immediately starts pawing and banging on his stall door. He continues to do so until he gets his treat, and even afterward, until she indicates that treat time is over by putting on his halter and leading him out. What is really aggravating is that several other horses in the stable take up the chorus in hopes of getting a handout. Beth is beginning to feel it is time she did something about Max's behavior.

WHAT YOUR HORSE WANTS YOU TO KNOW

⋒ *Hurry up! I know you have a treat for me. You always do. Stop wasting time!* Horses are very quick learners, especially of things they like. They also like routine, and expect you to stick to it.

◠ *I know if I keep annoying you, you'll stop doing whatever it is you're doing and pay attention to my needs.* Horses are great manipulators, and once they find out how to control you, they'll keep using the same tricks.

WHAT TO DO ABOUT IT

◠ You use almost exactly the same technique as in Feeding Problems: Making Noise While Waiting (page 62) to teach your horse not to paw for treats. That is, when he paws, turn your back and totally ignore him—which is not easy to do if he has learned to paw in a determined way. As soon as the pawing stops, even for a moment, turn to face him again but don't move toward him immediately. If he starts again, turn away again. When he stops long enough to indicate that he seems to be figuring it out, walk toward him and give him one treat. Then go on with your preparation for grooming or whatever your intention was. If he paws again, repeat the sequence. If he stays quiet for a reasonable length of time, you can offer another treat.

◠ Using clicker training enables you to give a treat to your horse and teach him good behavior at the same time (see page 27 in the Introduction and Personal Space: Mugging for Treats, page 124).

WHAT NOT TO DO ABOUT IT

◠ As in the other pawing circumstances, punishment is not effective.

TALKING HORSES

I was told an amusing story of a horse who used pawing to manipulate an inexperienced young instructor. Mitch lived in a stall that faced the entrance to the adjacent arena. He had developed the habit of pawing, either from boredom or to attract attention, and pawed in such a way as to bang loudly on his door. When Bill was trying to give a lesson, the banging made it difficult for his student to hear him. His solution was to call to whoever was in the stable to give Mitch a flake of hay to shut him up. Mitch quickly realized that he had a good thing going, so every time he got a little hungry and saw Bill in the arena, he pawed. Bill swore a little and got someone to give the horse some hay. After awhile Mitch figured he could up the ante, so, after taking a few bites of hay, he started to paw again. Sure enough, after a little persistence on Mitch's part, Bill told the stable boy to give him some grain. Pretty soon Mitch had Bill so well trained that he could get food whenever he liked. Unfortunately for Mitch, the stable manager came in one day when Mitch was getting his third or fourth feeding of the morning, and Mitch soon found himself relegated to another stall far from the arena while Bill got a short lecture on who was supposed to be training whom!

PAWING FROM NERVOUSNESS

Teddy has been standing quietly on the crossties while Jeannette grooms him. It is fairly early in the day and other horses are being taken out for their daily turnout. Teddy usually gets turned out as well, but Jeanette came early today because of other obligations. When Teddy sees his buddies being taken out, he starts to show signs of worry. His head comes up, he begins to fidget, and then to paw. Jeannette ignores the behavior at first, but Teddy's pawing becomes more and more frantic as the other horses disappear from view. Jeannette is afraid to come near him, since he obviously is totally preoccupied with the other horses and doesn't even seem to know she is there.

WHAT YOUR HORSE WANTS YOU TO KNOW

⋒ *I'm upset, and I'm expressing my frustration with the situation.* Pawing is often an expression of emotion. Horses paw when they're angry or hungry or tense about any number of things.

⋒ *I'm afraid. My friends are leaving me behind and my instinct tells me this is dangerous.* Very few horses are really comfortable alone unless they have had some serious training. This is especially true when one horse is left behind when the others depart. In a wild herd, the horse who leaves may be feeling bold and resolute, but the one who is left behind may be the one who is weak or injured, and thus doomed.

⋒ *I don't know what to do.* The horse wants to escape and wants to be with the other horses. Nature is telling him to get going, to run and catch up. Since he can't, he moves in the only way he can.

WHAT TO DO ABOUT IT

⋒ If you are fairly experienced with the clicker, you can try marking the moment when his foot is on the ground, then treating. Continue to shape the behavior as the horse keeps his foot down for longer and longer periods. If the horse is not too far out of control, the act of playing the game may relieve his tensions enough to restore his self control.

⋒ Otherwise, if you haven't yet begun any sort of preparatory training for this problem, your first consideration is to keep the situation from escalating to where someone, person or horse, gets hurt. If the horse shows no signs of calming down, even though it seems like rewarding bad behavior, bring another horse back to the stable for now. If that is not possible, bring the nervous horse out to where the others are and, if he is manageable, walk him around or graze him in their company until he settles down, then lead him away from them.

⋒ You might find it necessary to turn him loose for awhile, then catch him and start again. If you make this decision, try to turn him loose at a time when he is being reasonable, controlled and attentive, rather than the opposite.

∩ Another choice might be to put him back in his stall where he can't get hurt (be sure the doors are fully closed and latched) and give him some hay to occupy him until he settles down. For most horses the stall represents security, while being on the crossties can make them feel exposed and threatened.

∩ Training techniques to help the horse deal with his insecurity are the same as those used in Panicking When Left Alone (page 114).

WHAT NOT TO DO ABOUT IT

∩ Unlike the other pawing situations, where the horse is trying to get attention, ignoring the behavior by turning your back or leaving won't work here. Like anyone who is truly frightened, a horse with separation anxiety needs help and support.

PAWING: MILD STRIKING

Roger is talking to his friend David, not paying a great deal of attention to his horse, Rudy, who has not been exercised in several days. Rudy begins to fidget, then to paw. He edges a little closer to Roger, who suddenly realizes that Rudy's hoof is coming uncomfortably close. Rudy doesn't actually make contact, but he looks as though he would like to. His head is up and his gaze is intent, and annoyance is apparent in his whole body. Roger chases him back, but Rudy continues to be a pest until Roger turns him loose to run.

WHAT YOUR HORSE WANTS YOU TO KNOW

∩ *Pay attention to me.* Mild striking—which is the horseman's term for kicking with a front leg—often arises out of impatience. The horse starts to paw, trying to gain his handler's attention. When that fails, he starts to reach out further with one hoof, not so much to hurt as to make a contact that the handler will have to listen to. It is a desire to control, but not necessarily to injure.

WHAT TO DO ABOUT IT

∩ The training method you use to deal with mild striking will depend on what you have available and what suits you and the horse. If the horse is bored or perhaps tense from lack of exercise, Parelli games (page 29), especially yo-yo, will occupy his mind and body while asking for attention and obedience. If you have a round pen (page 34) available, working him back and forth, moving and changing direction frequently, will remind him that standing still politely is much easier than working harder than he really wanted.

∩ If he is not especially tense, and is just trying to attract attention without regard for your person, use the clicker (page 27) to mark the moment when his foot is down. Gradually shape his behavior so he is standing quietly for longer and longer periods. If he still has the tendency to paw when bored, attach a voice command to the click that tells him to stop. That is, once he understands that clicking means to stop pawing, use a word such as "down" —not in a pejorative way but as a command—at the moment his foot hits the ground, followed immediately by a click and treat. If the horse is accustomed to clicker work, he will figure this out quite quickly.

∩ If the pawing is due to tension, Tteam work on the front leg (page 34) may help to relieve it by relaxing the shoulder, neck and leg muscles.

WHAT NOT TO DO ABOUT IT

∩ Don't slap the horse or yell at him to get him to stop. Chances are the slap or yell will occur when the horse's foot is on the ground, so he won't understand what it is you want and he may just perceive it as part of the game.

PERSONAL SPACE: BUMPING, STEPPING ON OR WALKING INTO YOU

Tina has been free-longeing Mickey for a few minutes. She signals him to come in and he trots over to her and stops. She gives him a smile and a scratch, then asks him to go out again. But instead of moving away from her, he cuts in close to her body, so she steps out of his way. Occasionally, as he moves around the arena he runs quite close to her and again, she moves over. Later, when she is holding him while talking to a friend, he bumps her with his shoulder so she has to move. When she brushes him off after their ride, he steps toward her so that she has to pick up her foot quickly or be stepped on. Mickey has a habit of annoying behavior, which Tina tends to overlook since it doesn't appear to be aggressive.

WHAT YOUR HORSE WANTS YOU TO KNOW

∩ *I win again.* This is the same game as the horse who swings his head is playing (see Personal Space: Head Swinging, page 122), but a little more subtle. The horse usually isn't trying to step on you, because he doesn't know it would hurt. He just wants you to move out of his way, proving that he is in charge.

Allowing the horse to take charge means you are losing his respect, and eventually his trust in your ability to take care of him in threatening situations. Allowing him to push you around a little may seem like an unimportant detail, but can make the difference between a horse who listens to you when there's trouble and one who ignores you and panics.

WHAT TO DO ABOUT IT

∩ *Stand your ground!* This is hard to do at first, because most of us learn as beginners to keep our feet out from underneath the horse to avoid being stepped on.

∩ Flap your arms, look stern and, if necessary (especially if the horse is loose), swing a whip or lead line so that he can't come near you.

∩ If he walks by you very close, poke him in the girth area with your thumb to get him to move away.

∩ Some of the techniques in Personal Space: Head Swinging can be adapted to prevent bumping.

WHAT NOT TO DO ABOUT IT

∩ Don't get careless because your horse is soooo cute.

∩ Don't get too aggressive. The horse thinks of this behavior as a game. That's okay, as long as you always win it.

TALKING HORSES

Deliberately stepping on your feet is rare, since most horses won't step on something that feels odd or insecure. However, the occasional horse finds out that if he stands on someone's foot, especially a beginner, he wins big time. A short course in manners, which includes a lot of firmness, is called for!

PERSONAL SPACE: HEAD SWINGING

Mike is holding his horse, Candy, while he talks to a friend. When Mike isn't looking, Candy swings her head around and bumps him on the shoulder, knocking him off balance so he has to take a step to recover. He yells at Candy and slaps at her, but Candy just swings her head out of the way. A few minutes later she does it again. This is a particularly sneaky habit. The horse appears to bump you accidentally, but it's really a dominance game to make you move your feet.

WHAT YOUR HORSE WANTS YOU TO KNOW

◠ *Nyah, nyah, you moved your feet. I win!* It may seem as though the horse is swinging her head to get attention, but it is really an attempt at dominance. One of the games horses play is a sort of "King of the Castle" where they attempt to knock the other horse (or person) off balance. Whoever moves their feet loses.

◠ *I like playing games.* When the other player responds by moving or shoving back, that's just part of the game, so the horse continues to play.

WHAT TO DO ABOUT IT

◠ If your horse has the habit of playing this game, you need to learn how to block. You can use either a straight arm and curled fingers, or an elbow block—whichever works best for you. You watch the horse out of the corner of your eye, with your arm ready. When you see her head starting to swing, bring your arm up quickly, without looking at the horse. She runs into your arm, but since you aren't looking at her it appears to be accidental. If she keeps running into your arm it stops the game, because you're not shoving back. In fact, from her point of view you aren't responding at all.

◠ Another block you can use is the "chicken" block. This is a little more active and requires more energy on your part. Hold out both arms with the elbows bent so that your hands are touching in front of your chest. Flap them vigorously up and down when the horse starts to come into your space.

◠ If the horse is very persistent, ask her to back out of your space altogether. If you have been studying Parelli (page 29), you can use the porcupine, driving or yo-yo game to send her back. Or you could use clicker to teach her to stand three or four feet away and wait there until she is asked to approach.

◠ If she is very strong, quick and determined, she may catch you off balance and make you move. Regain your grounding as promptly as possible, then send her around you several times until she decides she would rather stop and turn to face you in a respectful manner and at a respectful distance.

◠ Once the horse understands that you aren't playing games, she will stand quite quietly nearby but not in your space. This is a secure thing for her to do, since you have made it clear that you are the authority but that you are still willing to have her near you.

WHAT NOT TO DO ABOUT IT

◠ When you slap at her or yell, she considers that just part of the game. You can't slap her hard enough to hurt, and she has succeeded in pulling your chain.

◠ If you get more aggressive with a not-too-bold horse, you will make her very tense, and thus less willing to stand quietly and less trusting of you as an authority figure. A very bold horse will take your aggression as a challenge and become more aggressive herself.

PERSONAL SPACE: MUGGING FOR TREATS

Tamara is very attached to Jonesy and loves to bring him treats. Unfortunately, he has now gotten so spoiled that he is constantly pushing and nipping at her clothes to get more. Slapping and pushing him away only works for the moment—he is soon bothering her again. She doesn't want to stop his treats altogether, as some people have suggested, but she needs to get his behavior under control.

WHAT YOUR HORSE WANTS YOU TO KNOW

∩ *You always give me treats, so I'm sure that if I'm persistent you'll give me some more.* A horse quickly learns how to get the results he wants. If the horse finds that being bothersome gets him treats, he will keep trying. Every time the handler gives in to his behavior, it just establishes the behavior more firmly.

∩ *Although I love you I don't really have much respect for you, so I feel like I can push you around to get what I want.* Lack of respect for personal space—pushing into your space, getting you to move—is an important horse game, because it establishes dominance. The more dominant the horse, the more safe he is, since the weaker horses get forced into positions where they are more susceptible to predators. Horses constantly play dominance games, and you have to play them too—and win—to gain their respect and thus their obedience.

WHAT TO DO ABOUT IT

∩ You can use Tteam, Parelli first-level games or round pen training to work on the respect issue (see the Introduction). The horse needs to learn to stay out of your space, but out of respect and affection, not fear. Flapping your elbows or swinging the end of the rope or the stick are examples of ways to chase or keep the horse out of your space by making him uncomfortable but not hurting him..

∩ Although it doesn't seem likely at first glance, clicker training (page 27), which involves using treats, is actually one of the better ways to teach the horse not to get pushy about treats. The first thing the horse learns about clicker training is that he has to figure out what *you* want in order to earn a treat. Once he makes the connection between performing an action (usually touching a target such as a small cone or plastic supplement lid), hearing the clicker and receiving a treat, you can quickly teach him that he only receives treats when he stays out of your space and waits politely. It's important that these first lessons take place in a situation where he can't chase after you. The best choice is with him in his stall, either behind the lower half of a dutch door or with a breast chain.

⋂ In association with the clicker, which marks what you *do* want, if you have the horse restricted by the door or chain you can mark the behavior you *don't* want by simply stepping away, turning your back and ignoring him. Part of the dominance game is the control he gains if he can annoy you. When you show him that you simply aren't interested in a particular behavior, the fun is over for him. If he was doing something noisy, when he stops you click and turn around and treat. If he is just pushing with his head, you face in his general direction using soft eyes (page 9) and when he swings his head away, you click. It's a little tricky handling the treats here, because as soon as he sees the treat he will try to grab it. If you hold the treat in your closed hand and run the back of your hand down over the front of his muzzle to his mouth, then roll your hand over and open it when his head and mouth are still, he will eventually learn to be more polite.

WHAT NOT TO DO ABOUT IT

⋂ When you are not actively working on clicker training, don't carry any treats on your person and try not to wear clothes that you customarily carry treats in, since your pockets will still smell tasty to your horse.

⋂ Don't slap or hit the horse for mugging. It just becomes part of the game. You can't really hurt him, and he will just dodge back and then bore in again. If you constantly slap at him, you may irritate him to the point where he starts nipping or biting.

⋂ Don't give in! Especially during the training period. It's easy to say, "Oh, he is looking sooo cute. I'll just give him one little treat." Many horses are experts at looking cute. If you want to give him a treat, insist that he offer some sort of polite behavior to earn it. Turning his head away and holding it there requires no props and reinforces the behavior you want.

REARING AS A GAME

Danny's owner, Shirley, had raised him from a yearling and was very fond of him. When he was young, she liked to play games with him when he was loose in the field. Unfortunately, Shirley did not show very good judgment in the games she played and the way she chose to play them. Danny has a natural tendency to rear when he plays and Shirley encouraged it, and also allowed him to strike at her with his front feet when they were off the ground. He always had his ears forward and was obviously not feeling angry or aggressive.

Like many horse lovers who lack experience, Shirley assumed Danny would never hurt her. And of course, he wouldn't do so on purpose. But he was never taught that humans are more fragile and less well coordinated than horses. So when Shirley moved Danny from her home to a public stable, he soon got into trouble. A groom was leading him out to the field and Danny decided to play his rearing game. The groom was inexperienced, and instead of joining the game, he tried to pull Danny down. Danny, still playing, struck out and broke the groom's collarbone with his hoof. The groom was angry, the barn manager was upset and Shirley was astounded that Danny would hurt anyone.

WHAT YOUR HORSE WANTS YOU TO KNOW

∩ *Come on, let's play a game!* Horses love to play games, and once they have learned a good one they want to play it a lot. Horses play fairly roughly with one another, but rarely hurt each other because they are the same size and understand the rules.

∩ *Betcha I can win!* As in any game, there are winners and losers. In some horse games, the one who gets his head above the other and keeps it there is the winner. By rearing, the horse makes himself much taller, giving him an advantage.

WHAT TO DO ABOUT IT

∩ Safety is the first concern. Using a long lead rope and wearing a hard hat are two essential precautions. And of course, no one but an experienced person should be allowed to handle the horse until the problem is solved. When the horse rears, let the rope run out so you are not pulled underneath him, and move off to one side. As soon as he comes down, take him in a small circle to prevent him from going up again.

∩ Make it plain that you aren't interested in playing any games, nor are you impressed by his antics. When he rears, position yourself safely, breathe and ground, and try to treat the incident very casually. You're not angry, it's more like being in the room with someone else's spoiled child. Mostly, it's just boring.

∩ When he comes down, *that's* when you make a fuss. If he is clicker trained, click as he hits the ground. If not, offer effusive praise and a treat. Lead him in a circle and praise and treat again, thus rewarding him for walking quietly, then do the same in a straight line. Keep looking for moments when you feel as if he is starting to settle down and stop thinking about rearing. If you keep yourself well grounded and breathing, it will help him stay settled and will also help you notice if he is getting tense, because it will make you tense as well. Conversely, if you find it easy to stay relaxed, that tells you he is relaxing too.

∩ The Parelli friendly game (page 30) might be useful, depending on how he reacts to it. If some activity causes him to rear, you can continue whatever action caused the rear until he comes down, then stop, stroke and praise, which is another way of reinforcing the action you want, which is "stay on the ground." However, do not face him in a confrontational way and swing the stick vertically, since this is the way to *teach* a horse to rear. This is rather confusing, because you do want the rear to occur so you can praise him for stopping, but you don't want to specifically *ask* for the rear. It just has to happen almost accidentally.

WHAT NOT TO DO ABOUT IT

⋂ Don't punish him for rearing. In this case the horse doesn't know it's wrong, so punishing is unfair. You'll just risk making him confused and angry, and possibly aggressive.

TALKING HORSES

Playful rearing is one thing; a horse whose ears are forward and who isn't really trying to hit you with his front feet is only dangerous if you are careless. A horse whose ears are back and who is trying to make contact is something else altogether. Truly dangerous horses are quite rare, but they can kill you. Even experienced professionals stay well away from such horses.

I have also heard of instances where an apparently normal and well-behaved horse had a brain tumor or other brain damage and suddenly became dangerous. So you cannot say with absolute assurance that any horse "would never hurt you." Never forget that horses are large and powerful, and as dangerous when out of control, for whatever reason, as a car on ice.

REARING WHEN BEING LED

Billy is a very cooperative horse in many ways, but when Nancy tries to lead him someplace he doesn't want to go, he stops and, if she persists, he rears. As he goes up, he swings his head around in a way that often results in the lead rope being pulled out of her hand. Sometimes he rears and comes down several times, then decides it's not so bad and comes along. Other times she either has to go another way or find someone with another horse to go first, so that Billy will follow. It really makes getting from here to there a chore, and Nancy has lost confidence in her ability to get Billy to follow her. She has also received some nasty rope burns from when he rears unexpectedly.

WHAT YOUR HORSE WANTS YOU TO KNOW

⋂ *I don't really trust you.* Horses are programmed to follow another horse whom they perceive as a leader. They hold the leader in high respect and trust her implicitly. If you have not established a similar relationship with your horse, he will be unwilling to follow you in situations that he perceives as threatening.

⋂ *I'm stronger than you, so I don't have to come with you if I don't want to.* Horses, like all herd animals, are always challenging the pecking order. You must be prepared to assert your leadership position regularly, thus ensuring your horse's trust and respect.

⋒ *The pull on the rope makes me want to resist.* One of the ways a predator tries to take down his prey is by grabbing his head, restricting forward movement. Prey animals thus instinctively resist any pull on their heads.

⋒ *The pull on the rope makes it hard for me to move.* Resisting the pull on the rope tends to lock up the muscles at the base of the horse's neck, which then restricts the forward movement of his front legs. With his front legs unable to move forward, the horse's need to move forces him upward into a rear.

WHAT TO DO ABOUT IT

⋒ If you know the horse has a rearing problem and you have to continue to lead him until you can retrain him, there are some things you can do to make leading safer and easier for both of you. First, wear gloves to protect your hands from rope burns if the horse goes up suddenly and unexpectedly. Next, use a longer lead rope—10 or 12 feet rather than the usual six or eight. Tie a figure-8 knot (page 189) in the end so the rope won't slip out of your hand, but won't trap it either. Keep some slack in the rope at all times, unless you are asking for a stop. Face the way you are going as long as the horse is on the ground, but if he goes up, turn and face him so you can see to stay out of his way. Keep your eyes soft and try not to be confrontational. Let the rope feed through your hand as much as necessary so that it never gets tight. With nothing to pull against it is harder for the horse to keep his balance, so he will come down quicker. As he comes down, try to move quickly into a position from which you can turn him in a circle. Also, smile and praise him for coming down. Circle him quietly a couple of times, then lead him in a slightly different direction before coming back to the direction you wanted to go in.

⋒ Retraining should begin as soon as possible, since rearing is a danger to both horse and handler. The first aspect to work on is gaining the horse's respect and trust—becoming his "lead mare." (The dominant horse in a herd is not, as one might think, the stallion, but the senior mare.) Trust must be established first, then respect. Techniques for building a good relationship are found on pages 26 through 35.

⋒ Besides dealing with the relationship issues, you also have to look at your own leading techniques. Rearing while leading is an extreme form of balking, and the techniques for dealing with that (Leading: Won't Go When Asked, page 91) will work equally well for rearing.

WHAT NOT TO DO ABOUT IT

⋒ Don't face the horse when you *expect* him to rear. The blocking and the appearance of confrontation may actually cause him to go up.

⋒ Don't try to pull him down with the rope. He will instinctively pull back and may go over backward, risking injury to himself and to anyone behind him.

⋒ Don't make a big issue of the rearing. That just tells the horse that he has gotten your goat.

SADDLING, MOVING DURING

Dave is not a very experienced horseman, but even he realizes that saddling his horse, Yukon, is more difficult than it should be. In order to put the saddle on, he has to crosstie Yukon to a couple of posts, then chase him around before he finally gets the saddle on the horse's back. Once the saddle is on, Yukon continues to move around, making it difficult to fasten the cinch. Altogether, saddling is a real production for all concerned, and takes away from both the time and the pleasure of the trail ride that follows.

WHAT YOUR HORSE WANTS YOU TO KNOW

⌒ *I've never really adjusted to this.* Anything coming down onto the horse's back from above can seem to him like a lion jumping on his back to deliver a deadly bite. If time has not been spent building the horse's trust and getting him accustomed to this frightening action, he will continue to have the fear.

⌒ *I'm afraid it will hurt.* Many people put the saddle on clumsily, especially if it is heavy or the person is small. As a result, the saddle lands on the horse's back with a crash, which is both painful and scary.

WHAT TO DO ABOUT IT

⌒ You have to begin by reintroducing the horse to the idea of being saddled. It's best to start at the most basic level of touching, patting and rubbing with your hands all over the horse's body, as in the Parelli friendly game (page 30). The horse should not be tied for any of this work. Hold him on a long lead line, so that he is free to move around and learn to stop by himself, as he realizes that you are not hurting him. Be sure to smile and praise as often as possible. This is especially important for a horse who is really frightened.

⌒ Unless you are quite tall compared to him, gradually introduce the horse to having a solid stool or box beside him that you can stand on, and use the same techniques you would use to teach him to stand for mounting (see Mounting, Moving During, page 102). Horses who are afraid of the saddle are often afraid of mounting as well, so you will be working on that problem at the same time.

⌒ Once he is comfortable with being touched in the saddle area and having you stand above him or reach over him, introduce him to a saddle pad. Allow him to smell it, then stroke him with it, using advance and retreat (page 27) if necessary. When he seems comfortable, quietly ease the pad up his side and lay it across his back. Repeat this until you're sure he is relaxed about it. Next, take the pad and swing it around as though it was a saddle you were preparing to put on. When he stands quietly for the swinging pad, swing it up onto his back. Be effusive with praise, treats and smiles.

⋒ When he is relaxed about having the pad "thrown" onto his back, he is ready for the saddle. Go through the same procedure of allowing him to sniff, and stroking him with the saddle as you did with the pad, before you try to put it on.

⋒ Swinging the saddle up onto the horse so it doesn't hurt him takes some skill, and is best practiced on a fence first. Stand with your left side nearest the fence, and grab the pommel or horn of the saddle with your left hand and the cantle in your right hand. With a western saddle, the right stirrup and the cinch should be hooked up over the horn so they are out of the way. With an english saddle, remove the girth and slide both stirrups up the leathers. Hold the saddle at your right hip. Your left arm will be across your body. Now swing the saddle up in the air, using both arms and turning your upper body, until the saddle is above the fence, then *let it down gently*.

⋒ Some people prefer to put the saddle on from the right side so the cinch is out of the way, and it is a good idea both for you and the horse to be able to saddle from both sides and have the horse accept it. Once you can put the saddle on smoothly from the left, practice doing it from the right as well. Then you can choose which way is easier. However, if you are saddling an unfamiliar horse always do it from the left, at least the first time.

⋒ Spend as much time as necessary on each step, returning to a previous one if necessary, until the horse will stand quietly with his head down, indicating relaxation and confidence, while you saddle him up. Be sure to read the next chapter, Saddling: Problems While Being Cinched or Girthed Up, so you don't undo all your good work.

WHAT NOT TO DO ABOUT IT

⋒ Yelling at the horse to stand still, jerking him up for moving or tying him very tightly will all make him more nervous and more firmly convinced that you are trying to attack him with the saddle.

TALKING HORSES

Many riding problems begin before you ever get on the horse. If he is made tense and uncomfortable by the tacking experience, it's going to be difficult for him to be relaxed and give you a pleasant, safe ride. And even if you enjoy the experience of a "spirited" (which nearly always means frightened!) horse, tension usually leads to unsoundness before long!

Saddling: Problems While Being Cinched or Girthed Up

Warily, trying to look both ways at once, Cindy reaches under Colonel for the girth. His ears are back and he fidgets uneasily, but she manages to get hold of it, bring it underneath him and stand up. As she brings the girth up against his barrel, his head swings around quick as lightning and he snaps at her. However, she is ready for it, blocks him with her elbow and yells, "Cut it out!" The rest of the girthing up proceeds in the same manner, until the saddle is secured. Cindy breathes a sigh of relief as she takes him out to be mounted, but both of them are tense and irritable—not a good way to start.

WHAT YOUR HORSE WANTS YOU TO KNOW

- *You're going to hurt me! Get away!* The girth or cinch passes under the horse's body across the end of his breastbone. In a young horse, this area is soft cartilage and can be compressed by a tight girth in a way that's very uncomfortable. The horse soon learns the cause of this discomfort, probably because he is still sore the following day, and begins to anticipate with fear the pressure of the girth. If the rider pays no attention to the horse's fears, he has no recourse but to try to drive her away.
- *I'm afraid I won't be able to breathe.* Many riders make the girth far too tight, and too soon in the process of saddling and mounting. This, of course, makes taking a deep breath very difficult, so the horse becomes uncomfortable and tense.

WHAT TO DO ABOUT IT

- Safety is very much an issue during girthing. You have to reach under the horse to take hold of the girth, and are in a position where he can easily kick you. Then, as you use both hands to fasten the girth, it is hard to defend yourself against a bite. If the horse is truly trying to hurt you, as opposed to just threatening, it is time to go back and work on trust. The friendly game (page 30) or some work in the round pen (page 34) are both good places to start. In the friendly game, particularly emphasize touching and rubbing in the girth area, using advance and retreat (page 27) as necessary. Throwing the lead over the horse's back and bringing it under, then sliding it off again, will help get him more comfortable with the touch of the girth against his body.
- With the actual girthing process itself, a combination of Tteam circles (page 34) and clicker training (page 27) can be very effective. Begin by making little three-finger circles all around the girth area. As the horse relaxes and accepts your touch, click and treat frequently. Then use advance and retreat with the girth or cinch itself. As a safety measure while you are doing this,

snap a lead line to the end of the girth and pass it under the horse, then use it to bring the girth toward you, rather than bending under the horse each time. Look for improvements in attitude that you can click and treat for.

∩ Once the horse is accepting the touch of the girth against his body without resistance, the next step is to fasten it up. *The girth or cinch only needs to be tight enough to hold the saddle down on either side of the withers. It is the withers that keep the saddle from turning, not the tightness of the girth.* (Of course, the saddle needs to fit the horse correctly.)

∩ When adjusting the girth, *only tighten it as much as the horse will give you at one time.* The correct way to tighten is to pull *down* on the girth or cinch strap, pulling the saddle down against the horse's back, then smoothly lift up and take up the slack created. This is exactly the way you tighten your own belt; the pressure as you tighten is against your back, not your more sensitive stomach. If you let yourself be aware of the horse's reaction, you will find you can adjust the girth in very small increments that the horse can deal with without any resistance

∩ Because it can only be adjusted from the ground, the western cinch should be adjusted at least four times before mounting, giving the horse an opportunity between adjustments to relax his muscles still further. First make the cinch snug when the saddle is put on, then walk the horse for a few minutes, then adjust the cinch again to take up the slack created as his muscles lengthen and soften. Repeat this, then adjust the cinch one more time just before mounting. If the horse is very tense you may decide to dismount after 10 minutes or so of riding for a final adjustment. This routine can vary, of course, with the individual horse. As long as he shows no signs of discomfort and the saddle stays in place, you have accomplished your goal.

∩ When checking the tightness of the girth or cinch, slide your hand under the saddle *at the widest part of the horse's barrel.* Most people slide their hand under the girth just below the pad or saddle flap, which holds the girth away from the horse's side, making it seem looser than it actually is. The english girth can be adjusted two or three times on the ground, then two or three times more after mounting, which is easily done in the english saddle. Snug up the girth when the saddle is put on, then check it again a few minutes later, before leading him out. Just before mounting, take up whatever he will allow. After mounting you can nearly always take it up one or two holes, because an english saddle compresses under your weight. Check it by bringing your foot—and the stirrup—*forward,* lifting the flap and pulling up on *just one* girth strap. If it comes up easily, set it on the new hole, then adjust the other strap. After about 10 minutes, reach down and check the girth again. Before you start any really vigorous work, such as galloping or jumping, check it one more time.

∩ If your horse has very flat withers or very flat sides, you should consider a breastplate, which helps to keep the saddle centered and also prevents it from slipping back off the withers. You must also work on your riding so that you can keep the saddle centered with your riding skills. It is perfectly possible to ride with no girth at all on level ground if you are well balanced and centered.

⋂ Use these same training and girthing methods with the horse who "blows up"—expands his lungs and his barrel as much as possible to keep the girth from being tightened too much.

WHAT NOT TO DO ABOUT IT

⋂ Never use any sort of force to get the girth tighter than the horse wants to give you. This is what causes all the problems in the first place.

TALKING HORSES

A horse with his girth too tight is frequently more dangerous than if the girth were too loose. I was once asked to look at a horse who had thrown his owner and broken her arm. When her father got on the horse to "teach him a lesson," the horse bolted through some trees with him and gave him a severe fall. The problem was that there didn't seem to be any cause for the behavior.

I began by turning the fully tacked horse loose in my outdoor ring to see what he would do on his own. He walked around like any sensible horse, looking at everything carefully but showing no signs of extreme timidity or nervousness. After a few minutes I asked him to trot, which he did quietly and willingly. Then suddenly he began to tense up, increasing his pace and looking as if he were on the verge of exploding, so I caught him before he lost it completely. I started looking around to see what the problem might be, and noticed that the saddle had slid back a couple of inches. Experimentally I pulled on the girth, and he reacted frantically.

When I had first tacked him, he had shown no particular response to the girth. But apparently he had had the sensitive end of his breastbone damaged in the past by being girthed too tight, so now the slightest pressure on it terrified him. We fitted him out with a snug breastplate, so that the saddle could no longer slide back. This solved the problem, but the original abusive girthing had resulted in at least two accidents that we knew of, and perhaps many more.

SPOOKING AT FAMILIAR OBJECTS

Suzy is bringing Foxy from his stall down to his pasture. It is early on a rather cold morning. As they approach a large rock beside the path, Foxy leaps sideways and rushes past it, knocking against Suzy in the process. She pulls him up firmly, saying, "Oh, for heaven's sake! What is it with you and that rock? We go by it every day. You'd think you would be used to it by now!"

WHAT YOUR HORSE WANTS YOU TO KNOW

∩ *Because I'm cold, I am feeling very tense and therefore threatened by anything that could conceivably hide a predator.* Like all of us, when a horse is resting or only moving slowly (which horses do much of the time), he builds up tension in his muscles. When you get up in the morning, you stretch to release some of that tension. Horses like to release it by running around and bucking, for the most part, but some horses seem to hold this muscle tension in, and then overreact to anything that might hide a predator. The fact that they spook at something with which they are quite familiar, and which won't bother them at all once they are warmed up, is an indicator that the problem is tension, rather than fear.

WHAT TO DO ABOUT IT

∩ There are two things to deal with here: the spooking itself, and the tension that is causing it. Looking at the second problem first, think about the times when the horse spooks. Is it every morning, winter and summer, or is it perhaps much worse on colder days? If it's the latter, the horse is telling you that he is uncomfortably cold—not all horses grow a really thick winter coat. Look for ways to keep him warmer. Maybe there are drafts in the stall, or perhaps he just needs another blanket on cold nights. Many horses become especially tense if their necks are cold, and are totally different animals if they wear a hood in cold weather. If you find the part of the hood that covers the head awkward to deal with and keep in place, you can have that part removed, or buy just the neck covering, since it is primarily the neck that needs to be kept warm. Ever wonder why horses have manes? Now you know!

∩ Another way to loosen the horse up is to groom him vigorously, increasing his circulation and warming and relaxing his muscles. Be careful not to use stiff grooming tools on cold, sensitive skin.

∩ Do some Tteam stretching exercises. The horse's legs can be stretched forward and back, worked in small circles and shaken out to release tension. For his torso, using your fingernails gently but firmly, go along his back on either side of the spine, from withers to croup, pressing down to get him to drop and relax his back. Arch your own back as you work on him, to help him feel what you want. Then do the same exercise from underneath, along his midline, to get him to raise his back and stretch it the other way, rounding your own back as you do so. Repeat the two exercises, first down, then up, three times. Finally, for his neck, do "carrot stretches," using a piece of carrot to encourage him to stretch his head and neck, first up, then right, then left, and finally down between his legs. Again, do these exercises three times. The exercises are also very useful if, for some reason, the horse can't go out at all.

∩ To deal with the spooking problem, first work on getting the horse to drop his head on command (page 14). A horse who drops his head is immediately more relaxed, and is much more inclined to listen to you. A horse whose head is up is blocking you out of both his sight and his mind, and is taking over.

◠ If the horse has not learned to lead with his head behind your shoulder, that is your next task (see Leading, Running Over Handler While, page 86).

◠ When the horse will drop his head and walk in the correct place while being led, he is ready to learn not to spook, using a technique similar to that described in Leading, Spooking While (page 89). However, because the horse is not truly frightened you don't have to worry so much about his fears—just about his behavior. Allow yourself plenty of time and lead him out as usual, making sure he stays where he belongs—which he may not want to do if he is expecting to be turned out. Place yourself so that you are between him and the scary place (he should accept leading from either side!). As you approach the place, watch for his head to come up. If it does, stop and ask him to drop it again, rewarding with praise or a click and a treat. Continue on, but keep insisting that he drop his head. If you get close to the place and his head is still coming up, and you feel he isn't really paying attention to you, turn and take him back to where he is calm and start again. After a while he will figure out that if he wants to get where he's going, he has to do it on your terms.

◠ Once he will stay behind you with his head down, the battle is pretty much won. Continue with the praise and treats. If he loses it a little, ask for the leading position and the dropped head again, ignoring the little slip. If he really loses it, that tells you he needs a bit more work on the head drop and leading.

◠ If you start to feel it's partly a respect issue, try spending some serious time on the Parelli games (page 29) or in the round pen (page 34), until he is willing to give you his full attention all the time.

WHAT NOT TO DO ABOUT IT

◠ Punishment will only make the horse more tense and will fix in his mind the thought that the "spooky place" is a place where bad things happen to horses.

◠ Be careful not to make a fuss over him when he is being flaky. You don't want him to think that's a good thing to do!

STALL PROBLEMS: BREAKING OUT

Brittany decides to pay her new pony, Jerry, a visit in his stall. It is late morning and he has finished his breakfast. When she unlatches the door, he shoves it violently with his nose, flinging it open and knocking her down in the process, then runs out the stable door. He races around excitedly for a few minutes, then stops to eat grass. When Brittany's mother tries to catch him, he runs away, fully expecting to be punished for his behavior. Eventually they capture him, but Brittany is upset and discouraged by his actions.

WHAT YOUR HORSE WANTS YOU TO KNOW

∩ *I want to go out now, and I am accustomed to getting my own way and doing whatever it takes.* This is a really obnoxious and dangerous habit, and results from the handler opening the door and letting the horse run out on his own, instead of teaching him to wait politely. If the horse is one who really needs to live outside, then his compulsion to get out is even greater.

WHAT TO DO ABOUT IT

∩ First you have to get the horse's attention. Using heavyweight screw eyes, install a short, strong chain with a heavy snap, from the door to the doorpost. The height should be just above the horse's shoulder points—which will necessitate some acrobatics on your part when entering or leaving the stall, but is a necessary part of the training. The chain should be adjusted so it is just long enough to allow a person to squeeze through, but not a horse, and should have extra links so that you can gradually increase the opening. Keep the chain fastened at all times, except when you are actually leading the horse out. When the door is opened, he will try to force it the rest of the way, especially the first few times.

∩ If the horse already has this habit, chances are he will try the same trick when you go to lead him out. Therefore, always be sure all outer doors are closed as well, while you do some retraining. A horse with this mind-set has learned that he can get his own way if he is determined enough, so you have to really think ahead to avoid giving him any opportunity to escape while you work on his attitude.

∩ Clicker training (page 27) is probably the best way to approach this problem, with some Parelli (page 29) on the side. With a horse like this, it is important to spend time first teaching him not to mug for treats (see Personal Space: Mugging for Treats, page 124), since he is accustomed to using force to get what he wants.

∩ Once he understands the basic clicker concept, teach him to stand while you open the door, using the chain to control the door. Be sure any outside doors are closed. Open the stall door using about a foot of chain. If he lunges forward, step back out of the way and let him hit the door. Then use the Parelli porcupine game (page 30) on his nose to get him to back away. When he has backed away and stands still, however briefly, click and treat. Then close the door, open it, and repeat until he stops rushing the door and stands waiting, when you click and treat with a jackpot (page 27). Repeat this step, though not necessarily with a jackpot, a number of times until he seems really secure and happy to stand and wait. Then adjust the chain a few inches longer, so the door opens wider, and repeat.

Be very careful not to stand right in the doorway. If the horse lunges forward and hits the chain, the door will close on both of you!

When the horse will wait while you open the door wide, with the chain still up, close the door and unfasten the chain. Then start again, opening the door only about a foot and rewarding if he stands and waits. If he reverts to pushing his way out, don't fight about it, just bring him quietly back and put up the chain again. He will soon figure out that pushing out nets him nothing, while waiting gets treats. Eventually work your way to the point where he will allow you to open the door all the way without trying to get by you.

⋂ The next step is to teach him to be led out of the stall, a step at a time, and stop and wait in the aisle. Read the chapters on leading and breaking away (pages 83 to 92), so that you don't accidentally provoke more unwanted behavior.

WHAT NOT TO DO ABOUT IT

⋂ Don't get careless with a determined horse. Every time he wins, he tries harder the next time.

STALL PROBLEMS: CROWDING

Jill walks into Andy's stall, where he is eating his hay in the corner. She wants to check his water, so she starts to walk by him to get to the bucket. He is standing a bit close to the wall, so she gives a little push to get him to move over so she can get through. Instead of moving away, he leans into her, pressing her uncomfortably against the wall. She pushes at him again, but he just leans harder. Now she starts to get a little panicky, but is able to control it, and decides to just stand still and see what happens. After a minute, the pressure relaxes and she is able to slip by and out of the stall, but she is understandably upset by the incident.

WHAT YOUR HORSE WANTS YOU TO KNOW

⋂ *Hey! Quit shoving!* If the horse has not learned how to move over, a push will put him off balance and he will push back. This can develop into a dominance game, where one horse tries to shove the other out of his way. The horse, of course, doesn't realize that you can't get out of his way. He thinks you are challenging him, so he keeps pushing.

WHAT TO DO ABOUT IT

∩ Working in a larger space, use the Parelli porcupine game (page 30) to teach the horse to step over easily in response to light pressure. When you are applying pressure, keep your weight very centered over your feet and *don't lean into the horse*. That becomes pushing, rather than pressure, and the horse will try to push back. It is rather a subtle difference, and is at least partly in your intent. You need think of applying pressure at a certain point, so that the horse will move *himself* over, rather than thinking *you* will push him over.

∩ If the horse seems to get locked up when you use steady pressure, try using a repetitive press and release—rather like trying to get someone to move out of your way at a crowded party.

∩ Turning the horse's head slightly in the direction you want him to step will help him understand the concept of moving his front feet. Turning his head quite far in the opposite direction will help him with moving his back feet. Teach him to move his whole body over a step in response to a tap given from in front of his shoulder, or from behind his hindquarters, so that you can move him over without being in a position to be crowded.

∩ Because the horse has an attitude problem, beyond just lack of comprehension, add a clicker element (page 27) by clicking or praising when the horse starts to give, and rewarding with a treat when you get a good step. Thus, getting your approval becomes more desirable than pushing you around.

∩ Even when your horse has become good at moving over in the open, for a while he may still be a challenge in a confined space such as the stall. Ask him to move well over before you pass close to him, and try not to touch him in passing.

∩ If the horse is a determined crowder and you will need to go into the stall with him while you are working on retraining, carry a short, blunt stick, such as a sawed-off broom handle. The stick needs to be a bit longer than you are wide. Hold it crosswise, so if the horse moves over into you, he runs into the stick, which presses into the wall. Being blunt, it won't hurt him, and being passive, it won't cause him to push back. He may lean on it for a minute or two, but he will soon find it uncomfortable and move away, at which point he is praised and thanked.

WHAT NOT TO DO ABOUT IT

∩ When you are being crowded, any sort of muscling is only going to get you in further trouble. This is not the time to try to win!

∩ For safety's sake, don't allow anyone into the stall unnecessarily, or anyone who might panic and get hurt, until you are sure the horse is cured, even with strangers.

STALL PROBLEMS: FEAR OF DOORWAYS

Marcy has finished her ride on Surtees and untacked him. Now she is ready to put him back in his stall. The aisle outside the stall is a bit narrow, and as she turns him toward the stall his head comes up and he starts to sidle and fidget. Rather than leading him into the stall, she brings him to the door, unclips him and quickly steps back out of the way. Surtees enters the stall with a rush, and it's plain to see why Marcy didn't walk in in front of him. He might easily have knocked her down. He goes in and out of his stall like this every time, and occasionally bangs his hip or side in the process, making him even more nervous about it.

WHAT YOUR HORSE WANTS YOU TO KNOW

∩ *This doorway is trying to hurt me.* At some point Surtees has banged against the door jamb, probably with the point of his hip, which is unprotected, so hitting it is very painful.

∩ *If I go in fast enough, maybe it will miss me!* A horse's instinct in any threatening situation is to run, even when, as in this case, it is the worst thing he can do.

∩ *I feel trapped in this narrow space.* Horses like to have plenty of room to maneuver, especially when they feel threatened.

∩ *I don't want to listen to my person; she always seems to be right there when this happens to me, so I think she is doing it!* Since the horse doesn't fully understand what is happening, he may blame it on his handler, especially if she has tried ineffectively to correct him.

WHAT TO DO ABOUT IT

∩ Begin by practicing the turn from the aisle to the doorway, making sure the horse is placed to walk straight through the door, not enter at an angle. Don't actually take or send him in to the stall, just make the turn and stop him facing the door. This will also start desensitizing him about the approach. Try to keep him behind you and to one side, in a submissive position, but if he makes a dive for the stall just let him go in without restraint or punishment, then quietly turn him around and bring him out again. Use the clicker (page 27) or verbal praise and a treat when he stands quietly facing the door.

∩ Next, ask him to step forward one step, then stop, using the click and treat as before. Then have him back a step and repeat the exercise. Be sure you are not standing directly in front of him when you ask him to step forward, although you should be able to be somewhat in front when you ask him to back.

∩ Gradually increase the length of time he stands before backing, then eliminate the backing step altogether. Ask him to take another step forward, then back from that place, repeating the same exercise. If at any point he rushes through the door, quietly bring him out and start over. Your goal is to have him walk through the door one step at a time, waiting for your signal to continue.

⋒ If he rushes coming out as well as going in, repeat the exercise in that direction as well, although once he has the idea in one direction, the other direction should be much easier.

⋒ In addition, if you are experienced with Parelli, the squeeze game will help the horse to overcome his fear of restricted spaces.

WHAT NOT TO DO ABOUT IT

⋒ Don't get careless. Safety is an issue here, since the horse can easily knock you against the wall or step on your feet if he is thinking about that "horse-eating" doorway. As you work with him, be very careful where you stand.

⋒ Don't hurry, or allow him to hurry, when approaching the stall. This is especially important at mealtimes, when horses are often thinking only of getting to their dinner. *Most door problems are created because somebody didn't bother to take the time to make sure the horse was straight when he entered the stall.*

TALKING HORSES

Many handlers assume the horse can look after himself. He can, but only when he knows what to look for and how to deal with it. A young horse, especially, like a young child, doesn't look at a situation, analyze it and say to himself, "That could hurt me." He just thinks about his objective and the quickest way to achieve it: "My grain is in my stall and I want to get in there as fast as I can." It is up to the handler to keep the horse from hurting himself until he learns. Parelli and Tteam training (page 29 and page 34, respectively) both teach the horse to think more carefully about handling his body in different or tricky situations.

STALL PROBLEMS: GETTING CAST

Marjorie has just finished cleaning the stalls and is at the far end of the stable when she hears a tremendous banging and thumping in one of the stalls. She runs back and sees Murphy, flat on his back against the stall wall, with his feet banging and scraping it as he seeks purchase. He lay down to roll in the fresh shavings and rolled all the way over when he was too close to the wall. He is now *cast*, that is, he is stuck, unable to get his feet down to the ground on the side he was rolling toward, and unable to roll back. Luckily for Marjorie, since she is alone in the stable, Murphy manages to find a toehold, and with a final wiggle he flops back over, gets his feet underneath him and jumps up, looking terribly embarrassed.

WHAT YOUR HORSE WANTS YOU TO KNOW

∩ *Help! I've fallen and I can't get up!* Sometimes horses get really stuck, and if help is not available they can die, because horses are not designed to lie in one position for long periods. They can also die from struggling.

WHAT TO DO ABOUT IT

∩ First, wait a few minutes and watch to see if it looks like the horse will be able to work himself free. Sometimes they can, but sometimes they get themselves into deeper trouble—squirming into a corner, for example. If things are not progressing, call for help. You need grownups, and fairly strong ones, preferably experienced with horses, but your local rescue people are usually pretty good at solving all kinds of problems.

∩ After you have called for help, put the horse's halter on. Then, if the horse continues to thrash fruitlessly—as opposed to lying quietly for fairly long periods, then trying again—sit on his head while you wait for help to arrive. Put on your helmet first. Approach from about his fore-lock area and sit firmly on his cheek, leaning well forward so you keep your feet under you as best you can. Sitting on his head prevents him from thrashing around and perhaps hurting himself, because he uses his head and neck for leverage. You can also pat him and calm him. Try to breathe and ground yourself, as this will help relieve some of his stress.

∩ This is not exactly a behavior problem in the sense that it requires some sort of training to correct it, but it is certainly a problem that can happen to anyone, so you should know how to handle it. Since the horse is thrashing around, the safety of every one involved in rescuing him is paramount. First, everyone who goes into the stall should have a hard hat on. Second, no one should be in the stall except those who can help. One person should give directions and the others should be prepared to listen and ready to move when told.

∩ If the horse is up close to the wall, so that it seems it would be easiest to roll him back over, the procedure is as follows. One person, fairly large but agile, sits on the horse's head. Then an experienced person, preferably with long arms, positions himself at the horse's croup and passes either a soft rope or a leg bandage around the horse's hind pastern (if he can reach it), crossing the rope so it stays in place. If he can't reach the hind leg, he moves up near the withers and uses a front leg instead. The hind leg is preferable because it puts less strain on the horse. In the case of a very large horse, if enough help is available use a rope on a front and a hind leg.

Now have one or two fairly strong people on each rope. When all is ready, the person sitting on the horse's head gets up and immediately either leaves the stall or moves into a corner well away from where the horse could possibly hit her or trap her. On command, the people holding the ropes pull. As soon as the horse clearly starts to come over, everyone lets go and quickly either goes out if the door is nearby, or goes into the corner nearest the horse's tail. Under no circumstances should anyone be anywhere near the horse's head or on a line with his body as it rolls. When he comes over, his legs will be five or six feet to your side from where his back was lying, and they will be moving violently. Then he will fling his front feet forward to get up rapidly, and will strike anyone within reach—not on purpose, but because he won't even know they're there!

∩ If the horse has rolled too far the other way to roll him back easily, try dragging him away from the wall far enough so that he can get some purchase with his feet to help himself. If he is wearing a blanket, he can be dragged fairly easily with that, especially if he is on clean shavings, which are fairly slippery. Otherwise, you may be able to move his forehand away by dragging on his mane, or you may be able to pass a rope or bandage under his neck and one front leg and back to your hands. Don't try to drag him by his tail, because you risk injuring his spine. It takes a lot of strength to drag a horse, but you usually only have to move him a few inches, and he will help all he can. Again, don't get in front of him, because as soon as he thinks he can get up, he will try to get his front feet out.

∩ Take any opportunity you get to watch horses standing up from a lying position. This will help you to understand what the horse has to do to regain his feet.

∩ For some reason, horses seem to like to do their rolling close to things like walls, fences and even trees. I have known horses to get cast in all those places. Most horses get cast once, or perhaps twice, then learn their lesson. However, sometimes you have one who doesn't seem to be able to figure it out. I had one who cast himself three days in a row. The third time he didn't even struggle; he just lay there and looked at me and said, "Come on, Mom, get me out of this, please." If that is the case, you can cure him by building up the bedding on the insides of the stall a couple of feet in from the wall, on a slant. Then, if he tries to roll toward the wall, he will slip down toward the center of the stall, where he will be able to get up again.

WHAT NOT TO DO ABOUT IT

∩ Don't panic if your horse gets cast. Even though it is scary and noisy, virtually all of the time the horse gets out of it with no injury—except to his self-esteem.

TALKING HORSES

Once he is up, the horse will probably stand calmly. He should be taken out and walked until he seems to have recovered, and checked for injuries. If you don't know how long he has been cast, call your veterinarian, because there is a possibility of pneumonia. The horse should also be observed for signs of colic as a result of the stress, and not fed anything except hay for several hours.

STALL PROBLEMS: KICKING THE STALL

Margie keeps her horse, Gus, at home, along with her husband's horse, in a small barn they built not far from the house. Although the horses are usually out in a field during the day, there are times when the ground is so soft that they can only go out in a little paddock. This is when Gus tends to resume his habit of kicking in the stall. He is more likely to do it as mealtime approaches, but sometimes he kicks during the night as well. He is not kicking at the other horse, because the stalls are across the aisle from each other. Not only is this a disturbing habit, it is also causing the beginning of a capped hock—a soft swelling over the point of the hock. While this is not making Gus lame now, it may well do so in the future.

WHAT YOUR HORSE WANTS YOU TO KNOW

∩ In this instance the horse is not knowingly saying anything. Repetitive habits like this tend to be unconscious, like nail biting.

∩ This is a way of working off some sort of tension, which could be psychological if the horse was kept confined for long periods, perhaps next to another horse who kicked. It could also be the result of some sort of chemical imbalance.

WHAT TO DO ABOUT IT

∩ Check your feeding program to be sure the horse isn't getting too much grain for his size and the amount of work he is doing. Try cutting his grain in half on the days he has to stand in, and increasing his hay, which will also give him something else to do. Talk to your veterinarian about mineral imbalances, and perhaps do some research on the web or with horse e-groups. This is not an uncommon problem, and other horse owners may have some good nutritional ideas for you to try.

∩ If the horse kicks fairly frequently and consistently, the best solution is the clicker (page 27). The horse probably will not kick if you are looking right at him, but may do so if you are standing near the stall with your back turned. Kicking, by its very nature, is not continuous. The horse kicks, then puts his foot down, or at least brings it forward before kicking again. So if you click almost immediately *after* you hear the kick, you will be marking the moment when the foot is coming back down. The horse will then come for his treat, which will stop the kicking for the moment. But if he is very addicted to the behavior, he will soon start again. You should continue the click and treat routine until the horse has made the association between putting his foot down and being rewarded.

∩ Then you can begin to shape the behavior by waiting a few minutes, or whatever period of time you can be sure that he won't have started kicking again, and again click and treat. If you misjudge and he starts kicking, just start over with the click for stopping. Gradually extend that period of time until he is standing without trying to kick for a half-hour or more. If the habit is well established, it may take some weeks of repetition before the habit is finally broken.

∩ The difficult thing about curing a horse of stall kicking is that they almost never do it when you are nearby. Therefore, using the clicker may not be feasible. The classic remedy for this problem is the "kicking chain," which sounds like some sort of torture instrument, but isn't. It consists of a padded strap to which is attached a short length of chain. The strap is buckled around the offending hind leg just above the hock. Each time the horse kicks, the chain swings and bangs him on the leg hard enough to sting. Most horses figure out quite quickly that they only have to stop kicking to prevent the chain from hitting their leg. If the horse is extremely tense or spooky, it might be as well to begin by rubbing his leg lightly with the chain and swinging the chain against his leg very softly, just so he knows it's there and is not taken totally by surprise. The sting when he kicks will still be enough to bother him.

WHAT NOT TO DO ABOUT IT

∩ Yelling at the horse to stop doesn't do much, except perhaps tell the horse that he has got your goat, at least for the moment.

∩ Going into the stall and punishing the horse is counterproductive, because as soon as you open the door he stops, and then you are punishing him for stopping.

STALL PROBLEMS: MANURE ON THE WALL, IN THE MANGER OR IN THE WATER BUCKET

It sounds like a bad joke, but Kerry's habit of backing up against the stall wall when he lifts his tail is very annoying and has the potential to cause other problems. Not only does it make a mess of the stall wall, but the manure gets caked on his hindquarters, his legs and the underside of his dock. If he doesn't get cleaned up daily, he is liable to get dermatitis in those areas, especially if his stool is loose. Mary spends a lot of time with a bucket and shampoo, which she would rather spend riding or ground training.

WHAT YOUR HORSE WANTS YOU TO KNOW

∩ *I am an obsessive-compulsive neat freak.* Sounds like a contradiction in terms, since the horse is making such a mess, but he is actually trying to place his droppings outside of his personal space. Many horses will put their manure as far into one corner as they can get it, but for the occasional horse, even that isn't good enough. Quite different from the slobs who drop manure anywhere and seem to like to use it for a pillow, especially if they are light colored!

WHAT TO DO ABOUT IT

⋂ If there is a larger stall available, that might well solve the problem. The horse generally positions himself relative to where his head is in the stall, so standing in the same relative position in a larger stall will bring his quarters away from the wall. You probably want to try the larger space for a few days first, to see if it helps.

⋂ The other solution I have seen used is to fix either two-by-fours or two-inch heavy plastic pipe, on brackets, six inches or so below the level of the horse's buttocks and about nine inches from the wall. Use plastic pipe, if possible, since the horse won't chew on it, and it is less dangerous if he manages to get caught in it in some way. If the horse is fouling his manger or water bucket regularly, place a barrier across the corner where they hang, and again, far enough away so the manure won't reach them.

⋂ Usually a horse with this problem only goes in one spot, so you probably only need to put the railing along one wall. If the railing is placed at the right height, the horse backs up against it and lifts his tail, and the manure mostly falls over the rail. Make sure the rail is low enough so that his dock doesn't get caught against it, but not so low that he could get a foot through it, either pawing or rolling.

⋂ This is not a perfect solution, but other than keeping the horse outside, it is the only one I know of.

WHAT NOT TO DO ABOUT IT

⋂ Don't even *think* of punishing the horse for this. He wouldn't have any idea why you were punishing him, and it would only destroy any trust he had in you.

STALL PROBLEMS: PLAYING WITH THE WATER

When Mark goes in to clean Lark's stall, the corner nearest the water bucket is always a swamp. Lark has spilled her water again! During the day Mark can often hear a rhythmic thumping as Lark picks up the bucket and drops it again, splashing water out each time. Besides the mess and the noise, Mark is afraid Lark isn't getting enough to drink. He chases Lark away from that corner whenever he sees her playing, but he can't stand there all the time!

WHAT YOUR HORSE WANTS YOU TO KNOW

∩ *I am bored, bored, bored!* Horses are made to live in the open, with plenty of room to roam, run and explore, and lots of buddies to play with. Unfortunately, this is not always possible. Many horses can deal with spending lots of time in the stall, but others develop bad habits of one sort or another.

WHAT TO DO ABOUT IT

∩ Because of the health issue, the bucket must be fixed so that the horse can't spill it, but so it can still be removed easily for cleaning. There are several creative solutions for this. One is to bolt a heavy milk crate to the wall, place the bucket in it and firmly fasten the bucket handle down to the crate with a snap or tie. You can also build a solid frame to put the bucket in.

∩ If at all possible, the horse should be given more turnout time, preferably with other horses so she can fulfill her need to play games.

∩ There are a number of stall toys on the market that horses enjoy playing with. It's best to get a variety and change them regularly, because horses, like us, lose interest in playing the same game all the time. An easy and inexpensive toy is an old, small (two-gallon) rubber bucket, with the handle removed. It can be rolled and tossed around, and is safe.

∩ Spend as much time as you can with the horse, riding, grooming, playing ground games such as Parelli games (page 29) or inventing clicker challenges. Using her mind also uses up a lot of energy, so she has less need to play games on her own.

WHAT NOT TO DO ABOUT IT

∩ Don't punish. It's a waste of time.

∩ Don't remove the horse's water. Horses need water available just about all the time, and someone might forget to put it back.

STALL PROBLEMS: SOURING EARS OR CHARGING THE BARS

Whenever anyone, horse or human, approaches the outside of Zeke's stall, he charges at them with his ears back, and sometimes teeth bared. When someone actually enters the stall, if she is reasonably polite Zeke backs away and looks at her, then somewhat grumpily allows himself to be haltered, or the stall to be cleaned, or whatever is necessary. Coquette is less aggressive, in that she only puts her ears back and looks annoyed but doesn't make any overt attack—similar problems, just a difference in degree.

WHAT YOUR HORSE WANTS YOU TO KNOW

⋂ *This is my space. Private property. Keep out!* Certain horses become very protective of what they consider their turf. Even though horses are, by nature, prepared to live in the wide open spaces in large groups, when you put them in a more confined area, they feel the need to keep some private space for themselves. With most horses, the stall becomes their safe haven in any danger, the walls more or less taking the place of the bodies of other horses during times of threat. An example of this is horses running into a burning stable, trying to get back to their stalls where they believe safety lies.

WHAT TO DO ABOUT IT

⋂ Advance and retreat (page 27) is the best solution here. By not forcing the issue, you communicate to the horse that you are not a predator trying to attack him or a bully trying to push him away, but rather an equal who respects his needs but still wishes to approach. As you move toward the stall, keep your eyes soft and your glance casual. Don't pin the horse with your eyes as though he was a particularly tempting piece of chocolate! Watch for the least sign of tension or aggression, and immediately stop your approach. Look away for a few seconds, then look back casually. If the horse is watching you with ears forward, smile and praise. After a moment, take another casual step forward. If he seems very threatened, step back again. Think of retreating, not out of fear, but out of politeness and respect; that is, you are *choosing* to retreat, the horse is not *forcing* you to do so. Wait, then try another step. You may have to continue this advance and retreat for several minutes, but if you stay calm and grounded the horse will eventually accept that you have no ulterior motives and allow you into his space. When you are within comfortable reach, offer him a treat, with lots of smiling and praise, then leave him alone for awhile.

After a few days the horse should accept you in his space without question, as long as you approach politely. You can then proceed with patting and scratching and generally making yourself pleasant company, but keep your visits fairly short at first, and your moves quiet. If the horse has had this behavior pattern for some time, he needs more time to rebuild his reflexes, so you want to avoid setting off the alarm.

⋂ If the horse is in an area where many people are passing his stall, and especially if his stall is located so that people walking down an aisle are walking directly toward him, try moving him to a quieter stall.

WHAT NOT TO DO ABOUT IT

⋂ Don't run at him aggressively to chase him away. It only confirms his belief that you are trying to drive him out of his safe place.

TALKING HORSES

When I was young we kept many of our horses in straight stalls at night, and turned out most of the day. The stalls were large enough for the horses to lie down, but not by any means spacious. We also had some box stalls that were given to horses who needed them for reasons of size or condition. One mare, Bonny, had lived in the same straight stall for many years. We tried moving her to other stalls, but when she came in from the field she would chase any other horse out of "her" stall and occupy it herself. One spring she was due to have her first foal. Since she refused to live in a box stall, my mother bedded her down in the arena during the night, where there would be enough space for her to drop her foal. The time for her to produce came and went. One morning she showed every sign of giving birth at any moment, so my mother kept her in the arena and watched her like a hawk. Finally we decided that she would be all right for the short time it would take all of us to have breakfast; she in her stall and we in the house. When we came back 20 minutes later, there was the foal on the floor out in the aisle, wondering about the cruel world. But Bonny was happy. She was in her own stall—the only place she thought was safe enough for this great event.

STALL PROBLEMS: TURNING THE TAIL TO THE DOOR

When Keith goes to Arnie's stall to bring him out, Arnie, who usually stands with his head in the far corner, deliberately turns so that his hindquarters are facing the door. Although he makes no attempt to kick, he seems sullen and resentful at having anyone enter the stall. However, when Keith reaches his head, Arnie allows his halter to be put on without resistance and walks politely out of the stall.

WHAT YOUR HORSE WANTS YOU TO KNOW

◠ *You didn't knock!* Horses like their privacy to be respected, some more than others. Probably at some point early in his life Arnie had the sort of person cleaning his stall who came in too quickly, hit him with the fork to make him move, yelled at him and generally treated him extremely rudely.

◠ *I'm not stopping you. Have you got a problem with something I'm doing?* Nobody has ever explained clearly to Arnie what they would like him to do instead of turning his tail. He senses their annoyance at his behavior and it makes him feel uncomfortable, but he doesn't know what else to do.

WHAT TO DO ABOUT IT

⋒ This is a very easy problem to deal with, because there is no real fear or aggression involved. All the horse needs is to be shown a way to behave that doesn't make the people entering his stall uncomfortable. Once you are more relaxed, and not frightened of or angry with him, he will be happier too.

First teach the horse the clicker concept (page 27). Once he understands that the click means he did something good and will get a treat as a reward, stand at the closed stall door and do something to attract his attention. Use a tongue cluck or call his name or bang on the door with your knuckles. You want to get him to turn his head toward you, at least a little. As soon as you get the slightest movement, click, at which point he will probably turn around, expecting a treat. (If he doesn't, it means he doesn't yet understand the clicker.) Praise him extravagantly, not forgetting to smile, give him his treat, and walk away. Wait a little while, during which time he will probably turn away again, then return to the door and repeat. When he is turning his head consistently as soon as he hears his name called (or whatever signal you are using), delay the click until he turns his head further toward you. If your timing is good, within a very short time you will have him turning around to face you as soon as he hears you, maybe even when he recognizes your footsteps.

⋒ Make a point of waiting at the open door for a few seconds, letting your horse smell your fingers and talking to him before entering the stall. How would you like it if people just walked in and out of your house without even acknowledging your presence?

WHAT NOT TO DO ABOUT IT

⋒ Smacking the horse on the rear end to make him turn around is just asking for trouble. A horse who feels threatened and has no place to run to is very likely to kick!

STALL PROBLEMS: WALKING AND WEAVING

While the other horses are quietly snoozing, looking out the window or watching to see who comes in, Star is walking, around and around, incessantly. Every day he wears a path in his bedding with his monotonous movement. He doesn't stall walk all the time, of course, but he walks enough that it is hard to keep weight on him.

Buttons, who lives in another part of this large commercial stable, has a different but similar habit. He stands in one place but constantly shifts his weight from one front foot to the other, swinging his head back and forth as he does so, creating a sort of weaving pattern. Both horses appear to zone out when they are doing their thing. If you get their attention they will stop temporarily, but soon go back to the behavior. While neither of these behaviors is obviously destructive, they create a lot of wear and tear, because the horse isn't getting as much rest as he should, and are indicative of emotional problems.

WHAT YOUR HORSE WANTS YOU TO KNOW

∩ *I'm so tense and uncomfortable I just can't stand still.* Although he can't tell us about it, the horse probably experiences something similar to "restless legs" in women. No pain is involved, just an annoying discomfort that is relieved by movement.

∩ *I don't really know what I'm doing, or why.* The repetitive movement appears to be hypnotic and, like cribbing (page 151), is a form of stress management. High-energy horses who are kept confined too much are the most prone to this behavior.

WHAT TO DO ABOUT IT

∩ The best thing you can do to help a horse with one of these problems is to arrange for him to spend much more time outside. Ideally, he should be in a space of 10 acres or more, with grass to eat and other horses to play with. Being out in a small paddock doesn't seem to help, since the horse is still confined and bored.

∩ If the horse is getting high quantities of concentrates—more than four quarts a day is a lot, unless the horse is very large and is working hard every day—try reducing the grain and feeding more hay. Having hay to eat will also give the horse something else to do, but don't feed so much that he strews it around the stall and wastes it.

∩ Check into mineral supplements and homeopathics, which may help reduce tension and relieve stress.

∩ For the stall walker, it can be helpful to place an obstacle in the stall to break up the pattern, as long as you are also doing other things to relieve the stress. Use a bag of shavings or, if you can find one, a large foam block placed on the track where he walks. Watch the horse in the beginning to make sure he is not frightened. Sitting on the bag or block yourself, and giving your horse some treats or scratching, will help him accept it. If you are relaxed and casual, he should accept it fairly easily.

∩ One or two soft objects hung from the ceiling will serve the same purpose. They can also be hung in the head weaver's favorite spot. Tires can be used for this. Just be sure that whatever the objects are hanging from will break if the horse gets tangled in them. And don't put too many in the stall; they might panic him.

WHAT NOT TO DO ABOUT IT

⋒ Don't scold or punish the horse, or try to restrict him even further. He can't really help it, and will only develop other undesirable habits.

STALL PROBLEMS: WINDSUCKING OR CRIBBING

Barney's problem is cribbing, also called windsucking. He grabs a wood railing, or his manger, with his teeth, tenses his neck and emits an annoying grunting noise. He repeats it over and over, driving Jeannine to near insanity. She has finally decided to put a crib collar on him, but realizes that it doesn't get at the cause of the problem.

WHAT YOUR HORSE WANTS YOU TO KNOW

⋒ *If it feels good, do it!* It used to be thought that cribbing was a bad habit resulting solely from boredom at being confined in a stall for long periods. It is now known that cribbing releases endorphins, and so is a form of self-induced sedation. There is some evidence that it increases the production of saliva, relieving stomach discomfort caused by long intervals between feedings. Many people now feel that cribbing is the result of low-level, undiagnosed pain.

WHAT TO DO ABOUT IT

⋒ The same treatments used for stall walking and weaving (page 149) are appropriate for cribbers. I have been told that horses with sufficient turnout and a constant food source will give up the cribbing habit.

⋒ Mineral supplements, especially dolomite and copper, given with veterinary supervision, may help as well.

⋒ If you must use a crib collar, try to use the most humane one available.

⋒ Although most horses will not pick up the cribbing habit just from observation, it does happen. If you put a new horse, especially if he is young or tense, next to a cribber, keep a close eye on him for a week or so. If he shows signs of trying to figure out how to crib, move him to another stall. Thereafter, treat him the same way you would a confirmed cribber, except for the collar, on the theory that he wouldn't be trying it if he didn't have some need for it.

⋒ If the horse is actually chewing wood, as opposed to sucking wind, see Turnout: Chewing Wood, page 165.

WHAT NOT TO DO ABOUT IT

⋒ Punishment is ineffective and unfair. It only creates relationship problems.

TRAILERING: LOADING

Garry has finished his trail ride at the state forest and is in a hurry to get home. He brings Butch up to the trailer and tries to lead him in, but Butch slips out to one side and avoids the ramp. Garry tries again, and this time Butch goes out the other side. Garry shortens up on the line and brings him right up to the base of the ramp, at which point Butch plants his feet and refuses to move. Several people come by and offer to help, and finally, with the help of longe lines and a broom (and because Butch is, by nature, a cooperative horse), he is put aboard. On the way home Garry finds himself thinking, "There has to be a better way!"

WHAT YOUR HORSE WANTS YOU TO KNOW

⋒ *I don't want to go into that narrow, confining space.* Horses are animals of the open prairie. Getting trapped in a small space often results in getting eaten.

⋒ *I didn't like the ride over here.* Many drivers don't realize that there is a "snap-the-whip" effect in the trailer that is not apparent to the driver of the tow vehicle. Also, trailers are not sprung like cars, making the ride rougher, and the horse's high center of gravity makes him feel very insecure on turns.

⋒ *I don't really trust you on this.* If you hurry the horse and haven't done your preliminary homework, you make him feel pressured. The saying is, "If you allow all day, it'll take you five minutes. If you allow five minutes, it'll take you all day!"

WHAT TO DO ABOUT IT

⋒ Most ground training methods offer excellent information on loading, which you should read up on, since they go into great detail (see Appendix A). However, no matter which method you decide to use, they all have one thing in common. They all say, *You can't wait until the day you want to ship the horse to start teaching him to load.* Before you ever think about trailering, there is a lot of prep work to be done.

1. The horse must trust and respect you.
2. The horse must know how to drop his head.
3. The horse must know how to follow a lead line.
4. The horse must willingly move forward to a signal.

5. The horse must back easily on command, both from in front and behind.

6. You must be able to move the horse one step at a time in any direction.

7. The horse must be willing to step on strange objects on command.

8. The horse should know how to step up, over and down, off steps and over objects, both forward and backward.

∩ When you have all the above in place, you are ready to introduce your horse to the trailer. First let him walk all around it and sniff it. Put some sort of reward (hay in a hay net, or if there is a place for it, a little grain) at the front of the trailer, which he will find when he gets inside. Open the escape door if there is one and let him look in. Then bring him back to a point a few feet from the tailgate or ramp and let him stand and look from there.

I have always had good luck walking in before my horses, but the current thinking is to send the horse in on his own. Either one is okay. It is probably better to send the horse in on his own if there is no escape door up front. It's also a better method if you're alone, so you can fasten up the butt bar. If there is an escape door, be sure the breast bar is up so the horse doesn't try to follow you out, or jump out the front on his own.

Ask the horse to take one step toward the trailer, either leading or sending. In either case, look where you want him to go, don't pin him with your eye. Don't apply a lot of pressure. Look for a try, and praise and smile. You can give him a treat if you like, but with some horses it is too much of a distraction. If he takes several steps, allow it.

If one step puts his foot on the ramp, let him remain there a minute if he wants to, then back him off. Do that a couple of times, then ask for two steps forward and back. If he only moves his front legs and not his hind ones, make that the next request.

Continue this procedure, which teaches him both how to load and unload, until he will walk on quietly and evenly, and back off slowly and straight.

∩ Introduce the horse to the butt bar or chain by holding a rope behind him, fastened at one end. If he backs against it, resist fairly firmly. Look for the least acceptance of the pressure, and praise. If he gets upset, ease off and let him back out, then put him in again. Continue to do this until he is comfortable with the restriction before fastening anything fixed behind him.

∩ *Allow yourself and the horse days to learn loading, not minutes.* What you do now will affect the horse for the rest of his life, and affect you as well if you have to fight with him every time.

WHAT NOT TO DO ABOUT IT

∩ Don't try to force the horse to step forward. Especially, *don't try to drag him forward with a tight lead rope!* (See Leading: Won't Go When

Asked, page 91, and Panicking Against Crossties, page 107.) Many horses who won't load are resisting the lead rather than the trailer itself.

∩ Don't prevent him from backing out as many times as he needs to so he can find out he isn't trapped.

∩ Generally speaking, don't fasten his head until the butt bar is up and the loading door is closed. Even a horse who doesn't normally pull back may do so in such a confined situation.

TALKING HORSES

Some trailers are a lot easier to work with than others. The trailer should be solidly built so it doesn't bang and rattle when the horse steps aboard. Most horses will deal with a step-up more easily than a ramp, but backing off is a little harder if they haven't had any preparation. Wide is better, with partitions that can be moved over. Narrow trailers with a fixed post in the center are particularly difficult. Stock trailers are the easiest of all. The open work makes them light and airy, there are no partitions and plenty of room for the horse to turn around and walk out facing front. Most professionals who haul a lot of unfamiliar horses use stock trailers. They aren't as classy looking as some others on the market, but class doesn't mean much to a claustrophobic horse!

TRAILERING: LOADING WHEN YOU CAN'T DO IT RIGHT

Jan took her horse, Scotty, out for a trail ride. When she was several miles from home, enjoying a nice canter, Scotty stepped on a broken bottle. He injured his foot quite badly—too badly to walk home. Jan was able to stop the worst of the bleeding. Then she used her cell phone to call her friend Merilee, who owns a trailer, and asked if she could come and pick Scotty up. Fortunately, Jan and Scotty were not too far from a road.

Merilee arrived, bringing bandages and antiseptics. They fixed Scotty up as best they could, then prepared to load him. Unfortunately, Scotty had not had much experience trailering and was reluctant to load. The women didn't want to get into a fight with him, but they weren't sure of the best approach to use, either.

WHAT YOUR HORSE WANTS YOU TO KNOW

∩ *I feel pretty insecure anyway, and I don't see why I should have to do this too.* Everyone is going to be feeling a bit upset in these kinds of circumstances, so that needs to be taken into account.

WHAT TO DO ABOUT IT

∩ First, you have to make up your mind that, as long as the horse stays calm, you can probably load him eventually. Second, you have to realize that maybe you won't be able to load him, and that's okay, too. You'll figure something out. In other words, you need to feel relaxed and confident that you can deal with the problem. If you allow yourself to get upset and worried, the horse will know and will probably figure that you're upset about that big box you want him to get into!

∩ If at all possible, eat something before you start. Not caffeine and sweets, which will make you hyper, but something reasonably sustaining. It's hard to be patient and determined when you're hungry and tired. Go through your five steps (page 7) and try to be as grounded as you can.

∩ Start by using the same techniques as in normal loading (see Trailering: Loading, page 152). You may just find that if you give him "the time it takes," 10 or 15 minutes, he will load without trouble. In most demonstrations by experts of loading a "difficult horse," the horse walks on in a fairly short time, even though he doesn't know the handler. If you have a good relationship with the horse, you are already ahead of the game.

∩ If, after a fair amount of time, it looks like the horse has decided he doesn't have to go if he doesn't want to, and if he doesn't seem upset or frightened, you can get a little firmer—as long as you don't get impatient.

The technique that is least threatening to the horse is the war bridle (page 23). This is an awful-sounding name for something that, if applied and used correctly, is perfectly safe and kind, because the horse is the one who decides how hard to pull.

Once the horse is facing the trailer with the war bridle in place, be patient. Watch the horse out of the corner of your eye as you face into the trailer, but don't stare at him and don't stand directly in front, in case he comes forward quickly. Have a little smile on your face, like, "Whenever you're ready, kid." Keep yourself very grounded and flexible, so you can follow him if he goes back, and not jab him accidentally. Especially in the beginning, look for the slightest try, so you can ease a little.

∩ If you don't feel confident using the war bridle, you can use a more aggressive dingo (page 14) game. If you have to be more aggressive, it works best if you incorporate Parelli's four levels (page 29.) That way, you give the horse the choice of responding to a lighter touch each time, rather than feeling that you're just whacking away at him.

∩ If the horse is trying to dodge out one side, look for something solid, such as a branch or pole, that you can fix on the side he is running out on. People often use a longe line, but you need extra hands for that, and it is only as strong as the person holding it.

∩ Double longe lines, crossed behind the horse, are another technique frequently used to load a reluctant horse. It takes extra hands. The secret is to put pressure on the horse without trying to drag him (see the

porcupine game, page 30). And of course, reward the try by easing the
pressure a little without letting go. Be firm, not angry.

∩ Whatever technique you use, decide that you are going to give it a very
fair try. Determined horses are like whiny children. They figure if they
persist long enough, you'll give in. Act as though you'll never back
down—not that you are going to be mean, aggressive or unfair, just that
you know you're right and you're going to stick to your guns. It's amazing how well horses recognize this, as long as they aren't frightened, and
say, "Oh, what the heck, I might as well just do it."

WHAT NOT TO DO ABOUT IT

∩ Don't let yourself get discouraged. There's always a way. Maybe some professional help, or a different trailer, or a vet and some tranquilizer. Confidence and discouragement are both contagious. Try to stick with the former.

TRAILERING: PAWING OR KICKING WHILE UNDERWAY

Jeff is on his way to a ride on the beach with his trail riding group, towing his
horse, Cheyenne, in the trailer. He's a bit late so he is hurrying a little. He hears
some rhythmic banging in the trailer but it doesn't sound too serious, so he keeps
going. When they arrive at the beach, Cheyenne seems a bit eager and excited.
Jeff opens the door and notices that there are signs of pawing on the floor, and
Cheyenne is a bit sweaty. It's not a big deal, but Jeff thinks that if Cheyenne continues this behavior, especially on long trips, he might hurt himself.

WHAT YOUR HORSE WANTS YOU TO KNOW

∩ *I am upset and worried.* Horses paw for a variety of reasons, but in this
situation the only likely cause is nervousness. The horse is pawing to
relieve his tension. Some horses will kick rather than paw, but the cause
is the same.

∩ *You're scaring me.* Driving even a little fast on winding roads is hard for
the horse to adjust to, especially if the trailer stall is narrow or the floor
is at all slippery.

WHAT TO DO ABOUT IT

∩ Spend some time rebuilding the horse's trust, especially about loading
(page 152), so the horse begins the ride with more confidence.

◠ Having the horse eat some of his meals in the parked trailer doesn't necessarily help with loading, but it can help with riding in the trailer. The horse should be free to walk in and out, and the meal, of both hay and grain, will be an automatic reward for standing quietly in the trailer for long periods. Be sure the trailer is solidly fixed with the wheels blocked.

◠ Riding in a trailer involves balance and coordination. Free-longeing the horse for 5 or 10 minutes before starting your trip will enable him to warm up so that he can handle the ride more easily and be more relaxed about it.

◠ If the horse is really nervous about riding in the trailer, take him on a lot of short rides, just around the neighborhood. Drive very slowly and carefully—I always describe it as driving as though you were on black ice— and finish with lots of praise and treats before unloading. If time permits, take him for a short ride, leave him in the trailer for awhile, then take another short ride, or even several more.

◠ When you finish a trailer ride, don't unload immediately. Let the horse get accustomed to standing around for awhile, so he doesn't associate stopping with unloading and start fussing in anticipation.

◠ One of the best supports is a quiet companion. Having another, familiar horse along, who is obviously unflustered by trailering, is a big help.

WHAT NOT TO DO ABOUT IT

◠ Don't try to scare the horse into standing still by stopping or starting suddenly.

TALKING HORSES

As with loading, the type of trailer can have a big effect on how the horse rides. If he needs to take a wide stance, you don't want a center partition that goes to the ground. Many horses prefer to stand diagonally, so you want a partition that you can fasten off to one side. If you trailer more than one horse, you might want to look at a slant load. Many horses like to ride backward, because it is much easier to deal with sudden stops in that position. There are trailers that are set up for that, as well. Height is important, so the horse can use his head to balance himself if need be, and width is important both for stance and for larger horses, so they don't step on or unbalance one another if they sway. Appendix A lists a web site with information about all different kinds of trailers. Finally, if you frequently transport several horses you might want to think about a small van. As a general rule horses ride and load in them better than in trailers, and, well taken care of, vans have a long life. Of course, they are not as convenient for you for just driving around, but they do have their advantages. You can use them for transporting hay and shavings, for example.

TRAILERING: SCRAMBLING

Harry is driving Ben in his new trailer for the first time. He was very pleased at how easily Ben loaded. Suddenly, as he rounds a corner, he sees a large rock in the travel lane, so he brakes and swerves, as gently as he can, but there is still quite a whip. Then he hears some loud banging coming from the trailer, which also begins to rock. He slows down and pulls over, gets out and goes back to look in the trailer. Ben is leaning against the partition with his feet up against the outer wall, scuffling and slipping as he tries to get them back underneath his body. As Harry is wondering what to do next, Ben makes a final effort and rights himself, but is obviously frightened by the experience.

WHAT YOUR HORSE WANTS YOU TO KNOW

∩ *I can't, I can't!* Horses have a high center of gravity. If the horse's feet are confined and a sudden motion throws his body off to one side, he can find it difficult, if not impossible, to recover. Once a horse has done this, he tends to panic under the same conditions and repeat the behavior.

WHAT TO DO ABOUT IT

∩ This is another safety-first situation. The horse has lost control of his body, so stay out of reach of his legs. It's possible he may get hurt, but there is no point in your getting hurt as well. And horses have an amazing ability to get out of what seem to be impossible situations without coming to harm.

∩ If the horse is still scrambling and there is an escape door at the front of the trailer that you can use, first try pulling his head toward the side that his feet are on. That may be just enough help.

∩ If the horse still can't recover and continues to scramble, undo the butt bar and move the center partition, if it moves. If you have another horse on board, unload him first. Undo the scrambling horse's breast bar if he isn't leaning on it, and unfasten his head before opening the tailgate and taking the other horse out. Then undo the butt bar so the partition can move. The horse may go down, but will get right up again. If the partition doesn't move, you will have to try to unload the horse by fastening a long rope to his head and dragging him backward. If the trailer has a ramp, try to guide his hindquarters so his hind feet don't fall off the ramp.

∩ The only true solution to scrambling is to provide enough space for the horse to spread his feet. If there is a center partition, it should be cut off well above the floor. Most horses who scramble want to put their right hind leg out to the side, so they should ride on the left side of the trailer. They can then put the right hind leg somewhat under the partition.

∩ Tteam work on the front leg (page 34) improves the horse's balance and thus his ability to stand up in the trailer.

∩ If you usually haul two horses and one of them tends to scramble, you might want to accustom them to wearing wraps so they don't damage one another under the partition.

∩ Many horses ride better backward or diagonally (for trailers that are set up for this, see page 173).

∩ Drive especially carefully with a scrambler.

WHAT NOT TO DO ABOUT IT

∩ Don't cram the horse into too narrow a space.

∩ Don't try to right him by driving more aggressively.

TURNOUT, BREAKING AWAY DURING

Margie has reached the point where she is afraid to turn her horse, Roscoe, loose in the field. Every time she does, as she reaches for the snap he pulls back violently, sometimes dragging the line out of her hand. If she manages to make him stand long enough to undo the snap, he immediately wheels and bucks. A couple of times his heels have just missed her face.

Ordinarily, Roscoe is a perfect gentleman. He allows himself to be caught, he stands for grooming and tying and he never behaves in an aggressive manner under any other circumstances. But Margie is not comfortable with turning him out herself, and she is afraid to ask anyone else to do so, since they might well get hurt.

WHAT YOUR HORSE WANTS YOU TO KNOW

∩ *I want to get out and run around and play.* Horses who spend a lot of time in stalls really look forward to playing in the field. Not just the running around, but playing with other horses as well. Getting away in a hurry becomes important, and eventually becomes a habit that is hard to break.

∩ *I just can't wait!* Horses sometimes develop something called "stall courage," which is another name for tension that builds up from lack of exercise, too much grain or cold weather. Once they learn that being led out into the field is a precursor to being able to release that tension, they anticipate to the point of losing control—just like kids waiting for the final school bell to ring.

∩ *I'm afraid you're not going to let me go.* Once a horse starts the breaking-away behavior, you are likely to become more aggressive about holding on. You tend to increase the tension on the line, causing the horse to want to pull back. Frequently a more "experienced" handler will punish the horse severely for trying to break away, jerking painfully on the line. This may get the horse to stand at the time, but it also makes him anticipate the punishment the next time.

∩ *I've discovered that I can get away with this and be in control.* If the horse has either been punished or made stressed by the turnout procedure, he feels the need to take control. He has lost the desire to please you, at least in this situation.

WHAT TO DO ABOUT IT

∩ First, figure out how to defuse the situation. This depends on the circumstances and your horse, but there are several approaches, which you can use alone or combine with the others.

∩ If you have the space and you both have the skills, longe the horse for 5 or 10 minutes to get rid of his excess tension. If he still seems tight— head still up, tail tense—you could turn him loose in the longeing area and gently encourage him to run around a bit more. The only difficulty you might run into is if you continued this pattern for an extended period the horse might learn to anticipate the turnout after longeing, as well.

∩ Teach him to wait while you undo the snap. You do this in the stable aisle, or in the stall with his head toward the door. Stand facing him as if you were going to turn him loose, reach under his jaw and snap the trigger of the snap without undoing it. Be sure you aren't putting tension on the rope when he is standing quietly. When he accepts the snapping of the trigger quietly, which he probably will in the barn, praise him and give him a treat. Do this a number of times, even though he stands quietly, so he begins to associate the click of the snap with receiving a treat, which he will want to wait for. Also lift the snap off his halter, give him a treat, and put it back on again. Then, without lifting the snap off, do the same exercise outside, in an area that he doesn't associate with turnout.

∩ Some people like to remove the halter altogether when turning out. If you are one of them, rather than practicing with the snap, practice reaching up as though you were going to start taking the halter off.

(If you take if off by undoing the throatlatch rather than the crownpiece, see Bridling: Raises or Throws Head When Removing, page 44.) Gradually work through removing the halter until the horse will stand quietly with his halter completely off.

∩ Make the turnout pattern less predictable. With the gate open and no other horses turned out, walk him into the field, make a U-turn and walk him back out the gate again. Praise and treat. Do this a number of times until you can feel him saying, "Bo-o-o-rrring!" If he starts to wind himself up, take him back to his stall and leave him there for a while. If he still can't deal with going in and out of the field, try leading him just partway to the field, or even just in and out of the stable. Once he will walk into the field and out quietly, add a stop, without making any turning-loose moves.

Finally, bring him into the field, position him for turnout (see the Talking Horses box) making sure you are grounded and breathing, and click the snap. If he does anything but stand there looking eagerly for his treat, he needs more practice. If he waits nicely, give him his treat, repeat the exercise a time or two, remove the snap from the halter, give him another treat and walk quietly away. It's best to be fairly close to the gate, because he may follow you looking for more goodies.

∩ A variation on this is to use a treat such as grain pellets and drop them on the ground for him before you unsnap. If there is grass as well, he will be occupied with eating for at least a few minutes before he remembers it's playtime. You can reach down and undo the snap or remove the halter while he is eating.

WHAT NOT TO DO ABOUT IT

∩ Don't grip tightly on the lead rope in anticipation of his breaking away. This will only increase his tension. Also, while you might possibly use a chain across the halter nose (page 17) for training, don't use it for turnout. The time it takes to remove the chain builds up his anticipation even more, and if he tries to pull away it hurts both of you unnecessarily.

∩ If he does break away, taking the rope with him, don't punish him when you catch him to remove the rope. That will only teach him not to let you catch him! Instead, use it as another little training session. By the time you catch him, he probably will have gotten his running and playing out of the way, and will be willing to stand and do the snap-and-treat thing a couple of times.

∩ Don't make the mistake of thinking that because he does it right once after some training, he might not revert to his bad old habits. For several weeks, do some preparatory snap-and-treat exercises to remind him.

⋂ Don't make it harder for him by making him the last one out. If possible, he should be first. But if he gets frightened when he is alone, turn out just one other horse first—preferably the one who drops his head and eats as soon as he hits the field.

TALKING HORSES

Turning out horses can be one of the more dangerous things we do with them. I have known a number of experienced people who were severely injured during turnout by horses they trusted. That was their mistake!

The way to get hurt is to bring the horse through the gate, unsnap him and let him run by you into the field. Some people will even give the horse a slap to get him started. In his exuberance, or perhaps surprise, the horse will often buck or kick out as he passes the handler. It is sort of a "Yipppeeee" action that he often does with other horses, without intent to hurt. He doesn't realize that people are often klutzy and don't seem to know enough to duck! Broken arms or jaws are a frequent result.

Always turn the horse all the way around so he is facing the gate, in which you are standing. Unclip him, and as he swings around to head out to freedom, step back a step through the gate, so you are out of reach of his hind legs.

Horses are a little bit like guns in that you are most likely to get hurt by the one you thought wasn't loaded.

TURNOUT: BULLYING OTHER HORSES

Susan is very concerned about her horse, Clyde. Although Clyde is well mannered in company when he is being ridden, the stable where she keeps him refuses to turn him out with other horses because he attacks them. He is quite a large horse, and between his size and his aggressive tendencies has become something of a bully. The other horse owners complain that they find their horses with big chunks of fur gone, and occasional abrasions and bruises. While none of the injuries are serious, if they are in the area where the rider sits, she may have to miss her ride, which does not make her happy. Observations by the stable manager and other horse owners point to Clyde as the guilty party, and nobody seems to know quite what to do about it. Susan feels, quite rightly, that horses are herd animals and need to interact with other horses as much as possible, but she realizes that nobody wants their horse to be chewed up!

WHAT YOUR HORSE WANTS YOU TO KNOW

Ω *This is fun! I am bigger than the other horses so I can be boss! (Gee, I wonder why none of them seem to like me?)* Some horses are, unfortunately, very lacking in social skills. They probably grew up with either no other horses around, or smaller ones, so there was no one to smack any sense into them once they were weaned. These horses probably aren't very happy, because they would really like to play but don't know the rules. Then no one wants to play with them, so they get annoyed and play rough instead.

WHAT TO DO ABOUT IT

Ω This is a tricky situation for which there is no easy answer. If the horse only bites, one solution is to put the horse in a grazing muzzle. He can still eat, but he won't be able to get his teeth into other horses. However, a determined bully may find other ways to make trouble, such as punching with the muzzle.

Ω If kicking is a problem, the bully's hind shoes should be pulled, at least for a while. Unless the horse is truly nasty, he probably isn't kicking so much to hurt as to bluff, but even an accidental kick with shoes on can do a lot of damage if it connects in the wrong place.

Ω Try to find another horse who likes to play, but will make his feelings known if the bully plays too roughly. A larger horse or horses, who aren't aggressive but won't take any nonsense, can often put a bully in his place. Putting the teacher horse(s) in a strong turnout blanket will protect them from serious bites, although the blanket will probably suffer some damage.

Ω The safest answer, in terms of the well-being of the other horses, is to put the bully in a separate paddock for awhile, perhaps with another playful horse in an adjacent paddock so that they can play over the fence, but the other horse can get away from the bully if he gets too aggressive. Once the bully shows signs of learning how to play nice he can be gradually reintroduced to the herd, first sharing a paddock with his buddy, then, if that goes well, introducing other horses two at a time, to keep the social balance.

Ω Sufficient space can be a big help. Horses who fight in a one-acre paddock often get along just fine in a 10-acre field.

Ω If most of the bullying takes place at feeding time, you can take over the job of herd leader and keep driving the bully off, using a stick or swinging line, until he learns to eat from his own feed pile. This takes awhile, but the bully will find the atmosphere more comfortable when he isn't making trouble, and so will accept it.

WHAT NOT TO DO ABOUT IT

∩ Going out into the field and chasing the horse on foot when you see him biting other horses is pretty much a waste of time, and the only permanent result would probably be that he'd become difficult to catch. He won't associate the biting with your chasing him, and may consider it part of a game that he can win just by running away. I have heard of people having success when they were mounted on another, bold horse. Using a swinging rope and the force of the horse you are riding to drive the other horse away and keep him away until he shows signs of submission, can result in a reformed character, but you do have to be available very consistently until the problem is worked out.

TURNOUT: CHARGING

Caroline is on her way out to the field to get her favorite horse, Patch, and go for a ride. She is carrying her lead rope, of course, but not just to use for Patch. Buzzy, one of the other horses who is turned out with Patch, has become very dominant. Every time Caroline goes into the field, Buzzy tries to chase her out. Caroline has to swing the lead rope very aggressively to defend herself. Fortunately, Patch is more than willing to come in, so once she gets close to him she can catch him easily and, by keeping him between her and Buzzy, get them both safely out of the gate. But it is *very* annoying, and more than a little intimidating as well.

WHAT YOUR HORSE WANTS YOU TO KNOW

∩ *This is my herd. You don't belong here. I'm in charge.* In any group of horses, one will become the dominant horse. This is not a problem, unless the horse has never learned respect for people. It is essential for your safety that, even though you treat the horse with kindness and respect, he knows that when the chips are down, you are the leader and are not to be physically challenged.

WHAT TO DO ABOUT IT

∩ In working with an aggressive horse, the tendency is to get forceful to deal with the aggressive part and to forget that without trust, you don't get true respect—only grudging obedience. Horses are made dangerous by people who try to control them by force alone, rather than by earning their trust first, then asking for respect.

⋂ If he seems to be a bit sullen and resentful, begin with clicker training (page 27) to get him thinking about you more positively. Work on getting him to face you with his head down and his ears forward, which can be done in the stall or a small paddock. After introducing him to clicker principles, stand outside the door or gate and make some sort of sound to attract his attention. When he responds, perhaps by turning his head, perhaps only by a flick of an ear, click and treat. Then click for a head turn, for a full turn, then for a quiet approach, taking as many steps as necessary at each level. If his ears are back or his approach is not polite, withhold the click and turn away a little. Usually, as soon as he realizes that the goody train is leaving, his ears come right forward again and you can click and treat.

If he approaches slowly but his head is up, when he reaches you, rub and pat him a bit, then ask him to drop his head (page 14). If the horse is reluctant to give up control, you might have to spend enough time on the head drop to develop a verbal signal, so that you can ask him to drop his head before he approaches. The reason is that a horse who approaches with his head up is still thinking of himself as dominant, and so will continue to defy you.

The net result of this work will be that the horse starts to think of you as a friend who is coming to visit, rather than as someone who has come to challenge him.

⋂ If he just seems to be full of himself and bratty, use the first four Parelli games (page 29), until he is responding well to the yo-yo game, backing off respectfully as soon as asked and approaching politely.

⋂ Whether you use clicker or Parelli to start with, you should finish with some round pen work to make sure the horse will continue to be well behaved when he is free. If you don't have a round pen, try to find a place that is not too big, and where you can position yourself so that you can keep the horse working away from the stable, or other horses, or whatever he perceives himself as being in charge of. Each time he tries to get past you, chase him back. He will end up running from one side to the other to get by you, so your longe whip should be long enough, and you should be quick enough, to stay ahead of him. If he gets by you, just quietly but firmly chase him out again.

⋂ When he stops to think about it, make a sound that will attract his attention and get him to look at you, then smile and praise. Gradually work him toward discovering that if he comes up to you as quietly when he is loose in a large space as he did during the clicker or Parelli work, you will allow him to go to the other horses—but it must be on your terms, not his.

⋂ Because the horse has already shown a willingness to be aggressive toward you, it is better to do the round pen work last, so that you already have a fairly good relationship with him before you try to work with him free. Otherwise, it is all too easy to end up in a battle.

WHAT NOT TO DO ABOUT IT

♫ Don't pin him with your eye, which would be confrontational.

TALKING HORSES

There are very few truly dangerous horses around, but they do exist. And because of their size and speed, dangerous horses are life-threatening. For that reason, you shouldn't go into the field with any horse or group of horses about whom you know nothing at all.

TURNOUT: CHEWING WOOD

Constance and Jim put up beautiful wood fences for their two horses, Bernie and Allan. But after a year, the tops of the boards are gnawed to splinters. They've tried painting the boards with various things, but nothing seems to work very well.

WHAT YOUR HORSE WANTS YOU TO KNOW

♫ *I'm bored, but mostly I just crave this stuff.* Horses can have special nutritional needs that aren't always met by commercial feeds.

WHAT TO DO ABOUT IT

♫ First, do some research into nutrition, especially trace minerals. Your veterinarian may be able to help, and there is a lot of information on the Internet (see Appendix A for some suggestions). Some of the equine e-groups have very knowledgeable members. I have also noticed that horses seem to want to eat tree bark in the late winter, perhaps because the sap is rising and contains enzymes that they crave.

♫ In the field, placing electric wire over every plank will stop chewing. Electric wire also prevents horses from leaning against the fences, and from rolling too close to them and perhaps getting cast. There are now fence chargers that have solar batteries, so they can be placed anywhere. Electric tape has also become popular and is attractive, as well as being less expensive than wood.

∩ If your horse chews wood in the stall, placing heavy metal caps over the tops of the partitions will prevent it. However, the metal must be heavy enough not to bend. Angle iron works; aluminum does not, since it can easily be bent, leaving sharp corners and edges.

∩ Special chew-deterrent paints work for some horses, but not for all of them.

∩ A grazing muzzle is made of fairly heavy metal rods, wide enough apart so that the horse can get his lips through them to eat grass, hay and grain, but not his teeth to chew wood. Some horses do well in these, especially if they are well padded with sheepskin. Others get sores on their faces. A muzzle is not practical in a situation where the horse is usually unsupervised and there are things he could get caught up in.

∩ As with other habits that arise partly out of boredom, finding a larger turnout area is the best solution of all.

WHAT NOT TO DO ABOUT IT

∩ Don't ignore it completely. Besides the destruction to property, severe wood chewing is a symptom of deeper problems. It can also lead to colic.

TURNOUT: REFUSING TO BE CAUGHT

Jackie's instructor will be at the stable in an hour, so Jackie goes out to catch Dan, who is in the field with two other horses. When she approaches him, he lets her get about 20 feet away, then turns and deliberately walks away. She follows him and the same thing occurs, again and again. She gets more and more frustrated as the time for her lesson approaches. Finally, using a bucket of grain, she is able to coax one of the other horses into a smaller paddock, and Dan follows. In the smaller space she finally catches him, but she is now late and flustered and annoyed, which does not bode well for the success of her lesson. The most annoying thing is that yesterday, when she didn't have time to ride and just went out to visit, he came right up to her!

WHAT YOUR HORSE WANTS YOU TO KNOW

∩ *I want to stay with my buddies.* Horses, being herd animals, feel most comfortable with the herd.

∩ *I sort of think that if you catch me you might want to eat me.* Allowing himself to be caught, to be tied up, and to be loaded in a trailer are the three areas that present the most problems for a horse. Why? Because all of them arouse the horse's natural fear of predators. Being caught, or trapped in a corner, can mean death to a wild horse.

WHAT TO DO ABOUT IT

∩ As with trailer loading and tying, there are certain basics that must be in place before you can expect the horse to allow himself to be caught consistently. Therefore, the first rule is not to immediately turn a new horse out in a large space with plenty of food and water available. If he has not learned to allow himself to be caught, you haven't left yourself much in the way of control.

∩ Trust, of course, is the most important thing. All the training methods advocate first working with the horse until he is comfortable with you touching him all over. Using whichever approach you like the best, a combination of advance and retreat (page 27), patience and quiet persistence will eventually result in a horse who actually likes having you around.

∩ The next step is to teach the horse to turn and look at you, and eventually come toward you (see Turnout: Charging, page 168). It is fairly easy to pair a signal, such as a whistle—your own, not a device—with the act of coming toward you, so that the horse comes on signal. In the stall or small paddock, teach the horse to associate whistling with a treat. Always use the same couple of notes, of course. But you can use almost anything as a signal. I used to keep treats in a plastic bag in my pocket, and all I had to do was rustle the bag to bring the horses to me.

∩ The Parelli driving game (page 32) can also help teach the horse to turn and face you when you focus on or move toward his hindquarters from the side. You have to spend enough time with this exercise that it becomes a conditioned reflex, or it won't work for you when the horse has other priorities.

∩ However, none of these will work if your approach in the field makes the horse think "Predator!" He zones out, forgets who you are and only thinks of getting away. The best, most foolproof method is to devote some quality time to the problem. Stroll out casually into the field, and take along a good book. Keeping your center very passive (page 13), walk around a little and look around, including the horse in your soft-eyed gaze without focusing on him. If he looks at you, turn away a little, as though you aren't interested. Find a comfortable place to sit, with your back to the horse, and enjoy your book. After 20 minutes or so, go away for awhile, then come back. Eventually, his curiosity will override his caution and he will come over to see what you're doing. When he does, smile and say hello but make no attempt to touch or catch him. If he stays around for a little while and seems comfortable, offer him a treat.

Pretty soon he'll start coming right to you, looking for the treat. You can bait the hook by carrying a little bucket of grain or noisily eating a carrot. The next step is to withhold the treat until you have touched him, stroking his shoulder and his muzzle at first, and gradually moving to include more of his body. Try to find his itchy spots—places where he especially enjoys being scratched, such as the side of his withers. After a few minutes at whatever level you are working, walk away and leave him. If he walks away first, pay no attention. Go back to your book for a few minutes, then leave and come back later.

∩ If he doesn't wear a halter in the field, spend some time in the stall teaching him to put his head into the halter (see Haltering, Resistance to, page 76) so that he doesn't perceive it as a trap. (Many horses are put off by the approach of the halter.) Then start bringing the halter and lead into the field. At first, just put the lead rope around his neck and let it sit there while you dole out some scratches and treats. Next, put the halter on, play for a few minutes, then take the halter off and leave. Now you should have a horse who is comfortable with you coming out and putting on his halter, in preparation for leading him out of the field.

∩ If the horse continues to dislike being caught, think about what is happening when he comes in. Are grooming, tacking up and riding all pleasant experiences for him? Horses learn to anticipate pain and discomfort, and start worrying in advance. Does he have a buddy who he hates leaving? Perhaps you could bring the buddy in as well, then turn him out again later.

∩ It's a good idea always to have a treat waiting for him in his stall when he comes in, so he looks forward to it.

WHAT NOT TO DO ABOUT IT

∩ Don't look directly at the horse as you walk out.

∩ Don't walk right at him.

∩ Don't hurry.

∩ Don't try to catch him by making a sudden grab at him as he approaches.

∩ Don't let him feel that you're out to "get him."

∩ Don't *always* go out to the field just to bring him in to ride or put him in his stall. Sometimes, just visit and give him a treat.

TALKING HORSES

I once had a horse named Randy who was always reluctant to be caught. He was very comfortable with me in all other ways, but he had had a very clumsy handler and it was before I knew about all these good methods and theory. I could catch him eventually, but it usually took awhile. One day a friend, also a horse person, stopped by to visit. I had been telling her about Randy, so she asked to see him. He happened to be out, so I said, "He's up there in the field, but he won't let you catch him." "That's okay," she replied, "I'll just go up and take a look." She walked into the field, stopped and looked at Randy, who was grazing about 50 yards away. He glanced up, then swung around and cantered over to her, stopped dead in front of her and put his head into her hands! Talk about a horse making a liar out of you! But of course he had sensed her intent, which was entirely passive and nonthreatening, so he never thought about being caught at all.

TYING: CHEWING ON THE ROPE

Marguerite's three-year-old gelding, Spirit, is coming along very nicely with his training. He leads well, stands in crossties, picks up his feet and has learned many other basic skills. However, he still has one irritating habit that Marguerite hasn't been able to solve. If she puts him on the crossties and turns her back even for a moment, when she turns around he has half the crosstie in his mouth and has chewed it to rags. She tried using chain, but he took that in his mouth as well, and she was concerned that he might get a tooth caught in it and really get hurt.

WHAT YOUR HORSE WANTS YOU TO KNOW

♫ *I'm kinda bored standing here, and besides, it feels so good to chew on something.* Young horses, like all young animals, have a short attention span. They also go through a teething period as their adult teeth erupt through the gums. Rope seems to be a very satisfying thing to teethe on.

WHAT TO DO ABOUT IT

♫ If he stands well otherwise, fastening the ties to the upper rings on his halter, where he can't reach them, may solve the problem.

⋂ Mouth work may be of some help, but if the horse is seriously teething it's best to give him a safe toy to work on until he outgrows it. A simple solution is to take a short length of strong, chew-resistant (that is to say, synthetic rather than natural) braided rope, about half an inch in diameter, which you can find at a marine supply shop or some hardware stores. Melt the end so it doesn't unravel and attach a snap to one end. Fasten the snap to the upper ring of the halter on one side, then bring the rope down and through the lower ring on the same side. Leave about a foot dangling down. The horse can play with this to his heart's content, and the worst-case scenario is that you will have to replace the rope after awhile. You might also look around for a safe chew toy for him to have in the stall.

⋂ It's worth considering whether something bio-chemical is making him tense (see Stall Problems: Kicking the Stall, page 143). A tense jaw could also be the cause. His teeth should be thoroughly checked, and massage or chiropractic considered.

⋂ If the chewing is just an annoying habit in an older horse, you can use the clicker (page 27) to mark the moment when he turns away from the rope. You can also do the friendly game (page 30) or Tteam (page 34) to distract and relax him.

⋂ If he chews the rope when you are holding him or leading him, which some horses do as an attention-getting or dominance move, the usual correction is simply to stuff as much of the rope as you can into his mouth. This is not done in an aggressive or punishing way, but just to let him find out that a mouthful of rope is not all that comfortable. It can be followed up with some mouth work.

WHAT NOT TO DO ABOUT IT

⋂ Don't yell at him or jerk the rope out of his mouth. This just creates more tension and thus more desire to chew. If the horse has any tendency to pull back, he may do so, forgetting he has the rope in his mouth, and really scare himself.

TYING: WON'T TIE

Karen has left her pony, Toffee, tied to the trailer at a show while she goes to get a drink. There is only a small amount of hay in the net, but Karen doesn't expect to be away too long. She gets her drink after waiting in line, and as she is walking back she sees Toffee sit back against his tie rope, brace himself and pull hard. After a few seconds something gives way, Toffee falls back on his haunches and rolls onto his side, then gets up and starts calmly eating grass, obviously totally unflustered. It is apparent that he ran out of hay, got bored and took matters into his own hooves. Karen realizes that, even though she has never seen him do this before and had no idea he wouldn't tie, this is probably something he has done many times before and has down to a science.

WHAT YOUR HORSE WANTS YOU TO KNOW

∩ *Hey, I'm not as dumb as you think. I don't have to stay here if I don't want to, and I don't want to.* This is further proof that horses are nowhere near as stupid as tradition has it. Outwitting him isn't going to be easy. This is quite different from the panicky situation described in Panicking Against Crossties (page 107).

WHAT TO DO ABOUT IT

∩ Besides all the techniques described in Panicking Against Crossties, here are some that are more appropriate for the horse who is not scared but simply determined.

Method 1: This is similar to the dallying method (page 109), but leaves you out of the action so the horse doesn't connect you with the restriction. Take the crownpiece off a flat nylon halter and replace it with several pieces of coarse, fairly strong baling twine. Use a halter that has a snap on the throat latch so you can slip it on without undoing your temporary crownpiece. Put the horse in a stall that has been completely cleaned out, and with no other horses around. The more boring the stall, the better. Tie the horse fairly short to a strong ring or stall bar. He should be able to back up a step or two, but not come close to the far side of the stall. To tie him, use one strand of twine that is moderately strong. You should be able to break it by pulling hard on it with both hands in gloves. You want it strong enough so that when the horse pulls back against it, it will be pretty uncomfortable for him, but not so strong that he can't break it without going over backward. Have plenty of this twine available.

Now walk away and leave him, but stay nearby and out of sight. Wait. Read a book. If he is a consistent tie rope breaker, after awhile he will pull back and break the twine. But he'll still be in the stall, there still won't be anything to eat or to do, and it will have hurt a bit on his poll. Walk in, say nothing, and tie him up again. Continue this procedure as often as possible, each time leaving him as long as is possible and humane, until he decides that breaking his tie rope isn't as much fun as he thought. When he begins to stay for longer periods, praise and give treats when you go in to check up on him. When he seems willing to stay for awhile, end the lesson, then repeat it in a day or so, asking for a longer stay. Keep an eye on his poll where the string pulls to make sure he doesn't develop a serious sore during training. Also be sure he has access to water. A horse can go longer without eating than without water. Once he will stand tied for up to an hour without attempting to break loose, you can probably consider him trained. As a further test, try tying him up in a small empty paddock or round pen.

Method 2: This method and the ones that follow have the potential to cause damage to the horse's neck, probably fixable by a chiropractor, but still possibly dangerous. Therefore, they should be used with extreme caution, after all other methods have failed and only if it is essential for the horse's safety that he accept tying. If the horse has previously shown that he will fight and struggle violently without stopping except momentarily, do *not* try any of these methods. There are some horses who will fight until they kill themselves rather than give in, because they are in what they perceive as a life-threatening situation. This particularly applies to Thoroughbreds.

You must also be very calm, grounded and nonthreatening while you are setting up these tying arrangements. If you frighten or anger the horse during the setup, both of you could get hurt. Keep in mind that you are trying to help the horse learn something that is necessary for his own well-being, not trying to show him who's boss. Stay within sight, but far enough away so that the horse doesn't associate the tying with your presence. Don't watch too obviously.

Use a narrow but strong rope halter, rather than a flat nylon or leather halter. Pulling on the narrower halter is more uncomfortable, so the horse will stop trying sooner. The rope should be tied to the halter, not attached by a snap, which could break. Use a bowline (page 189) if you want to be able to untie the knot later on. All the equipment should be virtually unbreakable. Tie the horse to something strong and well above his head. Something that is also flexible, like a tree branch, is even better. If he can't get purchase with his feet on a direct line with the rope, and if the tie point moves, he can't break it.

Method 3: Using the same equipment, tie the horse to something very strong and solid, such as a tree trunk, at about withers height. Don't trust a fencepost. A determined horse may break it off or lift it right out of the ground, and then you *do* have a problem. Tie him very short, not more than a foot, so that thrashing his head around is kept to a minimum. A horse who is stubborn and determined, but not irrational, will fight briefly then give up, usually for good.

Method 4: Again, you need a solid support, such as a tree trunk or a heavy ring tied or bolted to a solid support, and the same halter on the horse, but now you need a long, thick, soft rope as well as the lead rope. Using a bowline (page 189), tie the long rope around the horse's body so that it fits snugly behind his withers, with the knot under his barrel where the girth would lie. It should not be tight, but should be snug enough that it won't pull forward into the tender area behind his elbows. Take the end of the rope from that point, pass it between his front legs, up through the halter ring and tie it to the support at a distance of about three feet. The lead rope should be tied six inches or so longer, so that the horse hits the belly rope first. The horse thinks he is tied by the head, but the pressure comes against his spine, which is uncomfortable but not as threatening.

Method 5: This is almost the same as Method 4, but the long line runs from his girth area through the ring and then back to the halter, where it is again tied with a bowline. With this method, when the horse pulls back with his head, he pulls against himself. The pressure against his spine makes him move toward the tying point, so he finds that coming forward relieves the pressure on his head.

   With Methods 2, 3 and 4, once the horse accepts the rope and stops fighting, be effusive with praise and treats as soon as he stands quietly. Gradually shape the behavior, as in Method 1, until the horse will stand for half an hour without any attempt to get loose, before trying to tie him normally. Then tie him in an enclosed space first.

∩ There are a few horses who never learn to accept tying. However, you can usually teach them to ground tie as long as you are nearby. Drop the lead rope on the ground and groom or tack up or whatever you need to do. Every time the horse moves out of position, simply put him back where he was without criticizing, praise and go on with what you were doing. After a while, he will decide that it is just as easy not to move in the first place. It's best to work on this initially after the horse has worked and is relaxed and a bit tired, rather than when he is eager to get out and get going.

WHAT NOT TO DO ABOUT IT

∩ Avoid situations that would seriously provoke him, such as leaving him tied for long periods under uncomfortable circumstances like extreme heat or cold, or without water.

∩ Don't give him any opportunities to break things until he has really resigned himself to staying tied. If he gets away with it again and again, he will become very hard to convince.

∩ Avoid leaving any horse tied in an exposed position entirely alone. This is very threatening, since he has no protection and no escape from a predator, so it is psychologically very damaging.

TALKING HORSES

There is always a debate about whether to use a long lead rope or a short one. I prefer one that is somewhere in the middle. When you tie a horse up with a rope that is only a foot or so long, he has to keep his head pretty much in one place. This is both unnatural and tiring, and I think it borders on abuse if it goes on for very long. However, if you use too long a rope, it is all too easy for the horse to get a leg caught in it and be seriously hurt. Generally, the rope should be just long enough so that if the horse stands as close to the tie point as he can, he can barely reach the ground with his nose. Thus he can raise and lower his head comfortably, but there is no room to get a leg caught.

A way to safely use a longer rope for long periods is to run the rope through a ring, with a heavy block on the end. When the horse pulls on the rope, it slides through the ring so he can move his head quite freely, but when he turns his head toward the tie point the block falls down and takes the slack out of the rope. The placement of the ring and the length of the rope are important, so that the rope always stays snug. It probably would not be safe for a horse who paws vigorously, since he could get a leg over it.

AFTERWORD

While this book has focused on solving the problems you encounter as you work with or around your horse on the ground, for most of you the important goal with your horse is to be able to *ride* him successfully. But of course, the ultimate use of the knowledge you have gained here *is* to develop your success in riding, since, as you are probably aware, the best way to deal with many riding problems is to work them out on the ground first. "You ride what you lead," as they say. In addition, when you are working out difficulties on the ground, you are not worried about the possibility of being thrown, and the horse isn't worried about dealing with your weight and movement.

Ground work is where you deal with any emotional issues you may have with a horse. That is to say, before you can even think about riding your horse, neither of you should be afraid of or angry with the other. You wouldn't want to ride in a car being driven by a person who was seriously upset, and you certainly wouldn't want to get on a horse in the same emotional condition. That's why there is so much emphasis on trust and respect in the What to Do About It sections of this book.

Many chapters in this book have direct applications to riding, especially the chapters that deal with dominance issues, such as the ones on leading. Unless the horse is comfortable with giving up control to you when he meets unusual situations, he will revert to his own instincts of "spook and run." In another area, trainers often skim too quickly over saddling and mounting during the horse's initial education, leaving him with insecurities that carry over into riding.

However, all the ground work in the world is not going to solve your riding problems if your riding skills are inadequate. Imagine a woman who takes ballroom dancing lessons with a professional and becomes very comfortable with what is a rather difficult athletic activity. She then goes to a dance with her husband, who, unfortunately, didn't want to bother with the dance lessons. (Too much work and time just to slide around on the dance floor.) So when they go out on the floor, his leading is clumsy, he gets in her way and steps on her feet, all the while grinning and enjoying himself and the music. His incompetence makes her miserable and frustrated, and finally she stalks off the floor and sits down crying. His response is, "What's wrong? I thought you *wanted* to dance!"

The horse who is out on a beautiful day on the nicest trail, but is being ridden badly, probably wants to go off into a corner and cry too. Sometimes he ends up doing the next best thing—bucking his rider off!

All too many people, involved in a skill of some sort, consider the learning process boring. They want to be out and doing, not home reading the manual. Every computer program has a Quick Start booklet, so you can start using it right away. And yes, this is important. But eventually, if you don't keep trying to learn, you become either frustrated because you keep failing, or bored because you can't progress.

The three basics that every rider needs to work on are:

1. Developing a good relationship with your horse (which is what this book is about).

2. The ability to sit on the horse in a way that does not disturb either horse or rider.

3. Understanding and using your aids to communicate with the horse.

All three take a great deal of time and dedication to learn well. But there are a great many resources available, some of which you will find in Appendix A, and some of which may well be in your own backyard. Good teachers can be found in many places.

Look for, and take advantage of, not just your riding opportunities, but your learning opportunities as well. Then you'll get the greatest enjoyment out of your horse, and he from you, both on the ground and in the saddle. Find that balance in your riding career and you can keep having fun *because* you keep learning.

Appendix A

RESOURCES

CLICKER TRAINING
Web sites, e-groups and contacts
www.theclickercenter.com
kurlanda@crisny.org
49 River Street, Suite #3
Waltham, MA 02453

www.clickertraining.com
(800) 47-CLICK

Clickryder@onelist.com

Introductory books and videos
Don't Shoot the Dog, by Karen Pryor, Bantam Doubleday Dell, revised edition, 1999.
Clicker Training for Your Horse, by Alexandra Kurland, Ringpress Books, 2001.
Clicking With Your Horse, by Alexandra Kurland, Sunshine Books, 2003.
The Click That Teaches (video series), by Alexandra Kurland, Sunshine Books.

PARELLI NATURAL HORSE-MAN-SHIP
Web sites, e-groups and contacts
www.parelli.com
pnhusa@parelli.com
Parelli Natural Horse-Man-Ship
56 Talisman Drive, Suite 6
Pagosa Springs, CO 81147
(970) 731-9400

Introductory books and videos
Natural Horse-Man-Ship, by Pat Parelli, Lyons Press, 2003.

There are numerous videos and other learning tools available. Call or visit the Parelli Web site.

ROUND PEN TRAINING
Web sites, e-groups and contacts
www.johnlyons.com
generalinfo@johnlyons.com
John Lyons Symposiums
P.O. Box 479
Parachute, CO 81635
(970) 285-9797

Introductory books and videos
Lyons on Horses, by John Lyons, Doubleday, 1991.

Many videos are available at tack stores and through the Lyons Web site.

TTEAM: TELLINGTON-JONES EQUINE AWARENESS METHOD
Web sites, e-groups and contacts
www.animalambassadors.com
info@tteam-ttouch.com
Tteam
P.O. Box 3793
Santa Fe, NM 87506
(800) 854-8326

Introductory books and videos
The Tellington-Jones Equine Awareness Method, by Linda Tellington-Jones and
    Ursula Bruns, Breakthrough Publications, 1988.
Ttouch of Magic (video), Linda Tellington-Jones, Animal Ambassadors.

RELATED EDUCATIONAL GROUPS
American Riding Instructor's Association
www.ridinginstructor.com
aria@riding-instructor.com
28801 Trenton Court
Bonita Springs, FL 34134-3337
(239) 948-3232
Find a certified riding instructor in your discipline and your area.

Centered Riding Inc.
www.centeredriding.org
P.O. Box 12377
Philadelphia, PA 19119
(215) 438-1286
Nonthreatening riding skills for all disciplines, and qualified instructors.

Centered Riding, by Sally Swift, St. Martin's Press, 1985.

ridingwithconfidence@yahoogroups.com
A support group especially for riders and owners with fear problems, moderated by Gincy Self Bucklin.

www.egroups.com
All kinds of equine discussion groups, including groups focused on all the training methods referred to in this book.

HORSE HEALTH AND WELL-BEING

www.naturalhorse.com
www.todayshorse.com
E-zines that are both well worth visiting.

www.abc.net.au/catalyst/stories/s545781.htm#transcript
Fascinating research about how horses see.

OTHER AREAS OF INTEREST

Specialized Parelli equipment is offered at the Parelli Web sites, and in tack stores and catalogs.

www.polocenter.com
Worldwide listing of trailer, float and van manufacturers and dealers (sometimes the right trailer can make all the difference in a horse's loading problems).

Appendix B

ILLUSTRATED GLOSSARY

PARTS AND FITTING OF THE HALTER

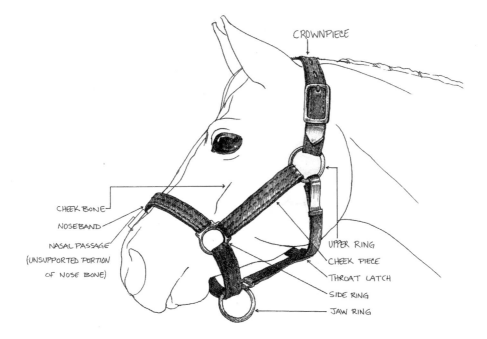

CROWNPIECE

CHEEK BONE
NOSEBAND
NASAL PASSAGE
(UNSUPPORTED PORTION
OF NOSE BONE)

UPPER RING
CHEEK PIECE
THROAT LATCH
SIDE RING
JAW RING

PARTS OF THE HORSE

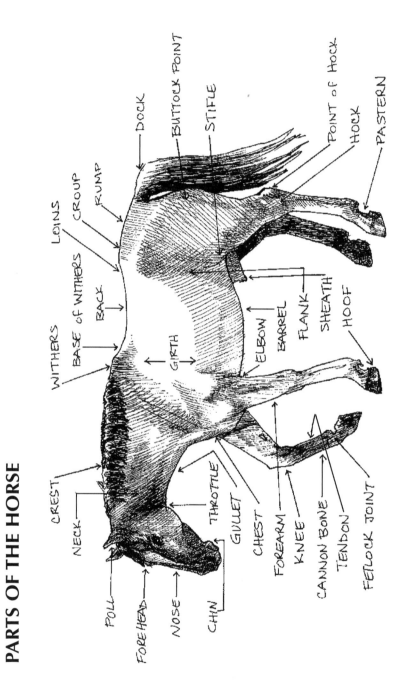

PARTS OF THE ENGLISH SADDLE

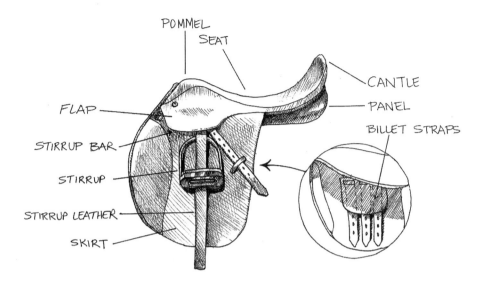

PARTS OF THE ENGLISH BRIDLE

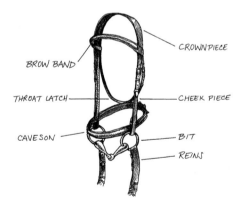

USEFUL KNOTS

Quick-Release Knots

Quick-release knots are used to tie a horse to any fixed object.

The **halter hitch** is the most common quick-release knot, and while it is easy to tie, it is not especially safe because if the horse pulls it tight before you can get to it, it jams and is very difficult to release. If you don't expect to have to release it in a hurry and just want a simple knot, tucking the end through the loop makes it less likely that the horse will undo it himself.

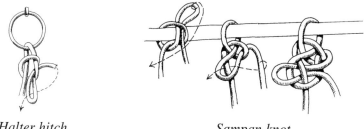

Halter hitch   *Sampan knot*

The **sampan knot,** which looks very similar to the halter hitch, will not jam no matter how hard the horse pulls, but can be pulled loose easily, even from a distance if you leave a long tail. A very useful knot, well worth learning.

The **picket line hitch** was used in the horse-drawn artillery. If made with a bight (loop) as the last turn, it is easy to unhitch, though it may jam if the rope is stiff.

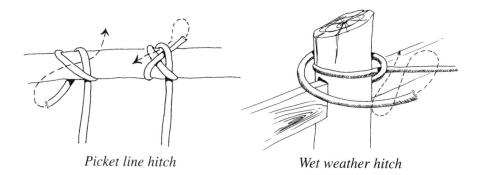

Picket line hitch   *Wet weather hitch*

The **wet weather hitch** was used by the circus to fasten the tents to the tent pegs. It never jams and is easy to adjust if you want to change the length of the rope without unfastening the horse.

The **chandler hitch** is a quick, safe knot to use if you aren't going to leave the horse alone, but it can work loose after awhile. Tucking the end through the loop will prevent that, although a playful horse could probably untie it.

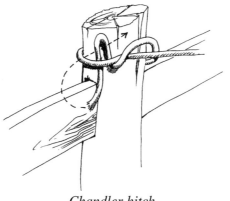

Chandler hitch

Other Useful Knots

The **bowline** can be used to make a loop that will not become a slipknot, or in any situation where you want a knot that absolutely will not come loose accidentally or jam. You can also use two bowlines to safely join together two ropes. The loop can be any size you need.

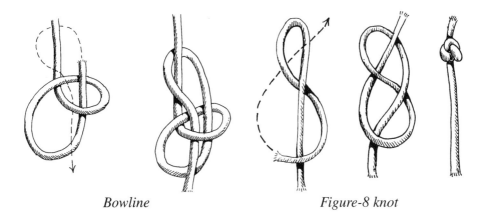

Bowline   *Figure-8 knot*

The **figure-8 knot** is used as a stopper knot, either at the end of a rope or in the middle. Like the bowline, it will neither come undone accidentally nor jam when you want to undo it.

The **square knot** and the **granny knot** are multipurpose knots. Although the granny is not held in high regard, it is actually in some ways a more secure knot than the square knot, which can be upset and slipped apart fairly easily if you pull on only one end. The arrows in the figure point out the difference in the knots.

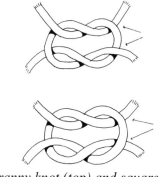

Granny knot (top) and square knot

The **becket hitch** is used to fasten the crownpiece of the type of rope halter that has no metal fittings.

The **neck halter** is a fast, safe way to put a nonslip loop around a horse's neck, either as a neck rope to ride with or to lead him by. It consists of two overhand knots (the same knot that you start to tie your shoe with), but figure-8 knots, which don't jam, could be used instead if the horse might pull against it. The knot at the end of the rope is put through the open knot in the middle of the rope, which is then tightened up against it. The knot in the middle can be moved up and down the rope to get the length you want.

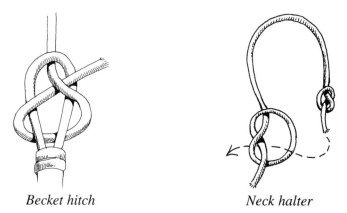

Becket hitch   *Neck halter*

Drawings of knots by Heather Holloway are based on designs in *Ashley's Book of Knots*, by Clifford W. Ashley, Doubleday, 1944.

INDEX